Wildlife Photographer of the Year

PORTFOLIO EIGHT

Designed by
GRANT BRADFORD

Competition Manager
LOUISE GROVE-WHITE

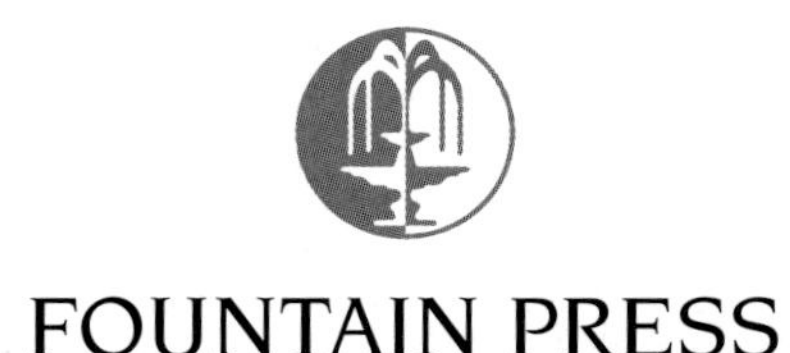

FOUNTAIN PRESS

Published by
FOUNTAIN PRESS LIMITED
Fountain House
2 Gladstone Road
Kingston-upon-Thames
Surrey KT1 3HD
England

Design & Layout by
GRANT BRADFORD
Design Consultants
Tunbridge Wells
Kent

Competition Manager
LOUISE GROVE-WHITE

Captions Editor
LINDA BENNETT

Colour Origination
Setrite Digital Graphics
Hong Kong

Printing & Binding
Die Keure n.v.
Belgium

ISBN 0 86343 303 0

Foreword

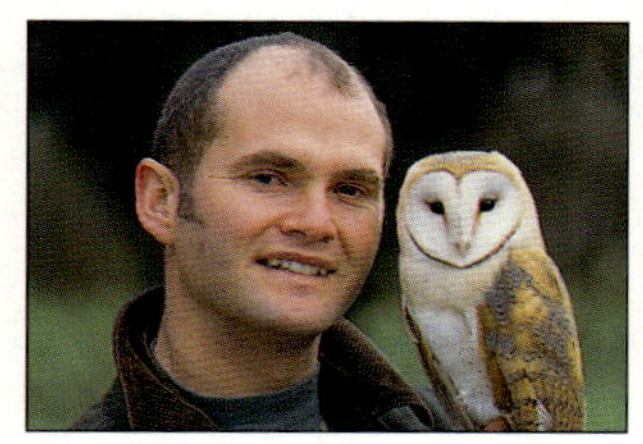

Good photography is, in many ways, like fine cooking. As you consider the prospect of poring over the images in this book, you develop a sense of expectation, an appetite if you will, for the contents. You may be uncertain if the meal will be entirely to your liking, but this only sharpens the edge of anticipation. As you turn the pages you are treated to a heady mixture, some of the elements familiar, others foreign. From time to time, you encounter an ingredient which challenges your preconception of what is good and bad, but with continued testing, discover its magic, its unique and exciting flavour.

Gathered within these pages is the cordon bleu of wildlife photography. Every course is a delight, stimulating the senses with a combination of aesthetic beauty and great theatre.

However you choose to dine on these visual delights, be it random picking or methodical progress from start to finish, you will find each image in harmony with the next, either by virtue of contrast or sympathy. This is a further illustration of the phenomenal standard of work here, the continuity of brilliance. And just as it is sometimes easy, when lost in the hedonistic pleasure of fine food, to forget the architect or the artist who created the work, so too you may find yourself so absorbed by the natural wonders within these pages that your thoughts for the photographers are few.
True, they have sought out the finest ingredients on earth, often with painstaking care and tenacity, but it is their skill and artistry which has converted these raw materials into the magnificent spread you are about to enjoy. Each of these artists shares an empathy with his or her subject, a pride in their work and most important of all, a love for the wild world.

This book is a celebration of the wonder and variety of natural splendour, served at your convenience to enjoy at your leisure wherever and whenever you choose.

Prepare for a visual feast.

Simon King Somerset 1998.

INTRODUCTION

This book displays the winning and commended images from the 1998 BG Wildlife Photographer of the Year Competition, which has been organised for the fifteenth year by *BBC Wildlife* Magazine and The Natural History Museum, London and sponsored for the ninth year by BG plc.

The Competition exists to encourage amateur and professional photographers around the world to record and document the beauty and wonder of the natural world. Each year the number of entries grows. This year over 20,000 slides were entered by photographers from 60 countries.

The photographers enter pictures on colour slides in 12 different categories which each carry a first prize of £500 and a runner-up prize of £250. Where competition is particularly fierce the judges award a specially commended or third prize. A number of the photographs that reach the final stages of the judging are highly commended. There are two special awards: the Eric Hosking Award for the best portfolio of pictures by a photographer aged 26 years or under, and the Gerald Durrell Award for Endangered Wildlife. This year the BG Young Wildlife Photographer of the Year Competition for photographers aged 17 years and under, consists of three age categories and a special award: the YOC Award.

The winning photographers are brought to The Natural History Museum in October for the presentation of the main awards and the official opening of the Exhibition of winning and commended images. Four sets of the Exhibition tour the UK, visiting some 35 different galleries, museums and nature centres. An international tour goes on display in Australia, France, Germany, Holland, Japan and the USA, amongst other countries.

THE JUDGES

Bruce Pearson
Wildlife artist

Heather Angel
Wildlife photographer

Dr Giles Clarke
Head of Exhibitions and Education, The Natural History Museum, London

Rosamund Kidman Cox
Editor, *BBC Wildlife* Magazine

Simon King
Wildlife film maker

Pierre Rouyer
Assistant Editor, Animan, Switzerland

WILDLIFE PHOTOGRAPHER OF THE YEAR 1991-1997

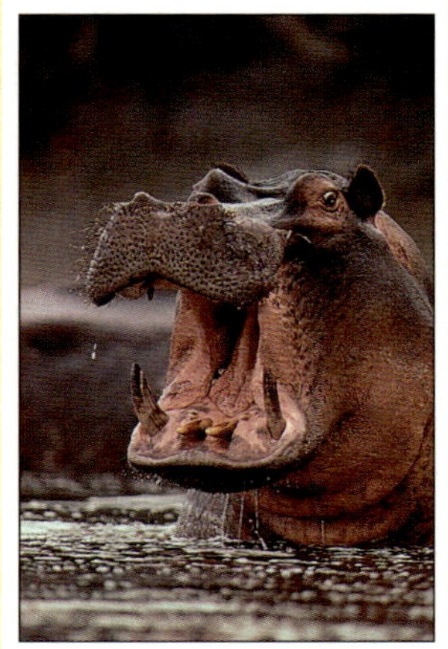

PORTFOLIO ONE
Frans Lanting
The Netherlands
1991

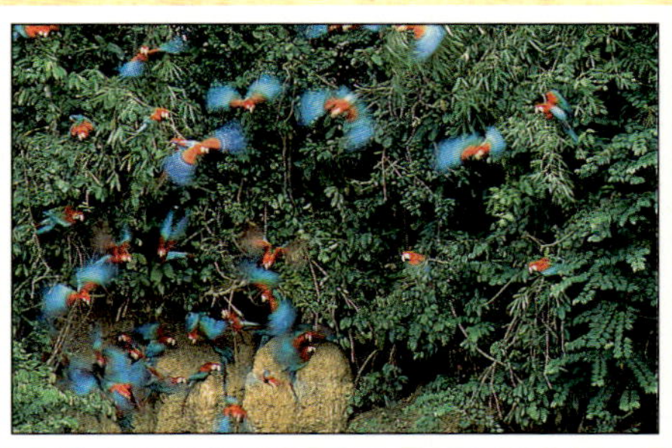

PORTFOLIO TWO
André Bärtschi
Liechtenstein
1992

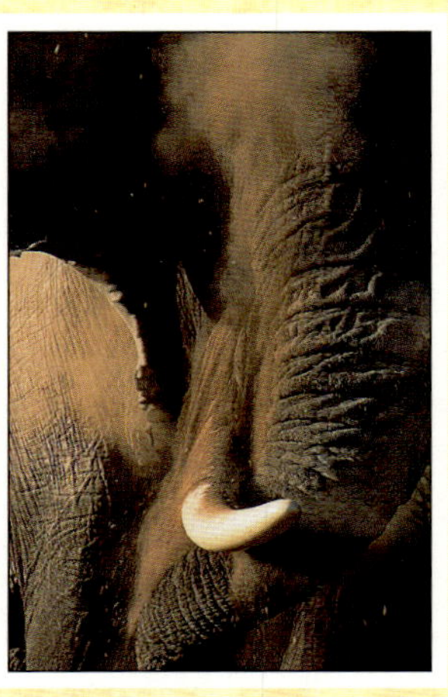

PORTFOLIO THREE
Martyn Colbeck
United Kingdom
1993

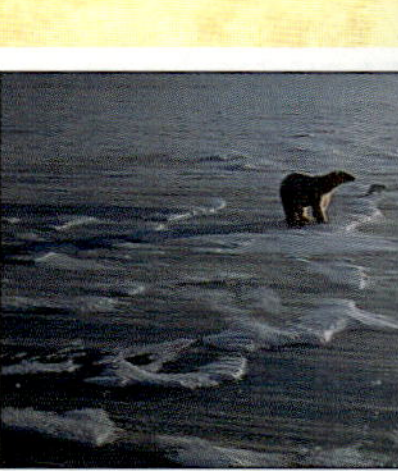

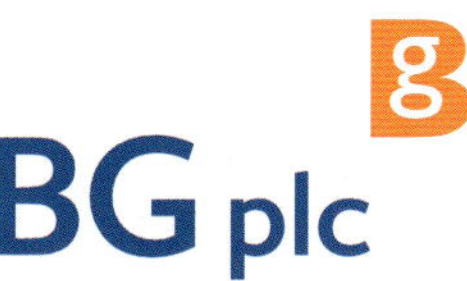

Wildlife Photographer of the Year

1998

"BG plc has a long association with the Wildlife Photographer of the Year Competition and has taken pride in seeing it grow to become a truly international event.

The skill of those behind the lens to capture, for all time, a vivid and significant image is stunningly illustrated in this collection of photographs. All very different in approach, style and outlook, they open up a unique window into the animal and plant kingdom, giving us a tantalising glimpse of the richness and variety of the wildlife on our planet.

They are also a timely reminder that nature is constantly under threat from us all. As a company whose business involves fossil fuels, BG plc takes its responsibility to the environment seriously. Both in the UK through Transco, our gas pipeline business, and overseas with British Gas International, we aim to ensure that our environmental performance is of the highest standard.

Our sponsorship of this competition is a further expression of our commitment to good environmental practice and we are delighted to be involved."

David Varney Chief Executive BG plc

PORTFOLIO FOUR
Thomas D Mangelsen
United States of America
1994

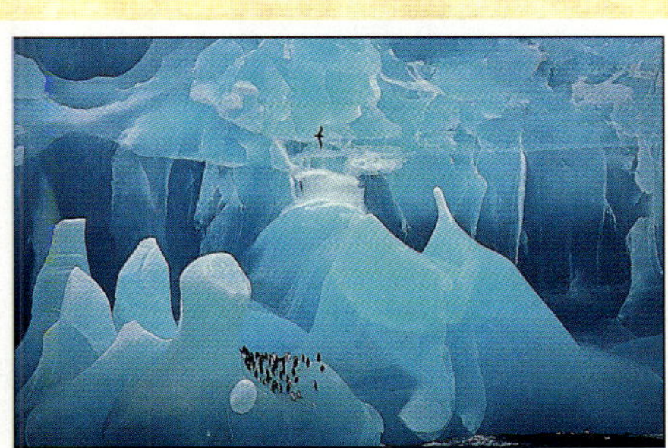

PORTFOLIO FIVE
Cherry Alexander
United Kingdom
1995

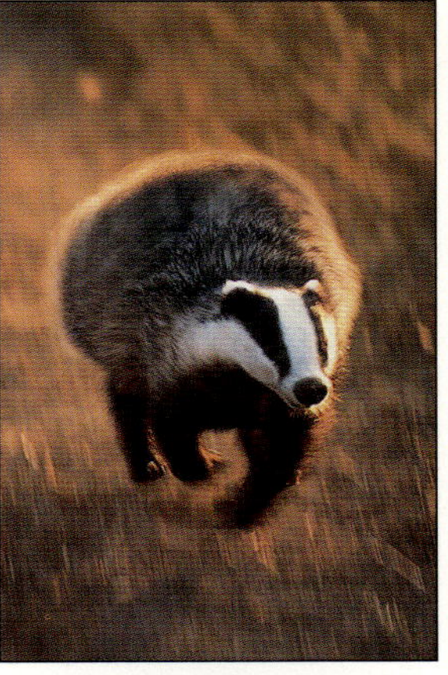

PORTFOLIO SIX
Jason Venus
United Kingdom
1996

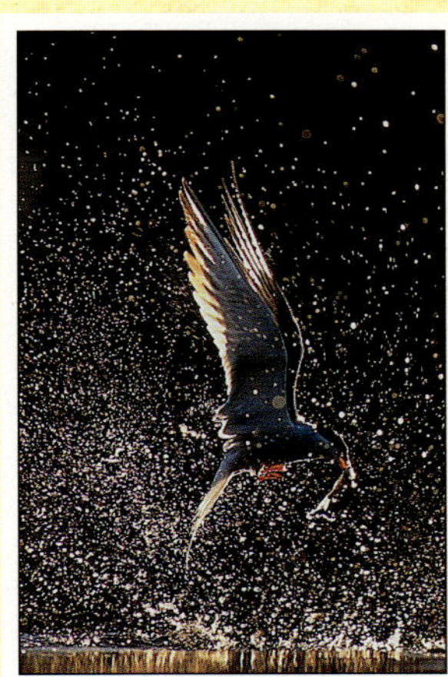

PORTFOLIO SEVEN
Tapani Räsänen
Finland
1997

Contents

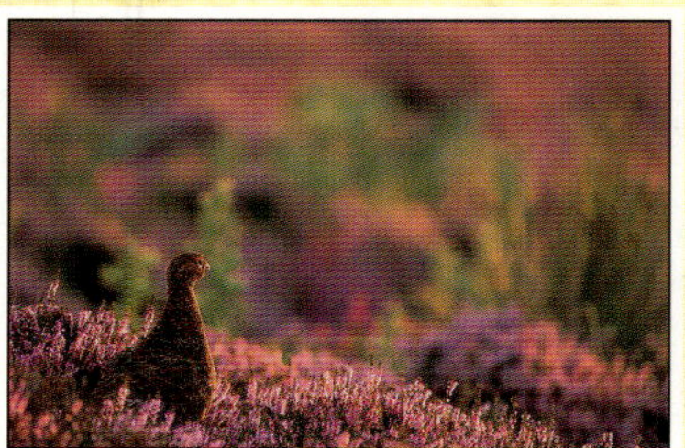

CONTENTS

Wildlife Photographer of the Year

The BG *Wildlife Photographer of the Year* title is awarded for the single image judged to be the most striking and memorable of all the photographs entered for the Competition. The 1998 winner, Manfred Danegger, received the BG Award - a bronze trophy of an ibis - and a cheque for £2,000.

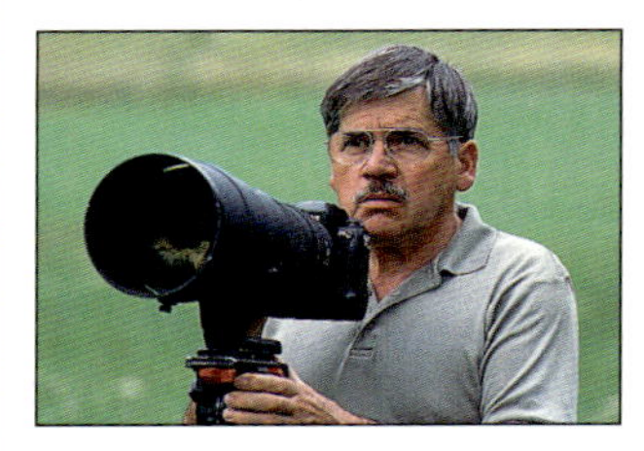

Manfred Danegger

Manfred was born in 1936 in Constance, in the south of Germany. He first developed a love for wildlife photography at the age of 16, but he actually became a professional photographer six years ago. He is married with one daughter who has followed in her father's footsteps to become a wildlife photographer. He travels extensively throughout Europe, Canada and Africa in search of suitable subjects for his work.

Manfred Danegger
Germany
WILDLIFE PHOTOGRAPHER OF THE YEAR 1998

Boxing hares

"I have been photographing hares for 20 years, but sadly such opportunities are now rare as the hare population in Germany has diminished significantly. During the breeding season, in March and April, I spend long periods of time at a number of 'favourite' sites along the edge of Lake Constance in southern Germany, hoping to capture the courtship behaviour of this shy creature. On this particular early morning I witnessed this female hare fighting off the advances of the courting male as a signal that she was not ready to mate. This is, in fact, a natural process that she has to go through in order to prepare herself for mating."

Nikon F4 with 400mm lens; 1/1000 sec at f2.8; Fujichrome Sensia 100

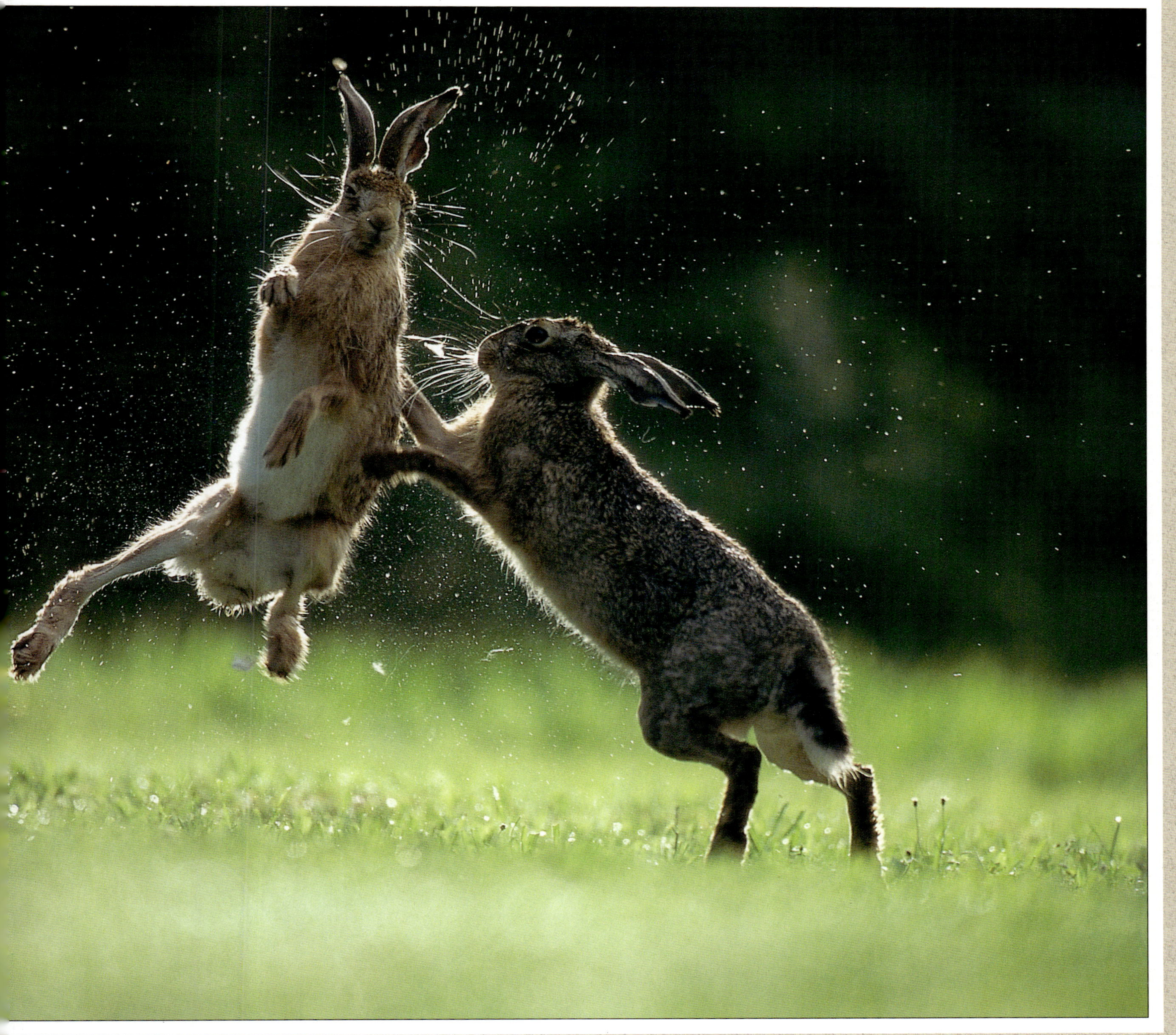

The Eric Hosking Award

This Award goes to the best portfolio of six images taken by a photographer aged 26 or under. The Award was introduced in 1991 in memory of Eric Hosking - Britain's most famous bird photographer. Eric was a supporter of the Competition from its earliest days. The prize is a specially commissioned trophy and a cheque for £1,000.

This year's winner, Jamie Thom from South Africa, received his first camera at the age of 17 while still at school. He had his mind set on a career in mechanical engineering but a friendship struck up with his neighbour, an avid wildlife photographer, had a deeper influence on Jamie's future. Over a number of years it became clear to him that his interests lay in photography and wildlife and not in mechanical engineering. In 1995 he joined the Mala Mala Game Reserve in South Africa where he now works as an assistant senior ranger. As can be seen in his portfolio of images, this environment has provided endless opportunities for superb photography. He would love to make photography a full time career.

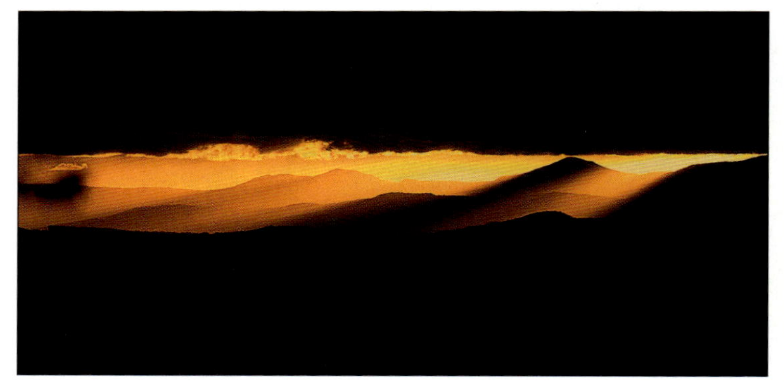

Drakensberg mountains

"Many beautiful silhouettes of this mountain range can be seen at sunset, but this particular one was unusual because of the rays of sunlight piercing the clouds and shining down between the ranges. I took this picture from my car in Mala Mala Game Reserve, South Africa, with my camera propped on a beanbag on the dashboard."

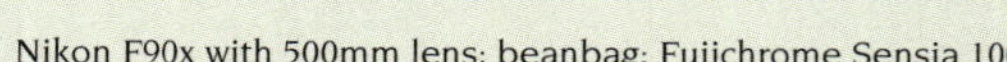

Nikon F90x with 500mm lens; beanbag; Fujichrome Sensia 100

Leopard cub in tree

Young leopards can be extremely nervous in their first few months, but are also sometimes strangely tolerant of human presence. This 5-month-old male cub was peering down inquisitively at our vehicle in Mala Mala Game Reserve. His mother was also in the tree with him, which was just a short distance from her recent impala kill."

Nikon F90x with 500mm lens; 1/125 sec at f4; Fujichrome Sensia 100

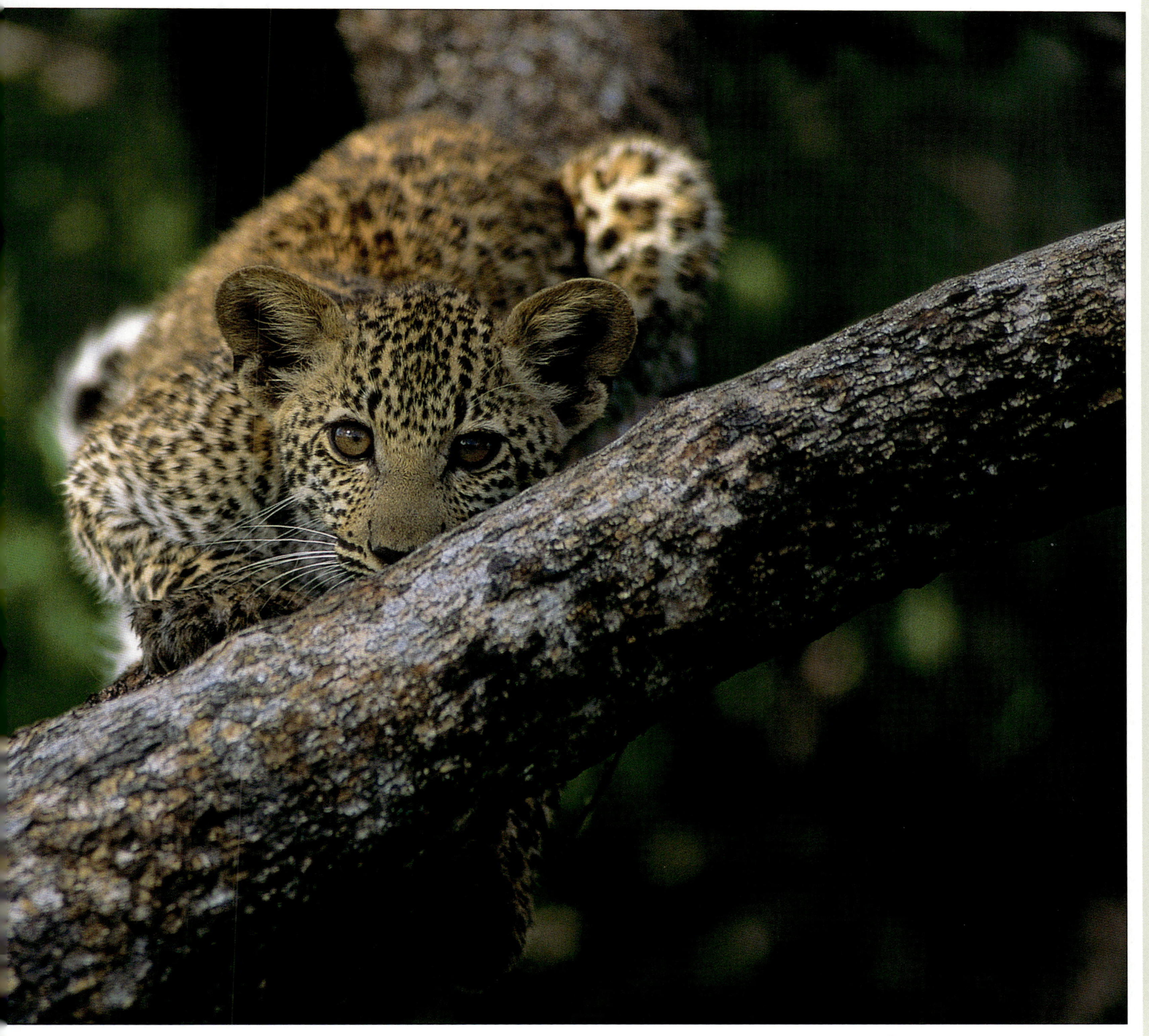

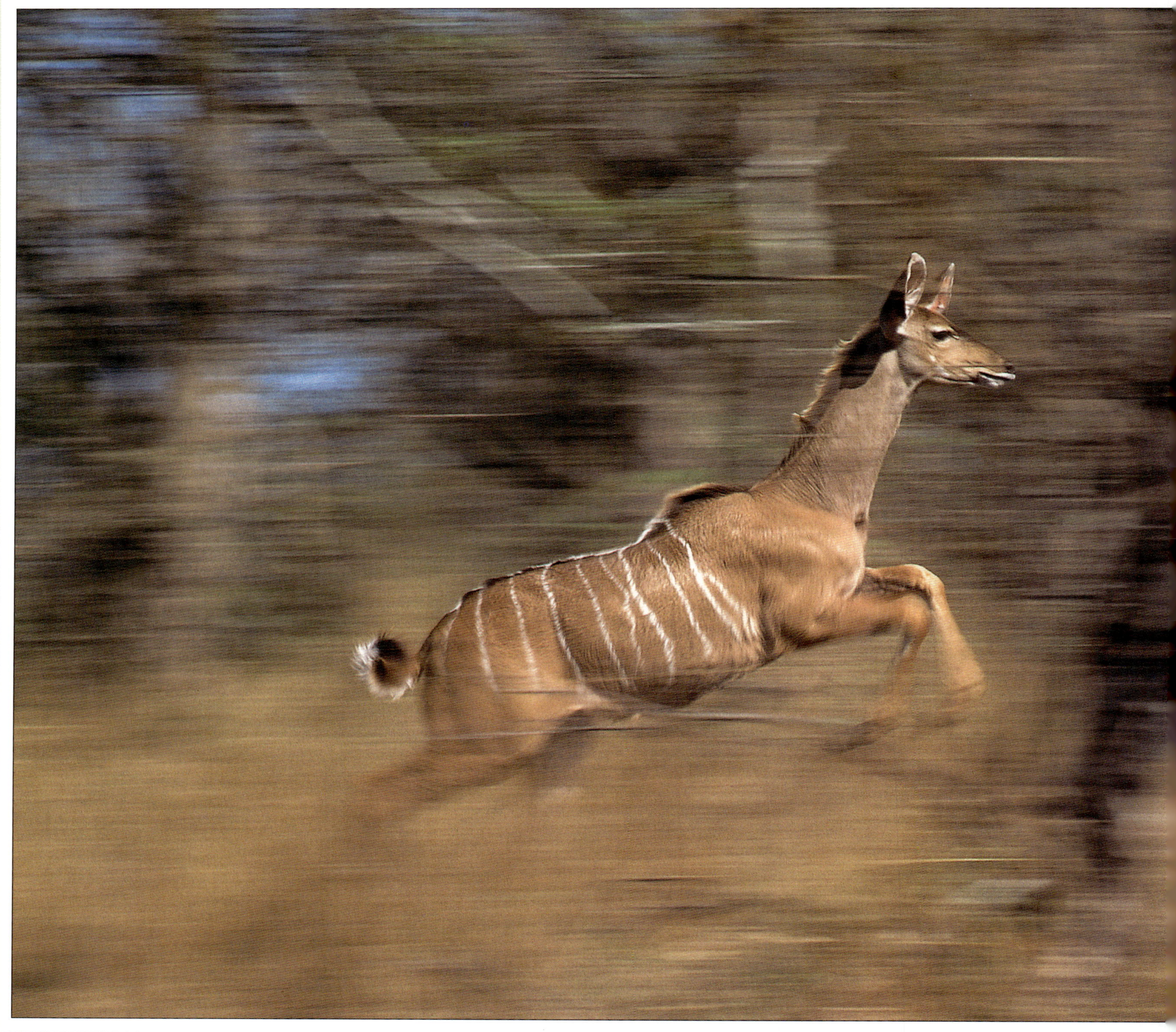

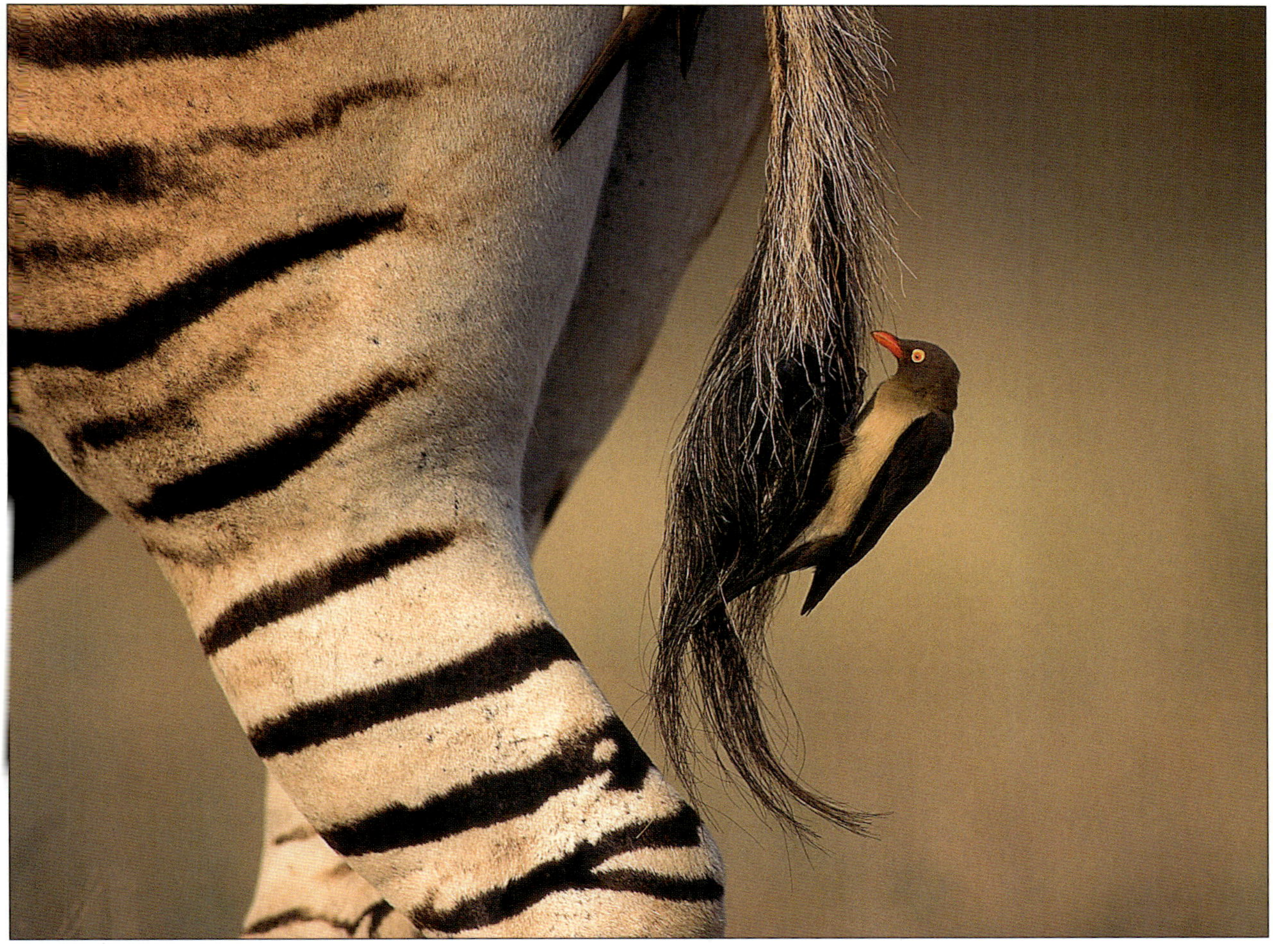

Jamie Thom
South Africa

Greater kudu

"Common in the well-wooded areas of Mala Mala Game Reserve, the greater kudu's long legs and neck enable it to browse the high foliage. They are exceptionally fast and nimble creatures, but still provide many meals for their predators. This female had fallen behind her herd and I was lucky enough to predict the route she would take when running to catch up. I pre-focused on a spot and the result was probably my best example of a panned photograph."

Nikon 8008s with 80-200mm lens; 1/60 sec at f4;
Fujichrome Sensia 100

Jamie Thom
South Africa

Oxpecker on zebra's tail

"The Kruger National Park is where I first learned to love the bush, and it still remains my favourite place to visit. Red-billed oxpeckers frequent this area and are often seen foraging for parasites on large species such as giraffes and rhinos. In this case, the contrast of colours between the oxpecker and the zebra provided that 'something extra' to make the shot."

Nikon F4 with 500mm lens; 1/250 sec at f4;
Fujichrome Sensia 100

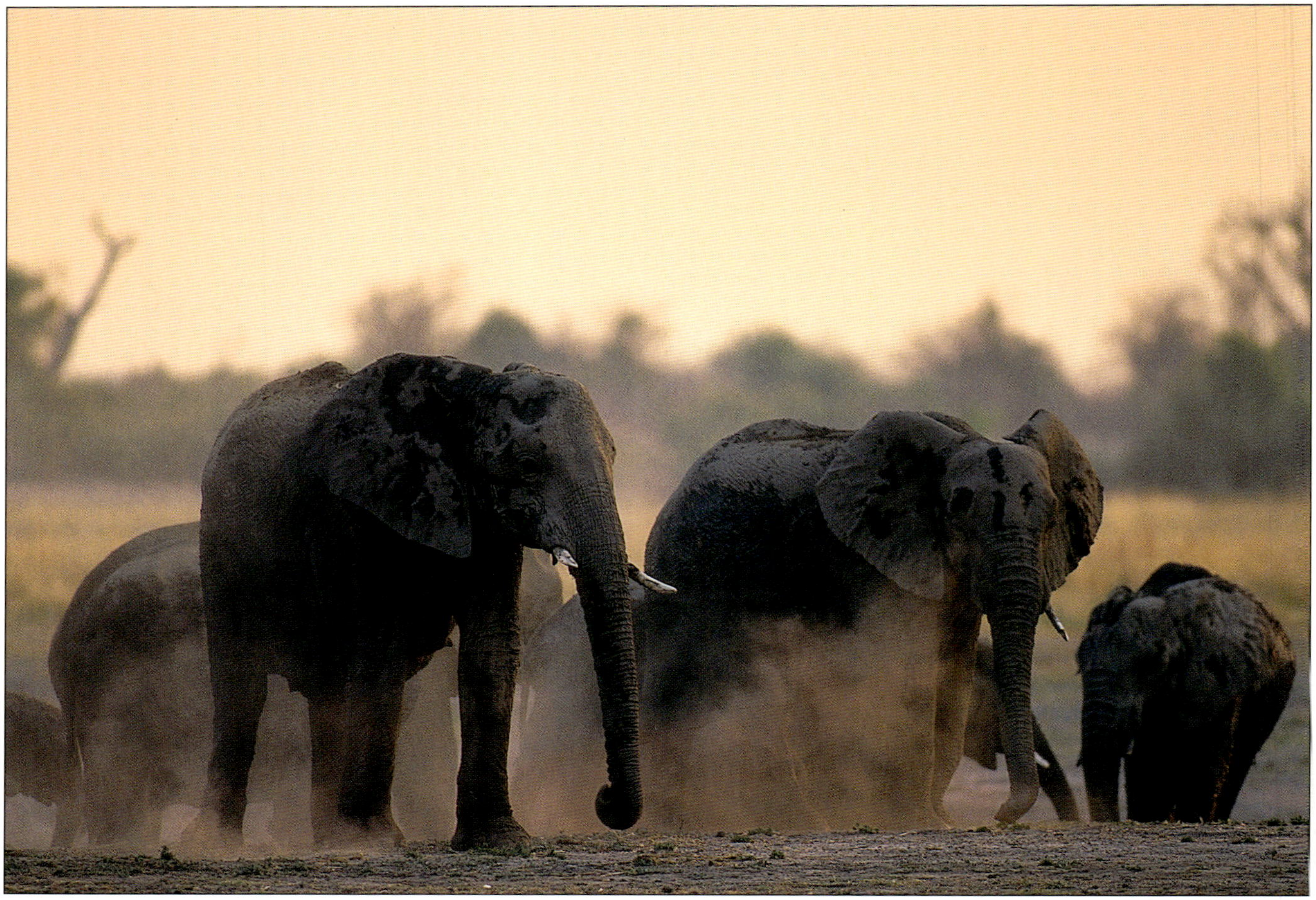

Jamie Thom
South Africa

Elephants

"Elephants are a common sight in Chobe National Park, Botswana, and are often seen moving through the open floodplains along the banks of the Chobe River. I had been photographing this particular herd for over an hour, when we drove ahead to get a different angle. As they approached, they created a dust cloud which caught the afternoon sunlight."

Nikon F90x with 500mm lens; 1/60 sec at f4;
Fujichrome Sensia 100

Jamie Thom
South Africa

Lions crossing river

"I watched a pride of lionesses stalk and kill a water buck by the Sand River in Mala Mala Game Reserve. After feeding for about 20 minutes, one of them left the kill to fetch the cubs. I was not sure where she had gone, so I waited by a frequently used river crossing point in the hope she would return that way. When she did, she started play-fighting with her year-old cub as they crossed back over the river."

Nikon F90x with 300mm lens; 1/175 sec at f4;
Fujichrome Sensia 100

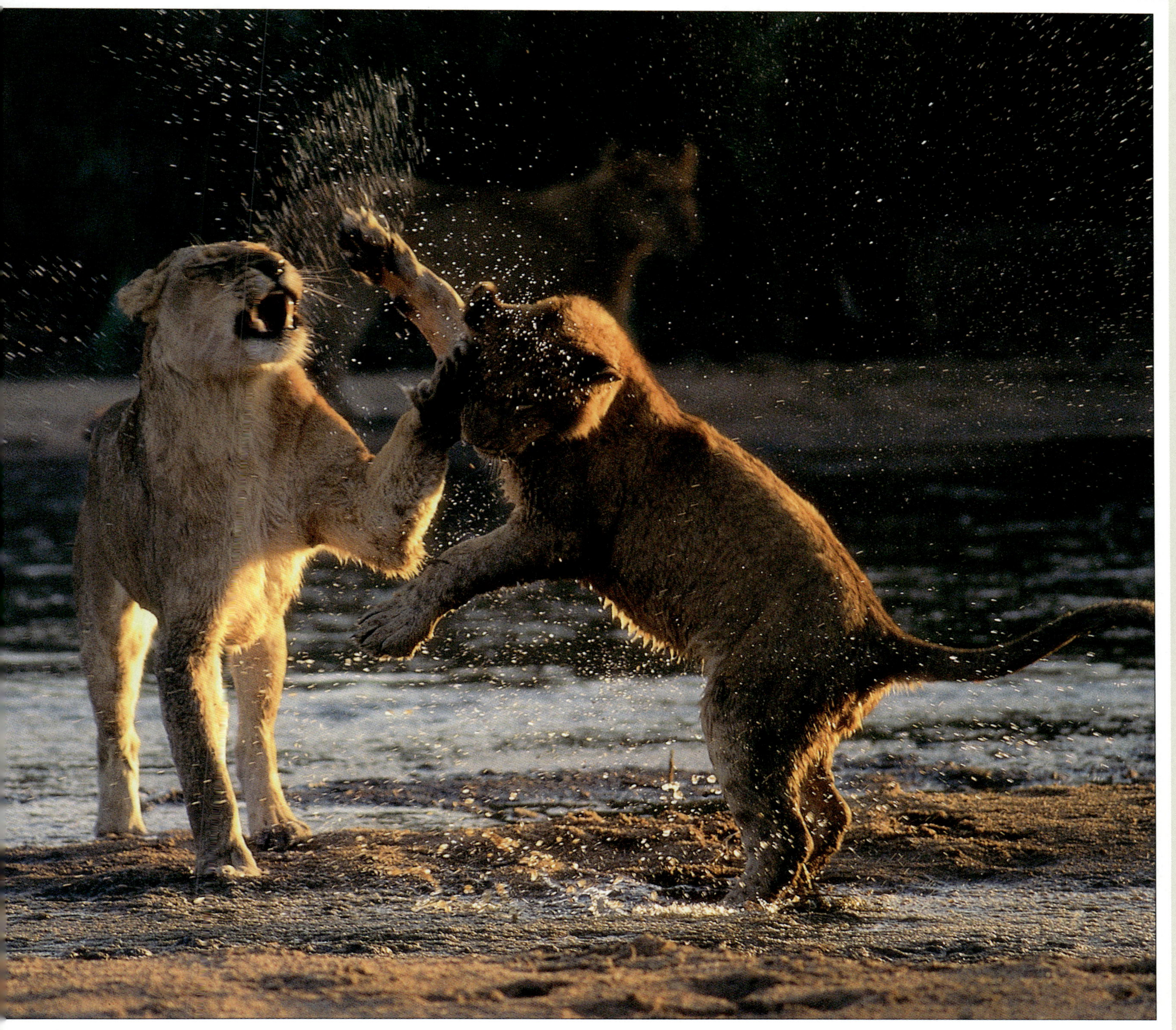

The Gerald Durrell Award for Endangered Wildlife

This Award was introduced in 1995 to commemorate Gerald Durrell's long-standing involvement with the Competition and his work with endangered species. The subjects illustrated must be officially listed as endangered or threatened at an international or national level. The winner, Dr Freek van Eeden, received a specially commissioned trophy and a cheque for £1,000.

Dr Freek van Eeden worked as a professional economist for 25 years. Following his retirement in 1995, he has devoted much of his energy to his love for nature and wildlife photography. As an Associate of the Photographic Society of Southern Africa, his work concentrates on wildlife in this region. He participates actively in national and international exhibitions for which he has received numerous awards and other forms of recognition.

Dr Freek van Eeden
South Africa
WINNER

Elephants in whirlwind

"These elephants had drunk from a waterhole, in Namibia's Etosha National Park, and sprayed their vast bodies with water. They had walked only about a hundred metres when a huge whirlwind appeared from behind and swept towards the herd. They huddled together to protect the small calves against the dust and wind."

Canon EOS 1 with 400mm lens; 1/125 sec at f5.6; Fujichrome Velvia 50

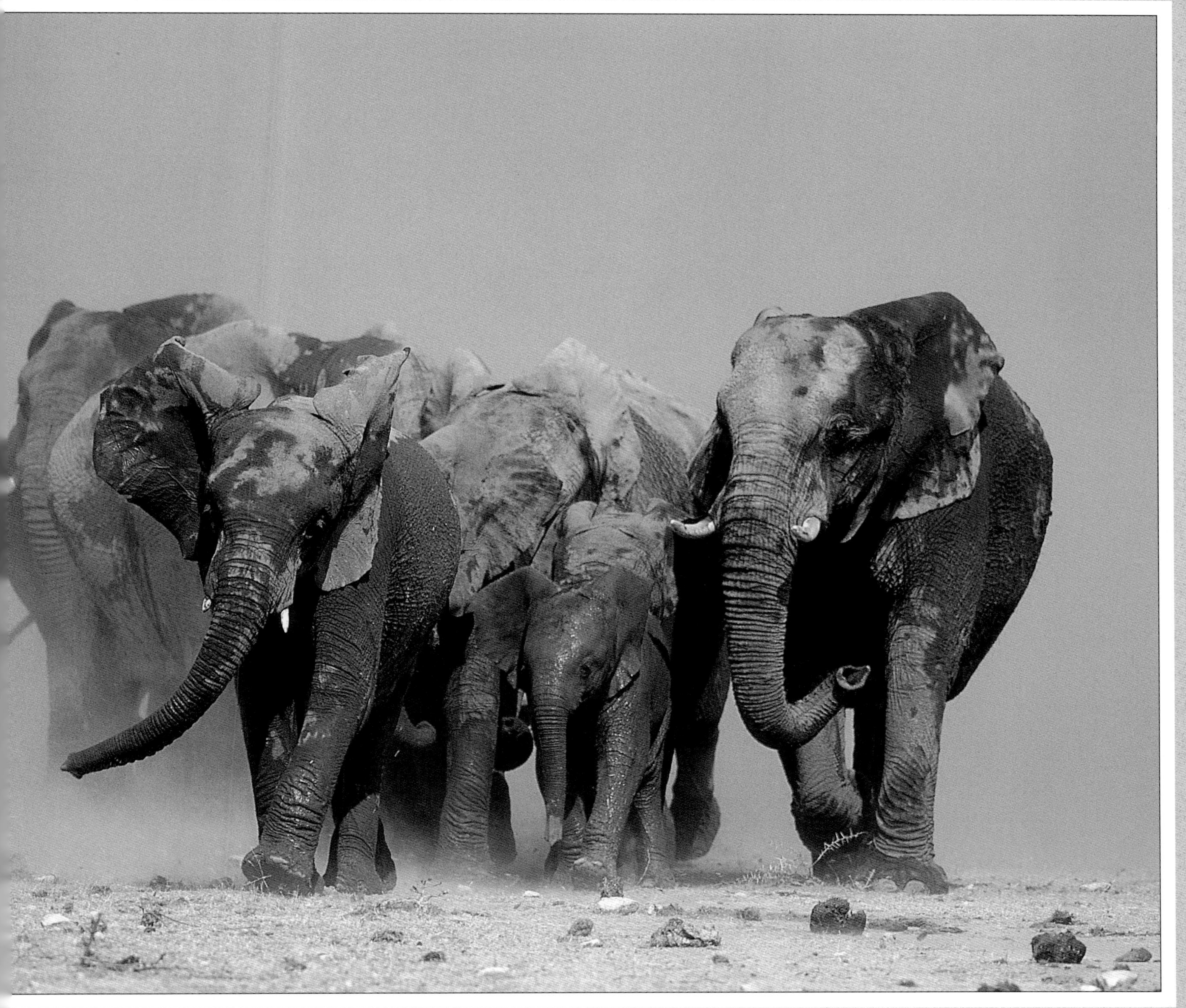

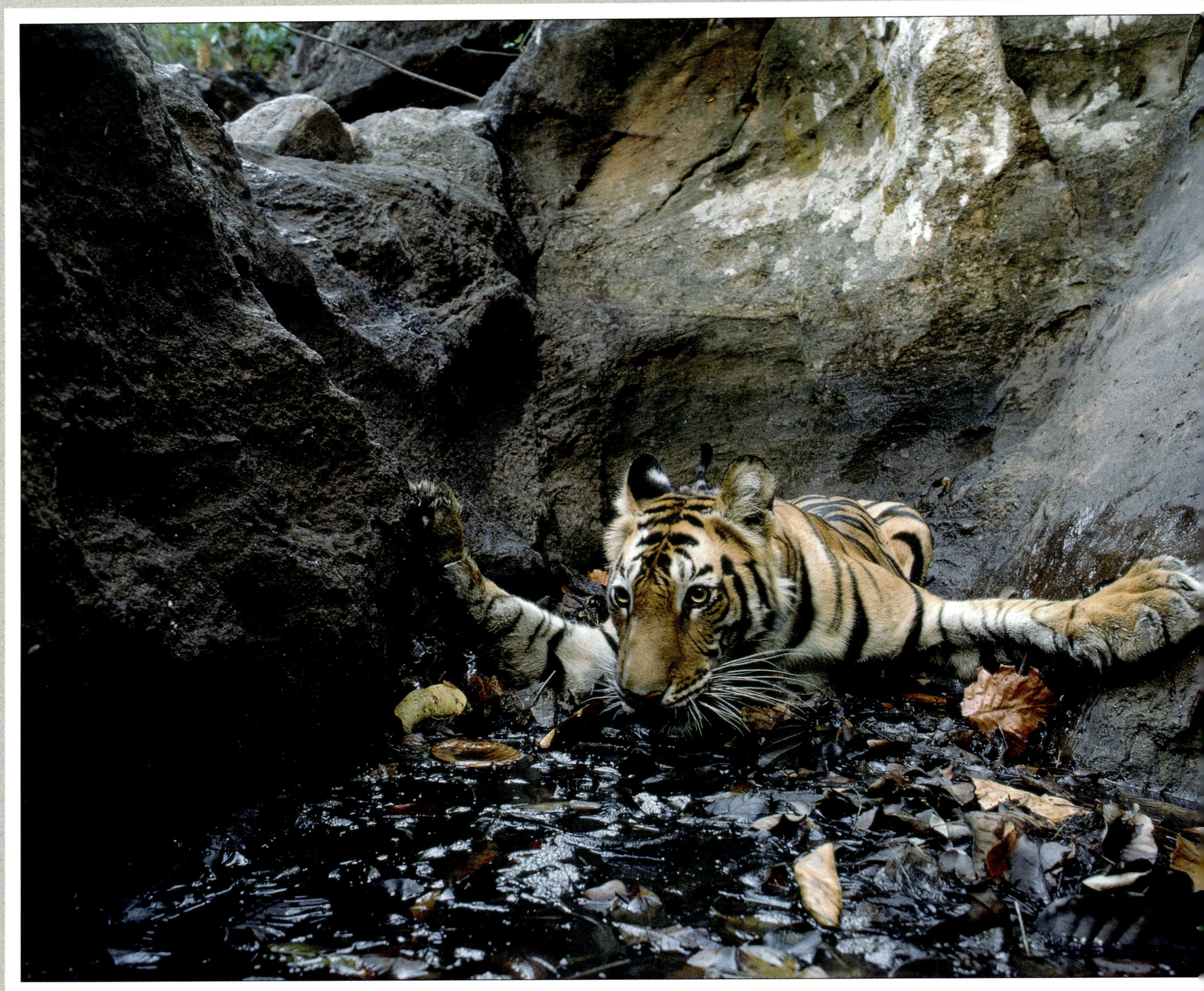

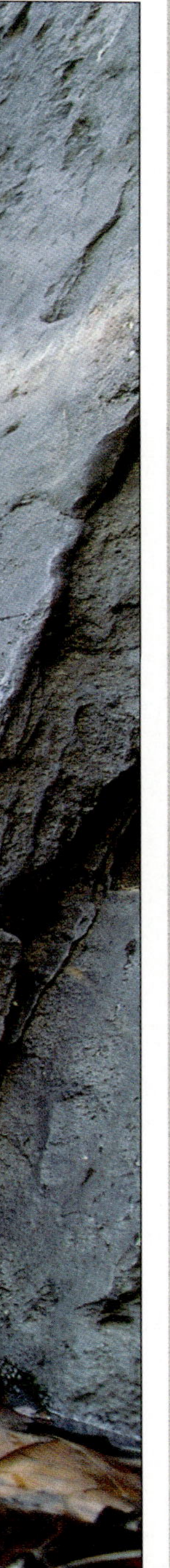

Michael Nichols
United States of America
RUNNER-UP

Tigress cooling herself

"The tigers of India's Bandhavgarh National Park, in Madhya Pradesh, are very elusive. So, using a remote camera system of my own design, I exposed a great deal of film to get a handful of images that provide a glimpse into their furtive lifestyles. Here, a young female cools herself in a pool reeking with the stench of monkey urine."

Nikon F4 with 300mm lens; 1/250 sec at f2.8; Fujichrome 100 rated at 200

Mary Ann McDonald
United States of America
HIGHLY COMMENDED

Leopard stretching

"This female leopard had been unsuccessful in her hunt of an impala in Buffalo Springs National Reserve, Kenya. She climbed onto a fallen tree, lay there for a while and then decided to follow her cub, who had gone into hiding in the bush after being disturbed by some baboons."

Nikon N90s with 500mm lens; beanbag; 1/30 sec at f4; Ektachrome 200

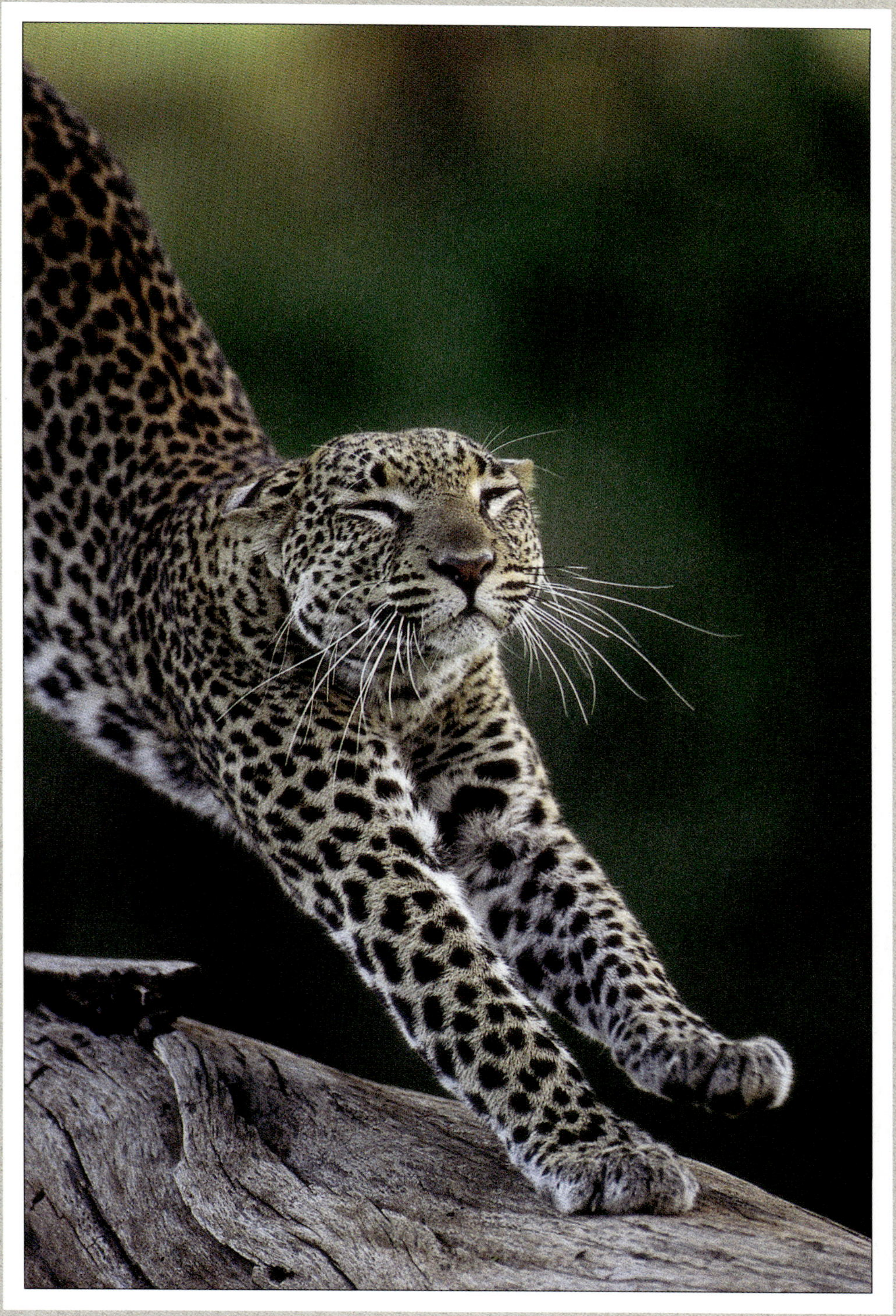

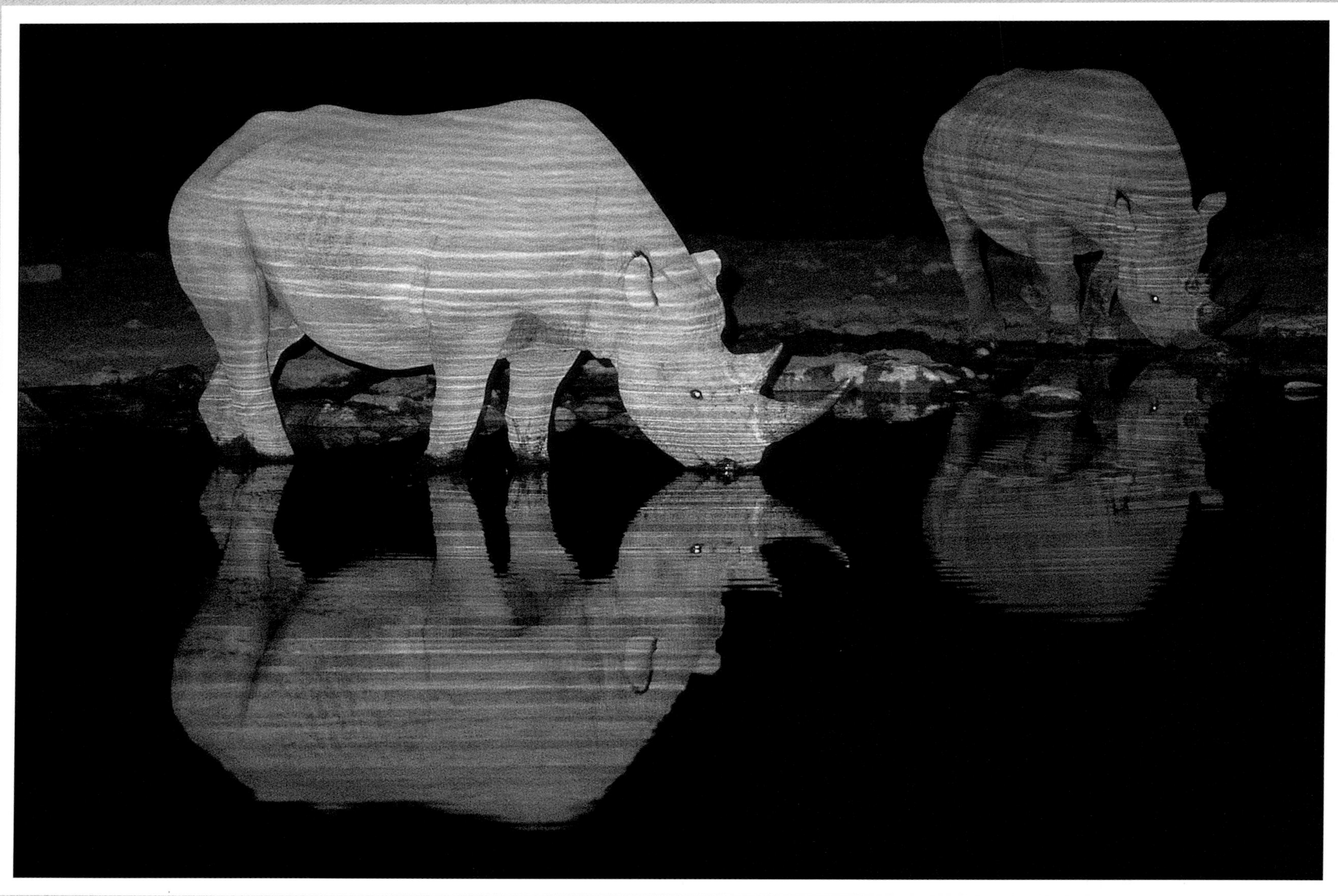

Wynand du Plessis

South Africa

HIGHLY COMMENDED

Rhinos drinking

"Black rhinos are usually solitary creatures, and in Etosha National Park, Namibia, mostly drink at night. However, at the waterhole interactions often occur between rhinos, as well as with other species such as lions and elephants, providing a fascinating insight into their social behaviour."

Nikon N801S with 75-210mm lens; hand-held flash; Fujichrome 100

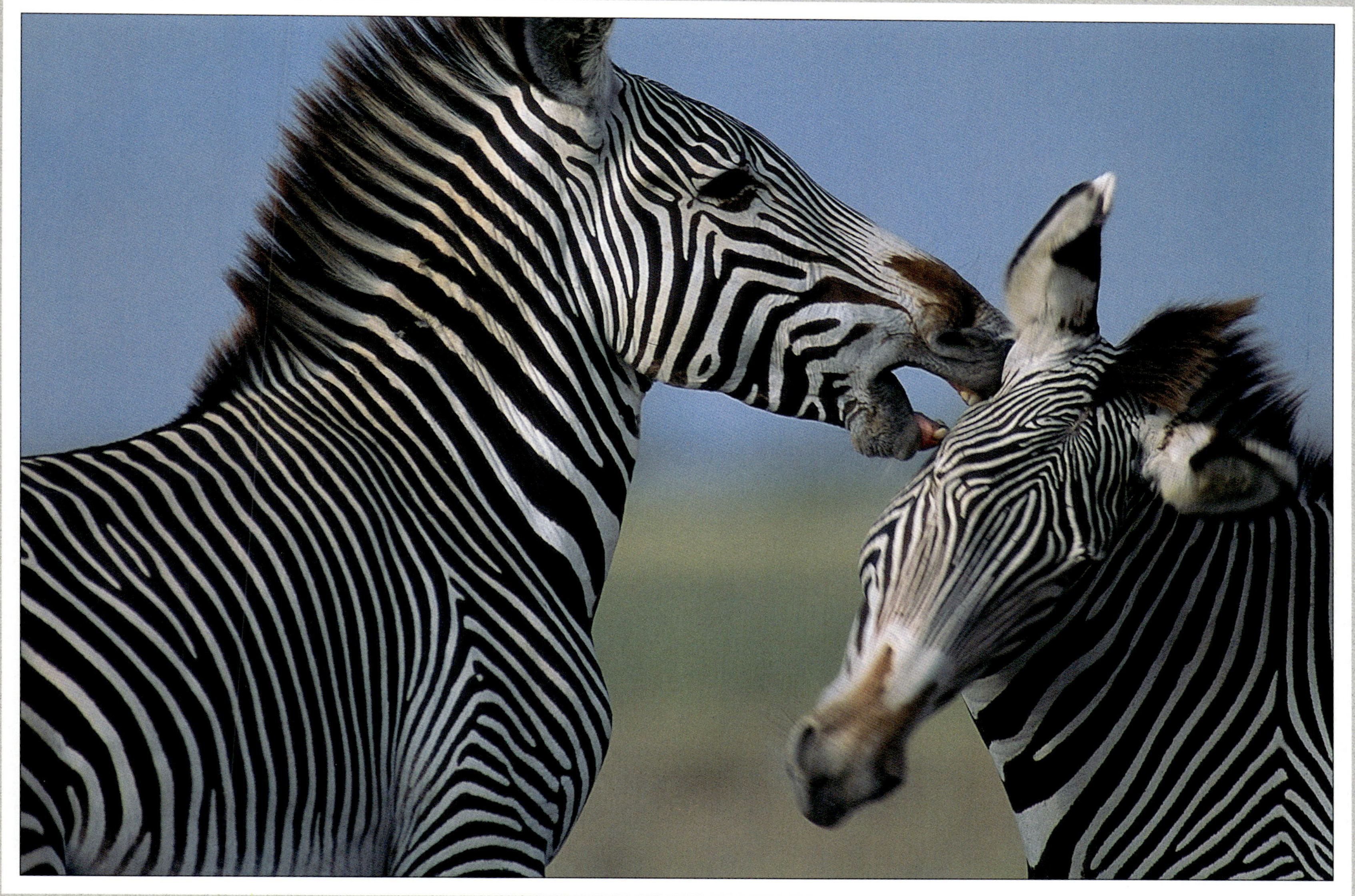

Karl Ammann
Switzerland
HIGHLY COMMENDED

Grevy's zebras sparring

"In spring the young stallions start to assert themselves and set up territories close to water. Grevy's zebras were once common throughout Africa, but are now only found in a few reserves in Ethiopia and Kenya. These were photographed at Buffalo Springs National Reserve, Kenya."

Nikon F5 with 800mm lens; f5.6; Fujichrome Sensia 100

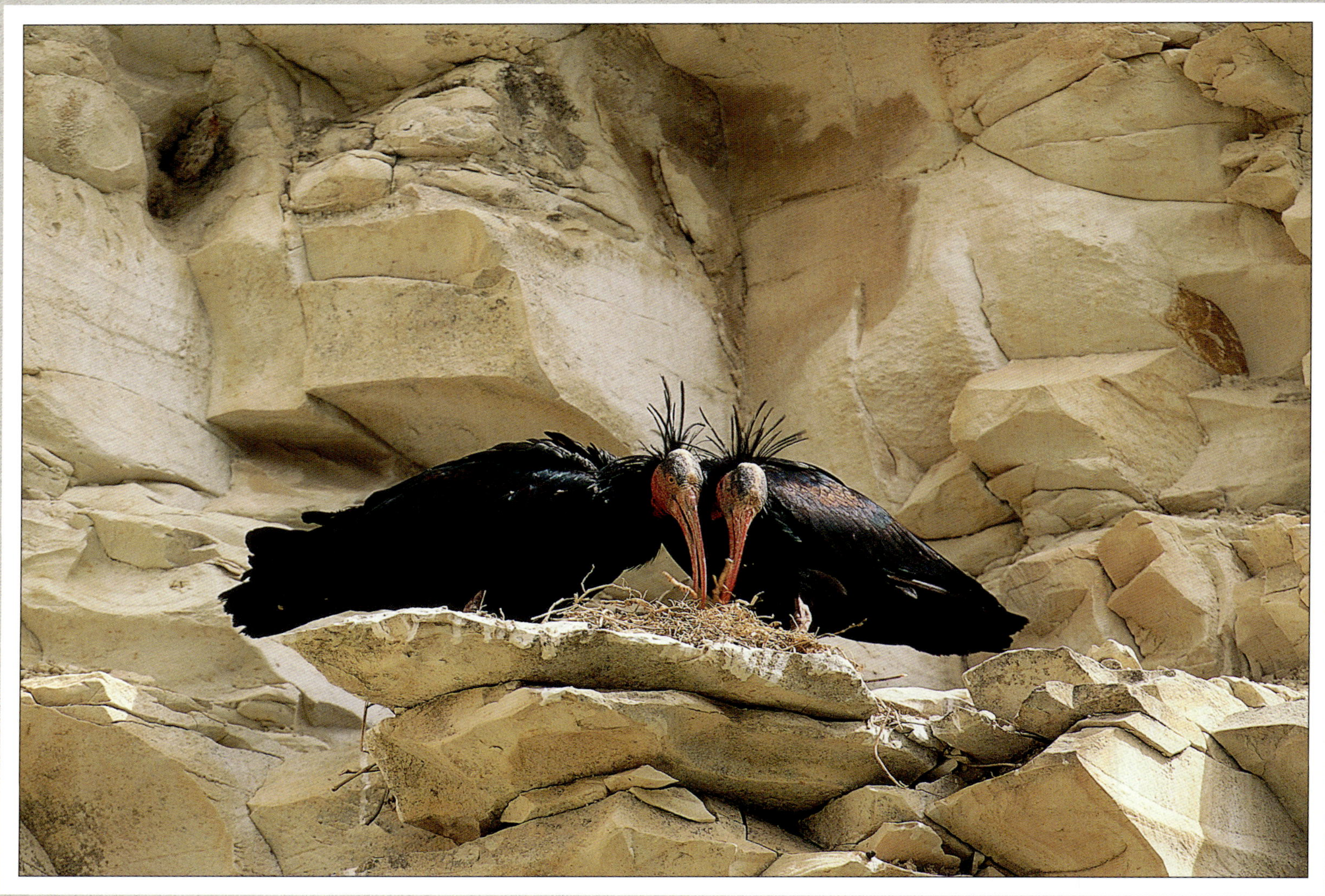

Carola Huhn
Germany
HIGHLY COMMENDED

Bald ibises

"These endangered birds were nesting on one of the special ledges set up by the World Wide Fund for Nature's breeding programme in Birecik, Turkey.
The project to re-establish the species, which died out in Turkey in 1989 due to pollution of the Euphrates, cannot be considered a complete success. Bald ibises are breeding again but they no longer migrate in the winter."

Nikon F4s with 500mm lens; tripod; Fujichrome Velvia

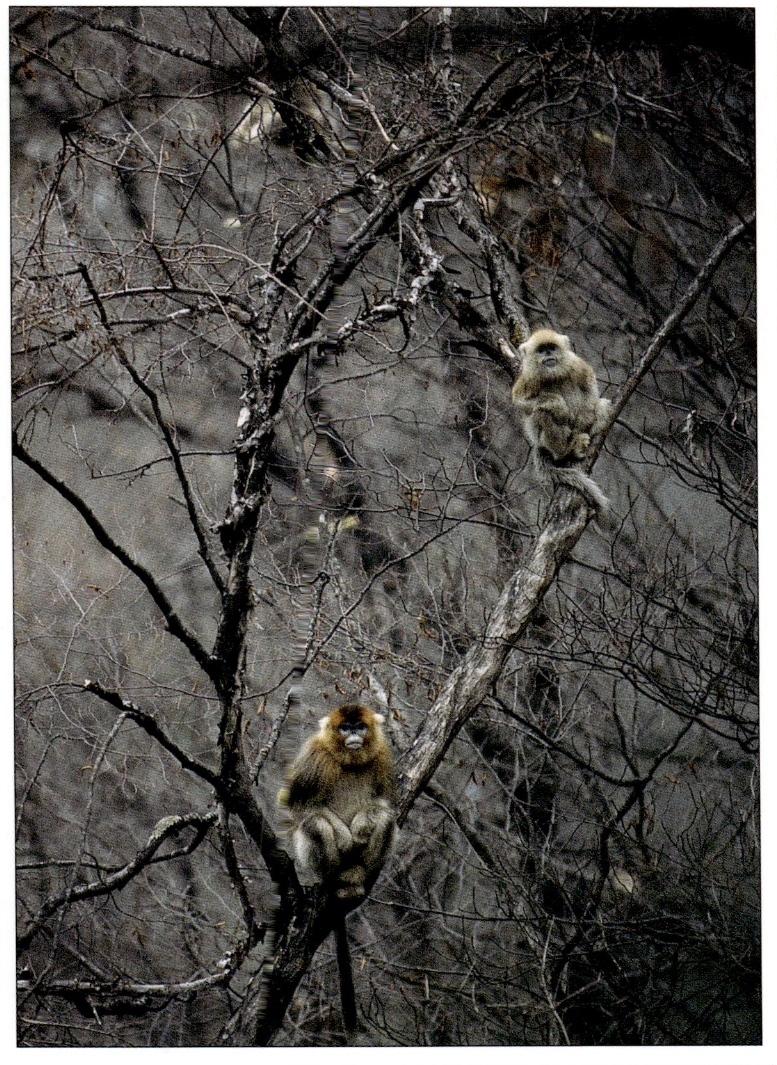

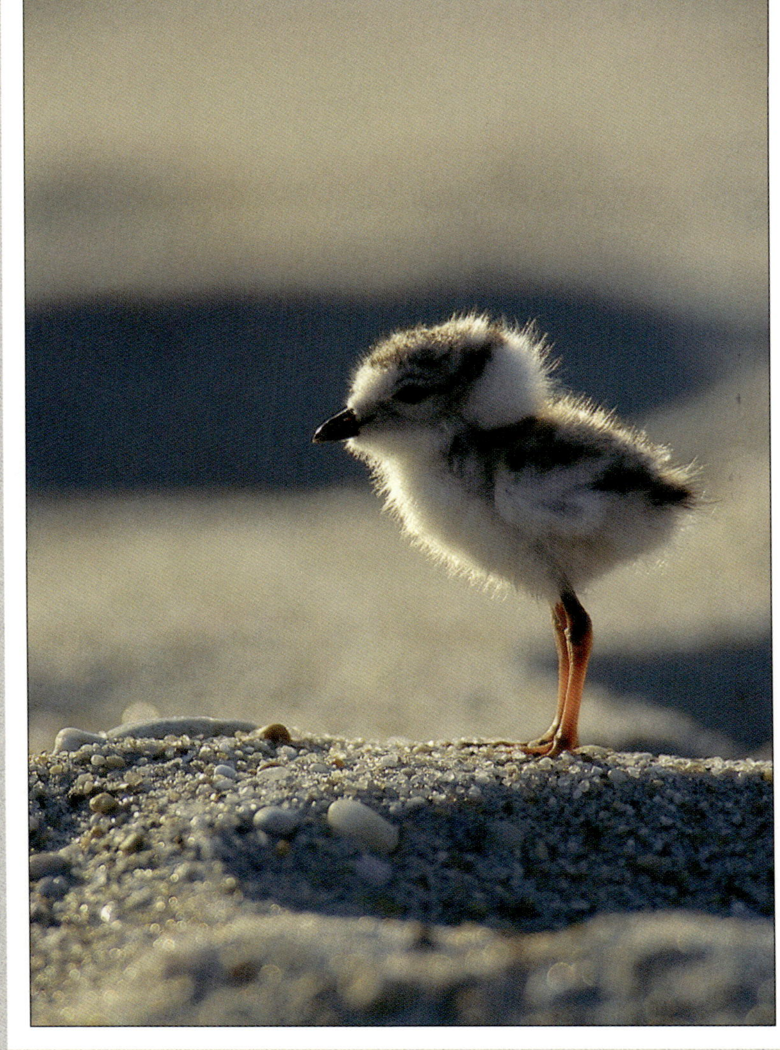

Roland Seitre
France
HIGHLY COMMENDED

Golden snub-nosed monkeys

"These monkeys inhabit the threatened bamboo and pine forests in the mountains of Sichuan, Western China, where temperatures can fall as low as –30°C. They are specially adapted to resist the cold. In the past they were hunted for their thick, warm fur, but despite 20 years of legal protection, their population still remains under 5,000."

Nikon F5 with 500mm lens; f4; Fujichrome Sensia 100

Richard Kuzminski
United States of America
HIGHLY COMMENDED

Piping plover chick

"While photographing the life cycle of the piping plover, in southern New Jersey, I was surprised when a clutch hatched two days earlier than expected. Just as the sun was setting, I managed to get close enough to this day-old chick. Eyes not fully open and unsure of each step, it must now fend for itself."

Canon EOS 1n with 400mm lens and x2 and x1.4 converters; 1/40 sec at f8; Fujichrome Sensia 100

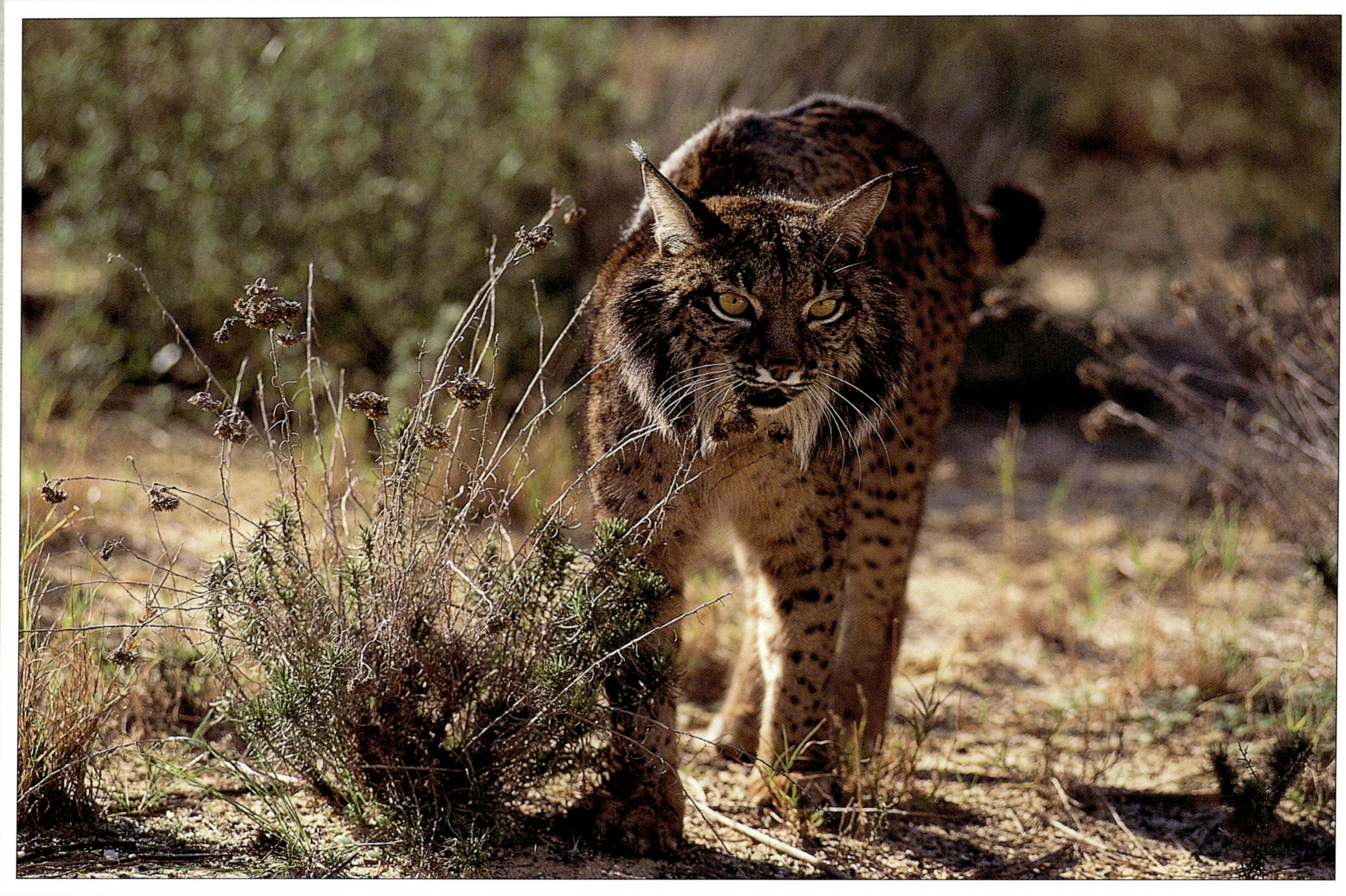

Juan Tébar Carrera
Spain
HIGHLY COMMENDED

Iberian lynx

"El Acebuche, an area in Doñana National Park, is very important for the endangered Iberian or pardel lynx. The park as a whole supports some 60 individuals. This species is smaller, has darker spots and a more pronounced beard than the common lynx."

Nikon F90x with 400mm lens; 1/250 sec at f8; Fujichrome Velvia

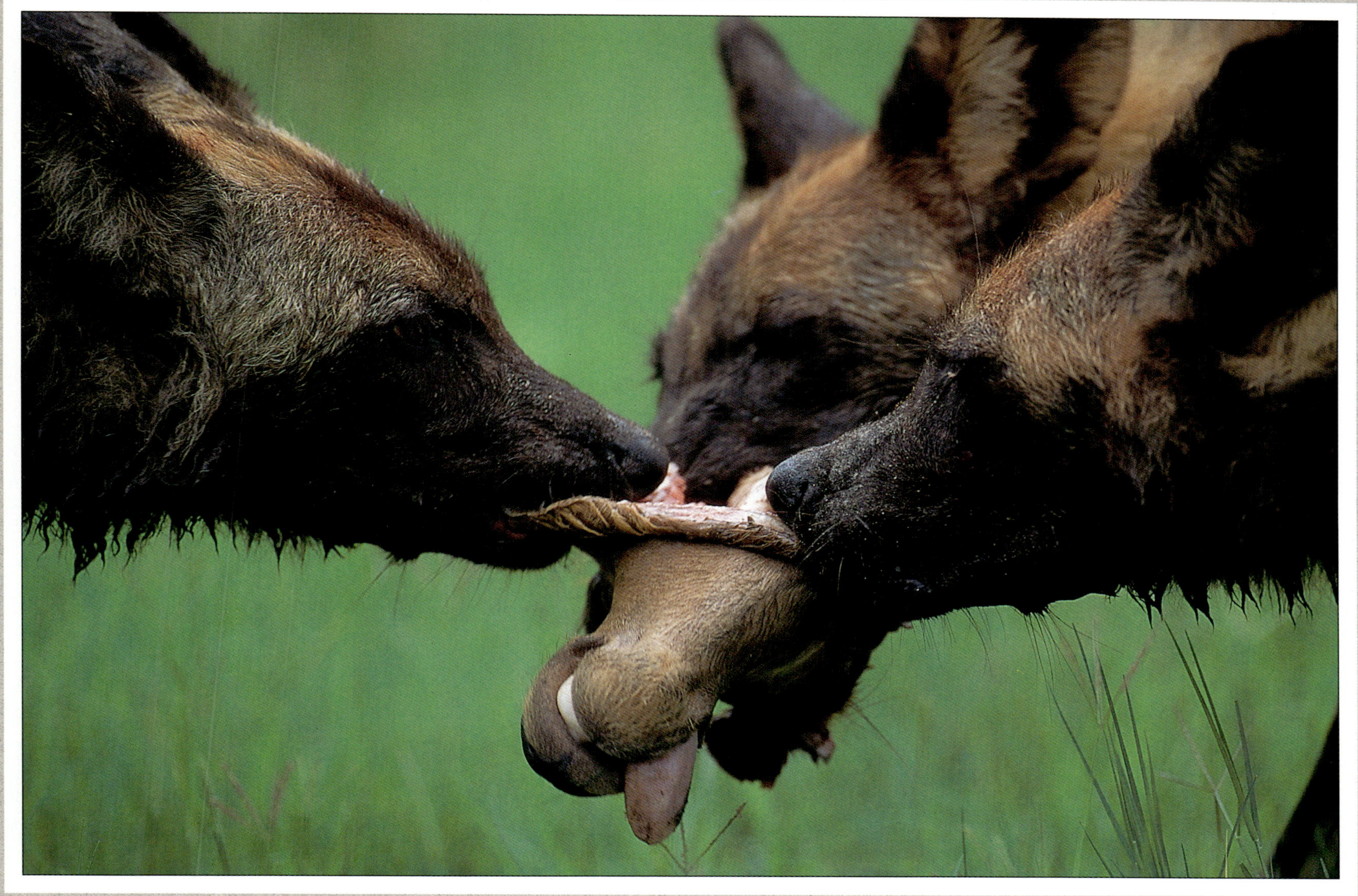

Adrian Bailey
South Africa
HIGHLY COMMENDED

Wild dogs with impala head

"These three yearlings were members of a pack of seven African wild dogs I photographed in Botswana's Moremi Game Reserve. After each kill, one of the youngsters would take a trophy from the carcass to carry as the pack moved on. Jealous of their sibling, the other two yearlings would constantly wrestle for possession of the prize."

Nikon F5 with 500mm lens; Fujichrome

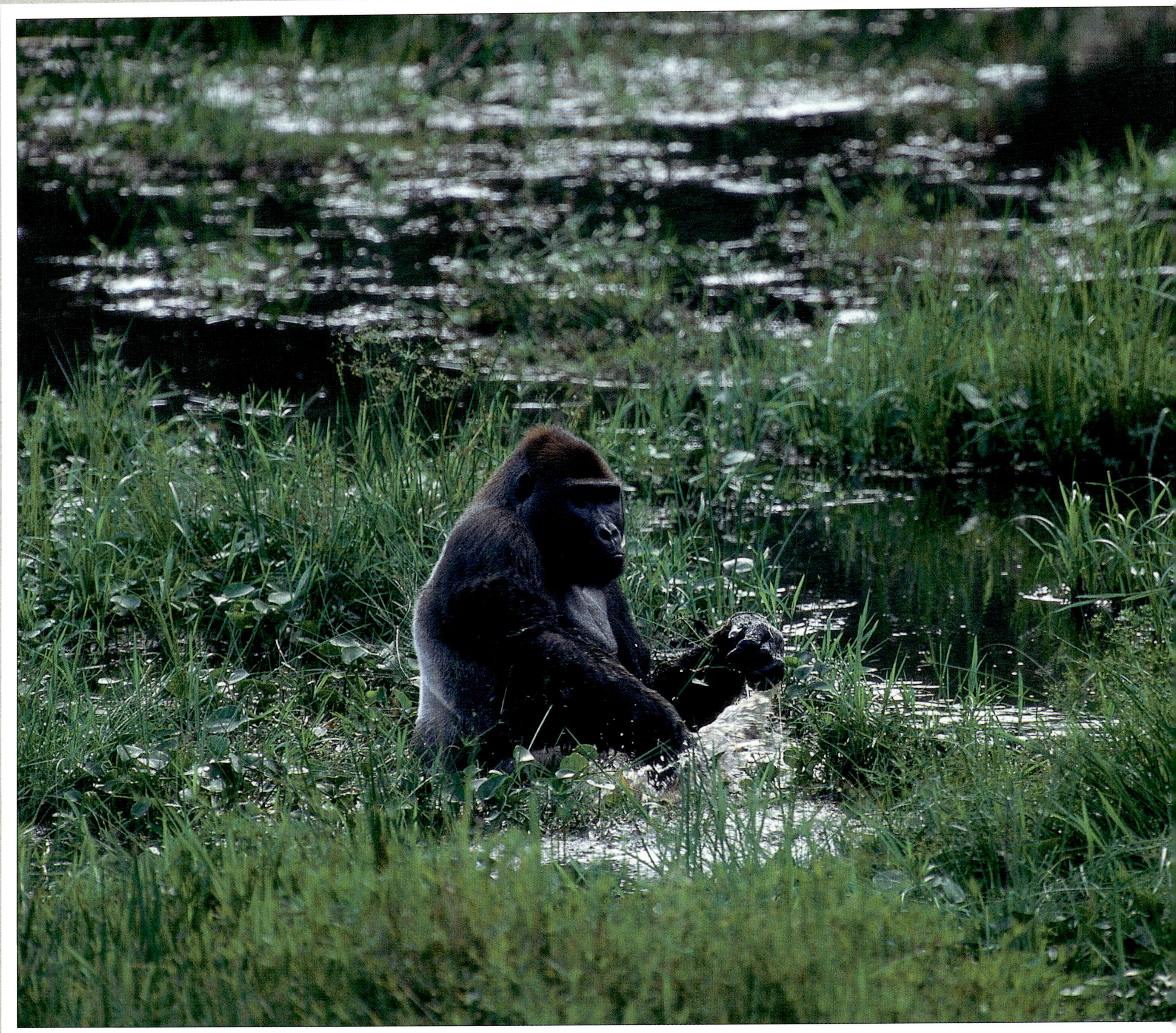

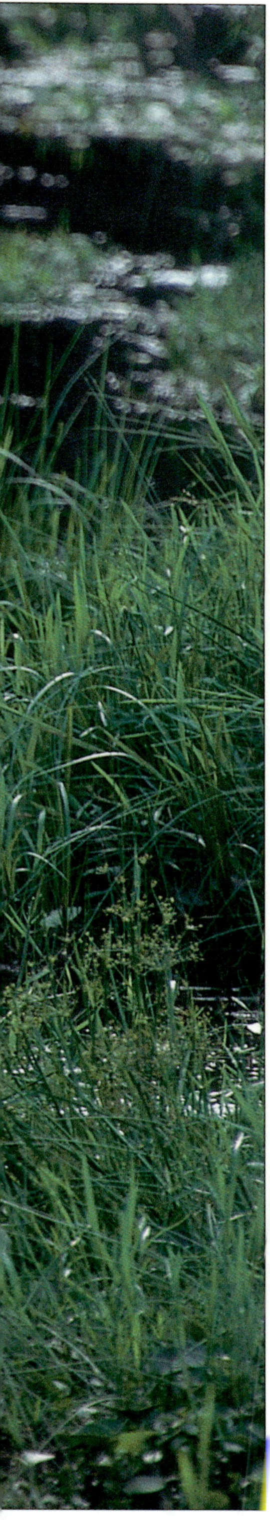

Michel & Yannick Stoffel-Willame
Belgium
HIGHLY COMMENDED

Western lowland gorilla feeding in water

"Until recently, it was believed that gorillas avoided water. But biologists have now discovered that lowland gorillas do not hesitate to wade into water to pick tasty aquatic plants. We spent ten days silently waiting on a platform in Nouabale-Ndoke National Park in the Congo before this silverback male approached close enough for us to take this picture."

Nikon F5 with 600mm lens and x1.4 converter; tripod; Fujichrome Sensia

Mike Hill
United Kingdom
HIGHLY COMMENDED

Young orang-utans

"These three young orang-utans came regularly to the feeding stations in the forest in Tanjung Puting National Park, which were set up by Birutė Galdikas as part of a long-term research programme. Sadly these individuals may no longer be alive as the forest fires in late 1997 killed many great apes."

Nikon F90X with 80-200mm lens; fill-in flash

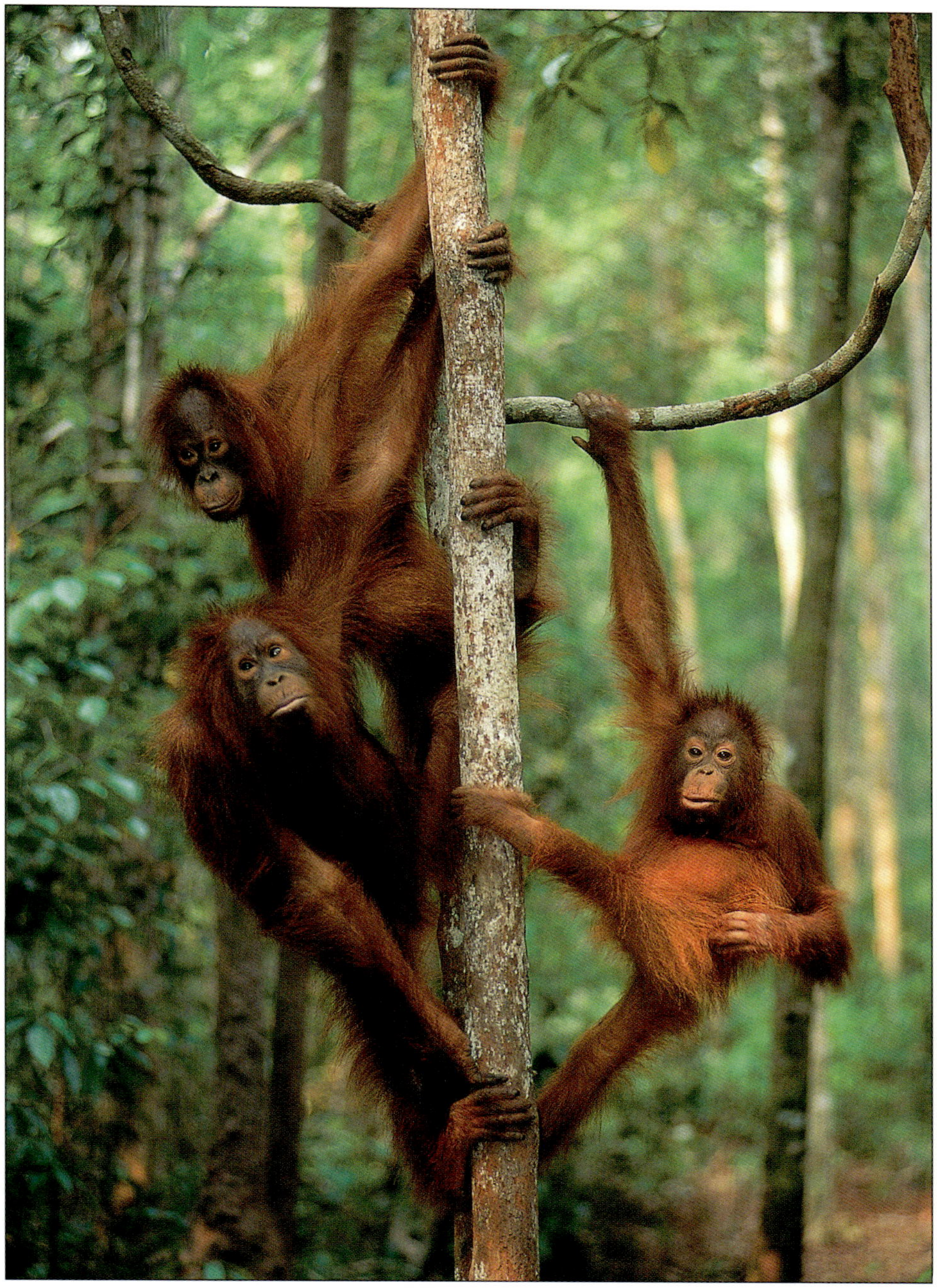

Animal Portraits

The photographs entered in this category should show the subjects in close-up.

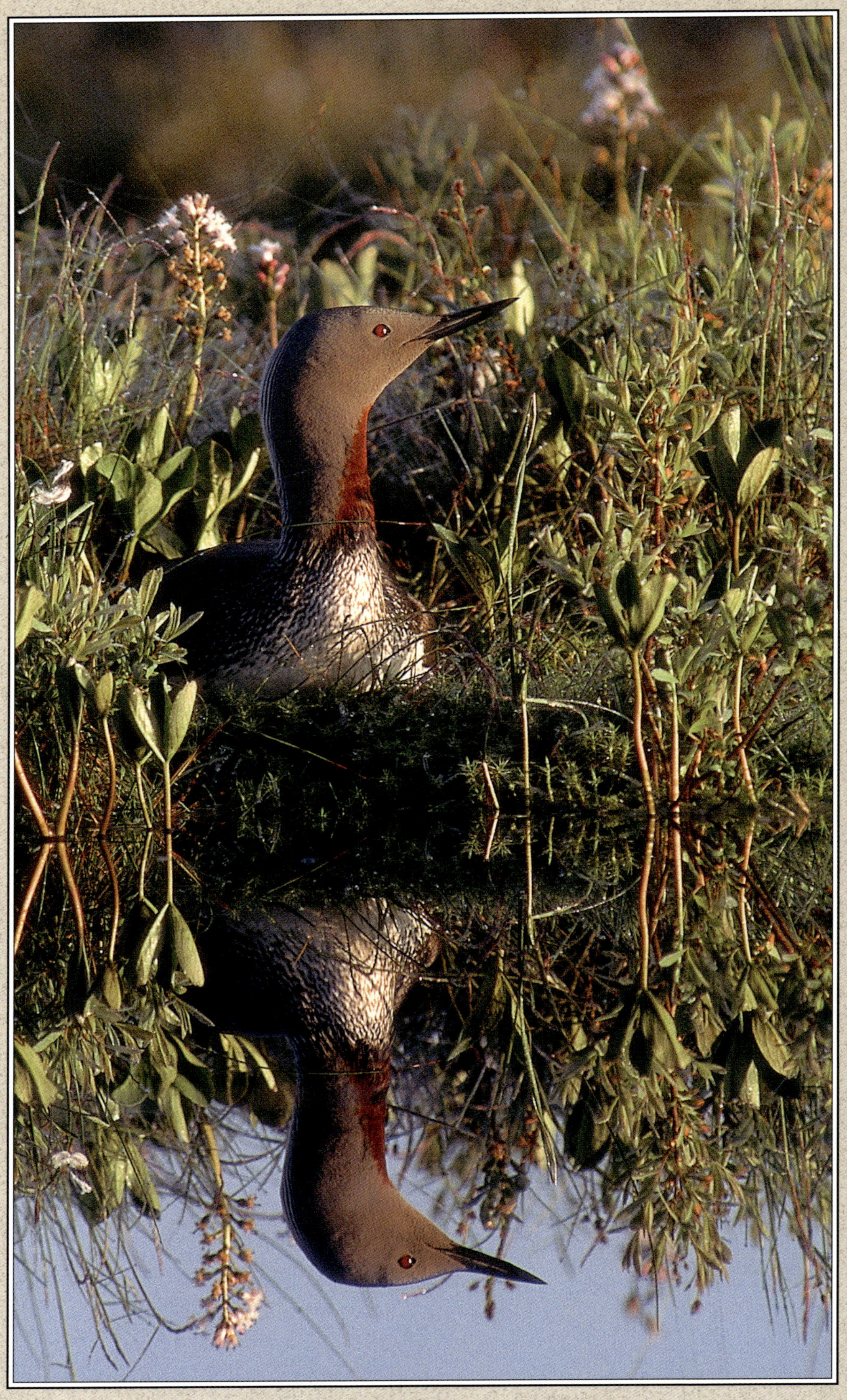

Geoff Doré
United Kingdom
WINNER

Red-throated diver

"I entered the hide under cover of darkness, and my wait for sunrise was rewarded by the striking position and pose of this diver as she brooded her two chicks among the bogbean. The whole portrait was reflected perfectly in the mirror-calm water of the lochan. Half an hour later the 'mirror' had disappeared as the breeze picked up and ripples covered the water."

Nikon F4s with 400mm lens and x1.4 converter; tripod; 1/30 sec at f3.5; Fujichrome Provia at 100

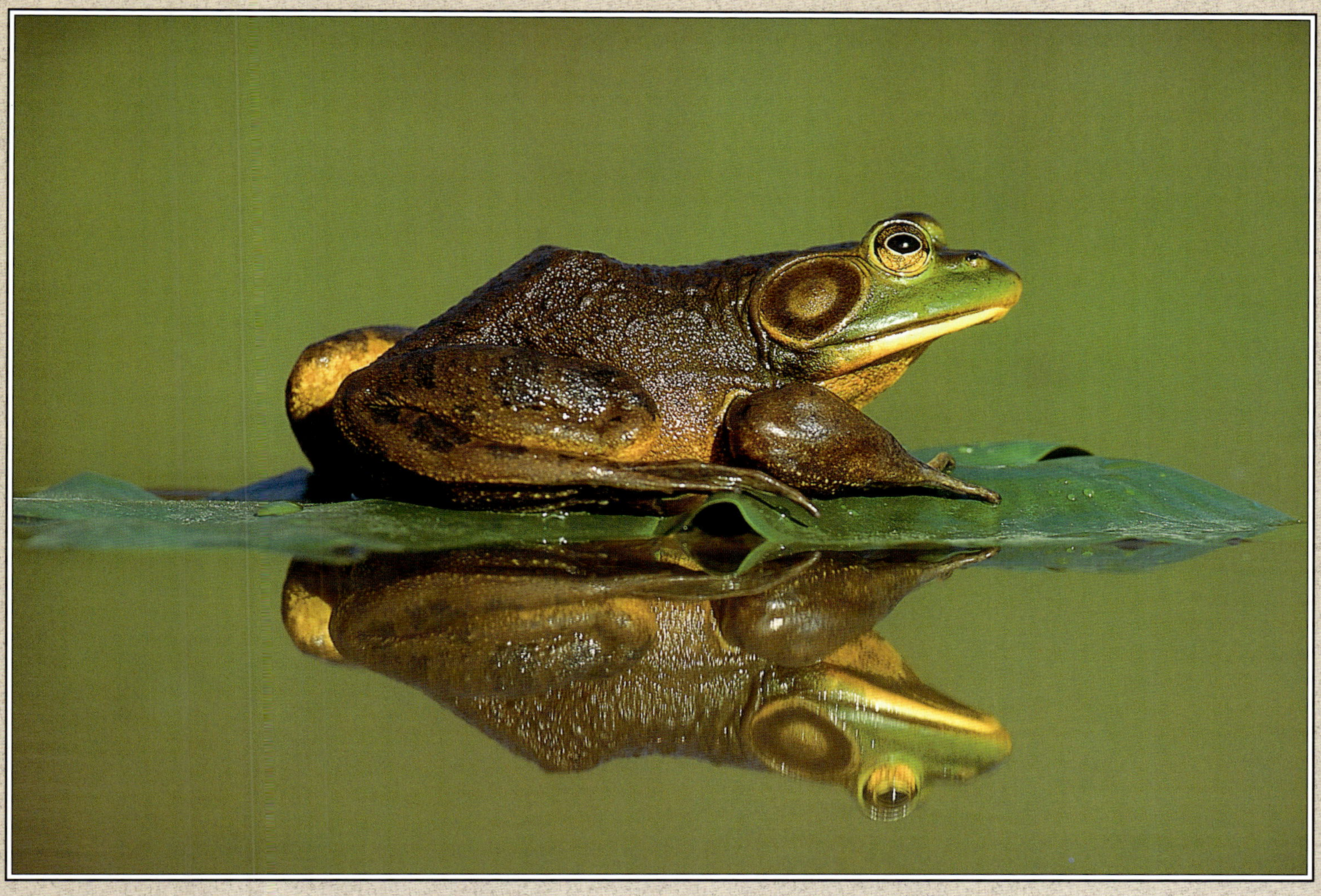

John Mielcarek
United States of America
RUNNER-UP

Bullfrog

"This male bullfrog regularly sunned himself on a patch of waterlilies, but would not let me get close. One afternoon I walked slowly into the pond right up to my neck, extended the tripod and crept nearer still. My lens was an inch above the water, and I was 20ft from him. I shot three frames, he jumped, never to be seen again."

Canon F1 with 500mm lens and 50mm tube; tripod; 1/125 sec at f4.5; Fujichrome 100

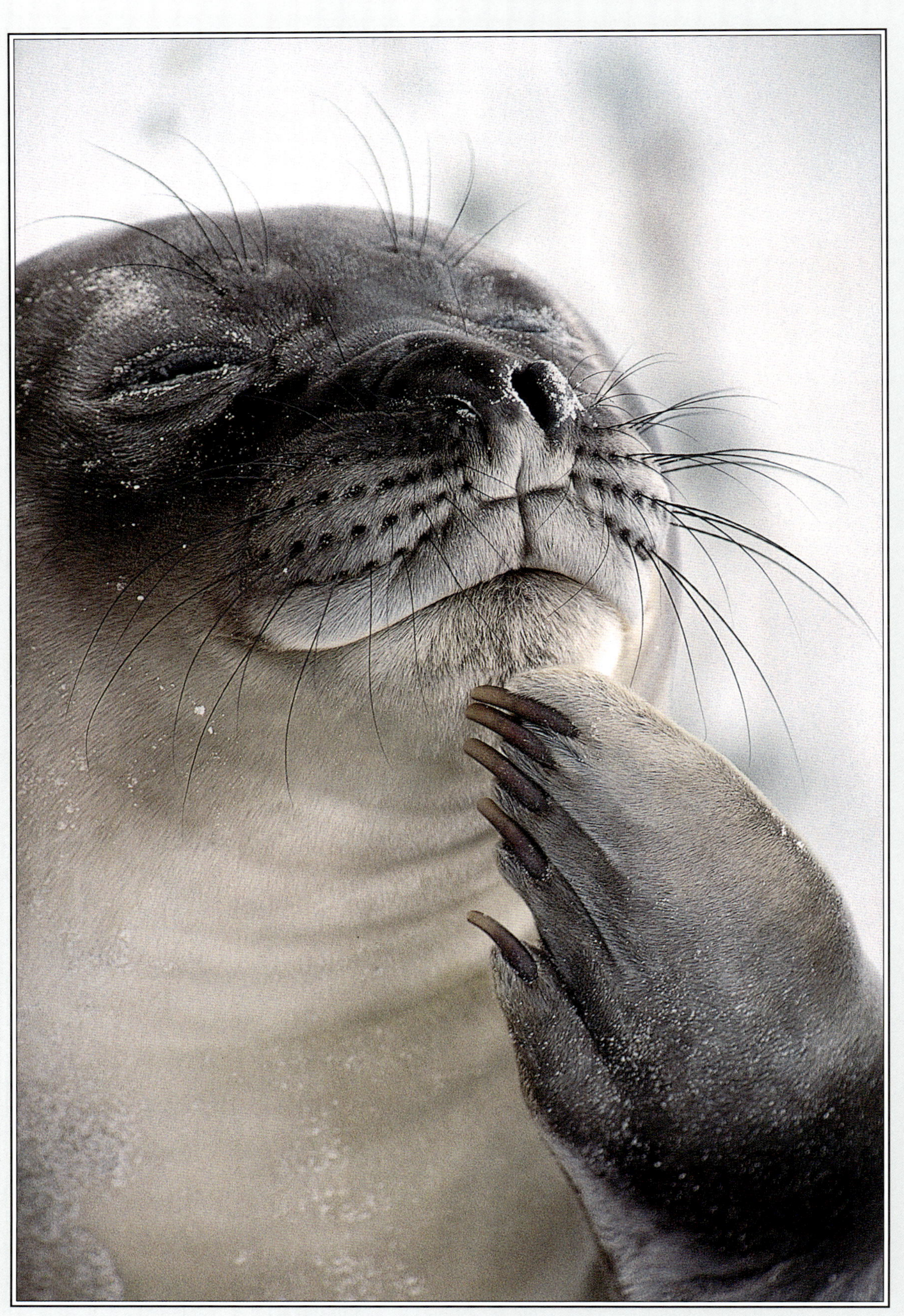

Edmund Fellowes
United Kingdom
SPECIALLY COMMENDED

Elephant seal pup

"I was photographing this pup on Sea Lion Island, in the Falklands, when it 'sat up' and scratched its chin. I just had time to swivel the camera to the portrait format."

Canon EOS 500 with 300mm lens and x2 converter; tripod; 1/125 sec at f5.6; Fujichrome Sensia 100

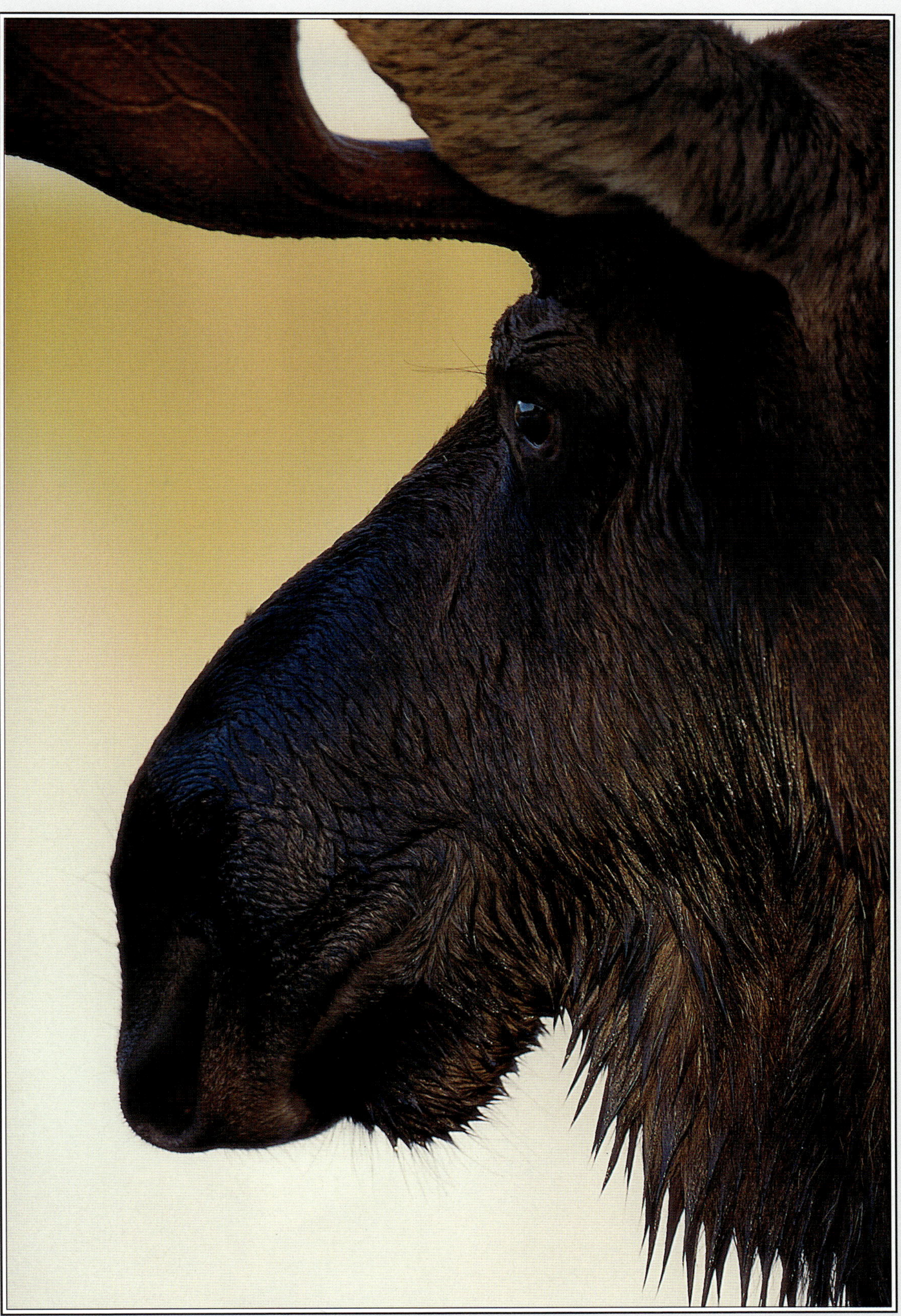

John J Mullin
United States of America
HIGHLY COMMENDED

Bull moose

"It was the rut in Baxter State Park, Maine, and a large bull came down to drink. He soon lost interest in his cows and moved towards me until he was inside my close-focus range (16ft). As I spoke softly to him, he plunged his head into the water and came up with a mouthful of vegetation. He then moved just far enough away to be in focus."

Canon T90 with 500mm lens; tripod; Ektachrome 100

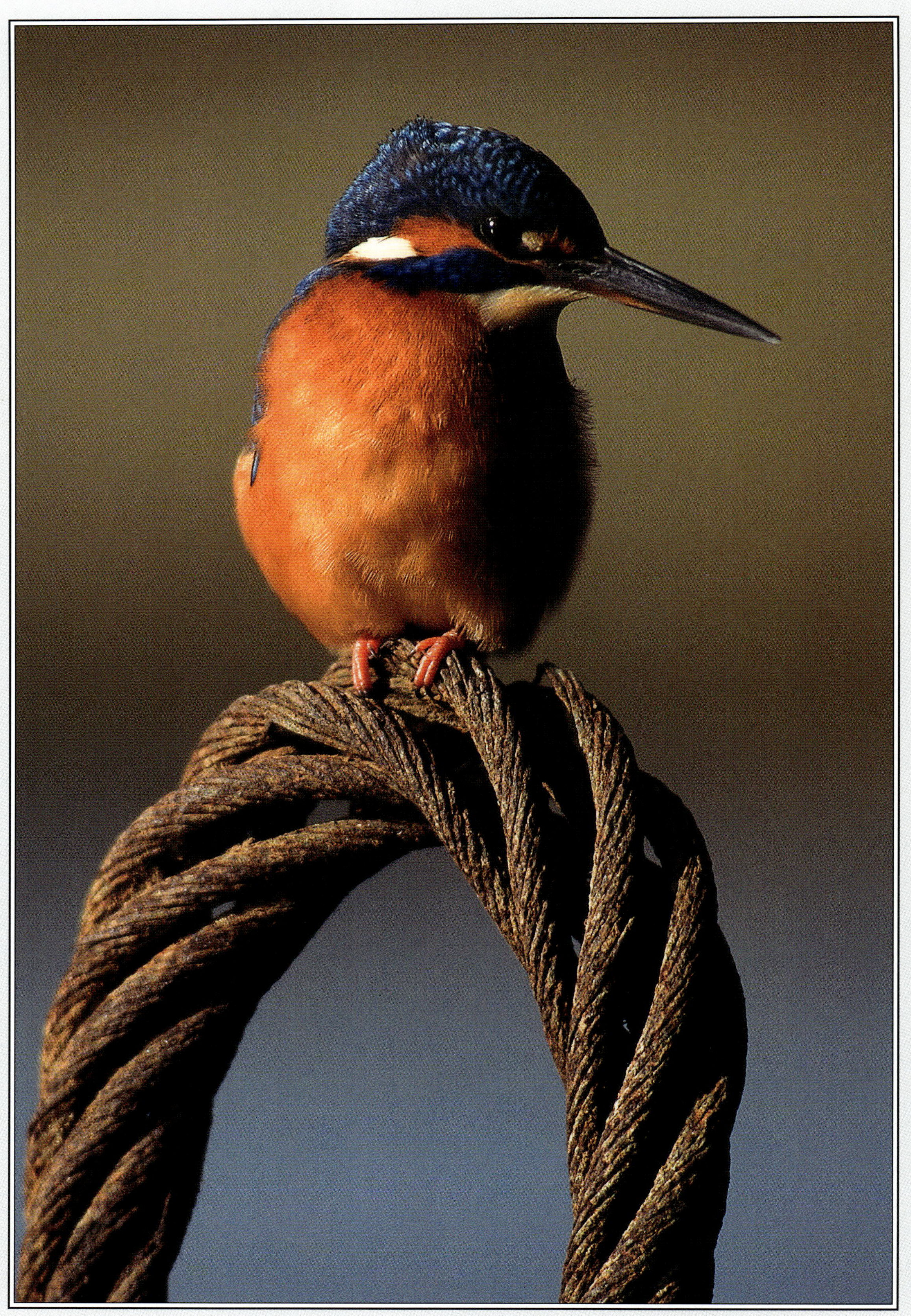

Russell Hartwell
United Kingdom
HIGHLY COMMENDED

Kingfisher

"Discarded metal hawsers, formerly used to tether barges at some flooded gravel workings in Buckinghamshire, offered this original portrait. The taut, twisted metal contrasts with the soft feathers of the kingfisher, with the rusting metal and russet plumage glowing in the winter sunlight."

Nikon F4 with 500mm lens and 25mm extension tube; tripod; 1/250 sec at f6.7; Fujichrome Provia 100

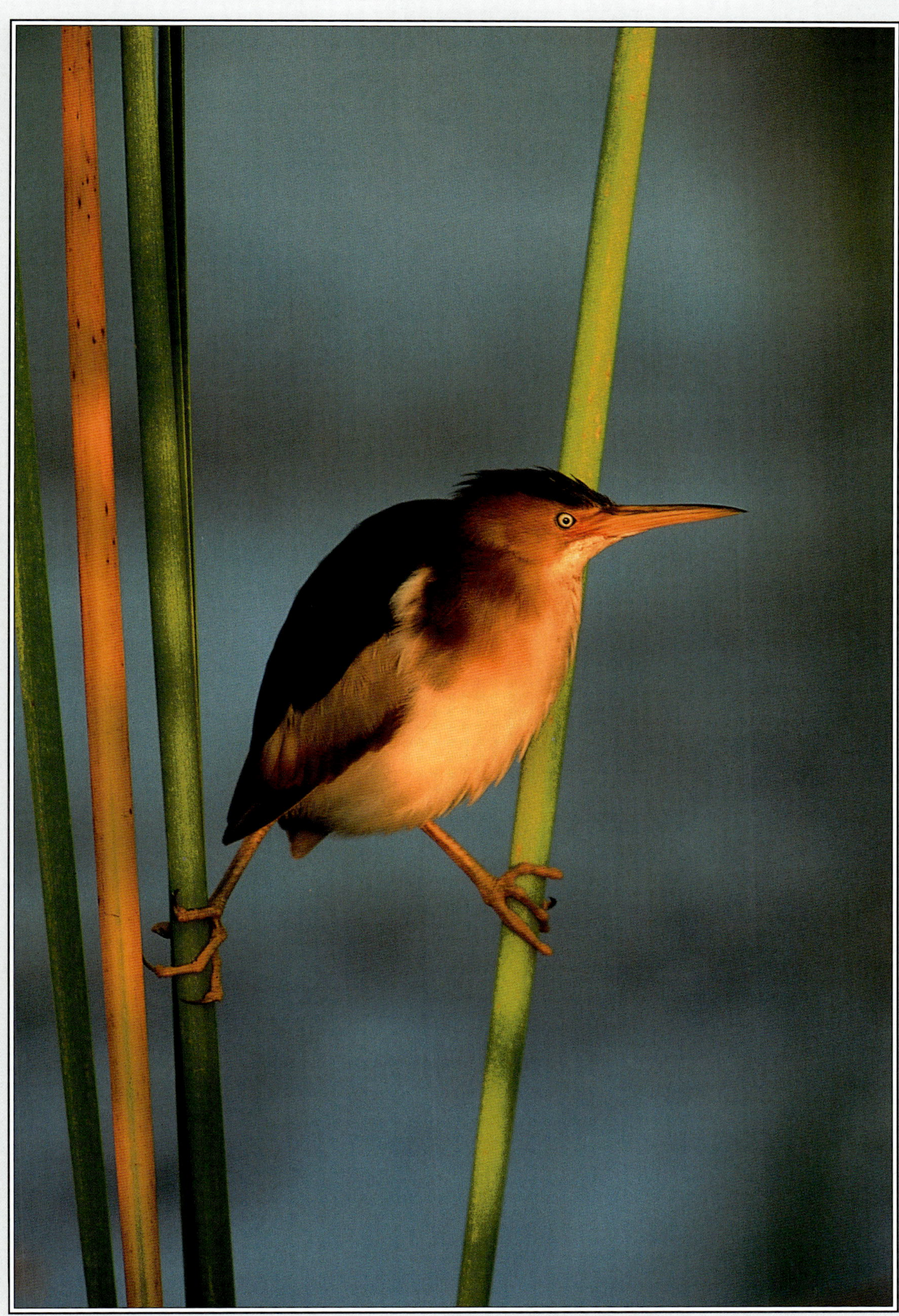

Dr Mamoru Yoshida
United States of America
HIGHLY COMMENDED

Least bittern

"When I came face to face with this shy, cryptic bird in Arthur R Marshall Loxahatchee National Wildlife Refuge, Florida, the early-morning light was poor. To minimise camera shake, I locked up the mirror and managed to get a few good shots before the bittern flew off."

Canon EOS A2 with 500mm lens and x1.4 converter; tripod; 1/45 sec at f6.7; Fujichrome Velvia

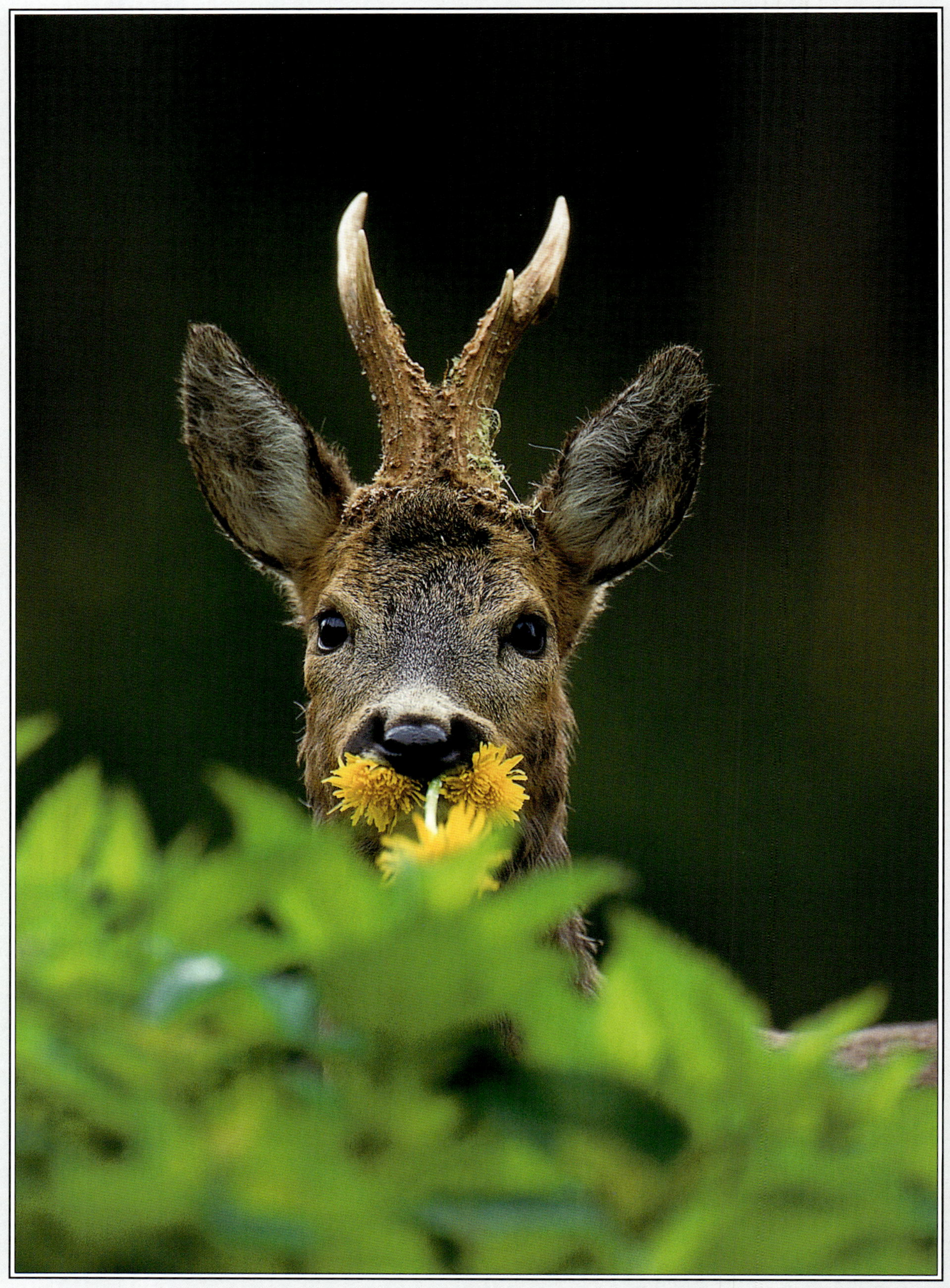

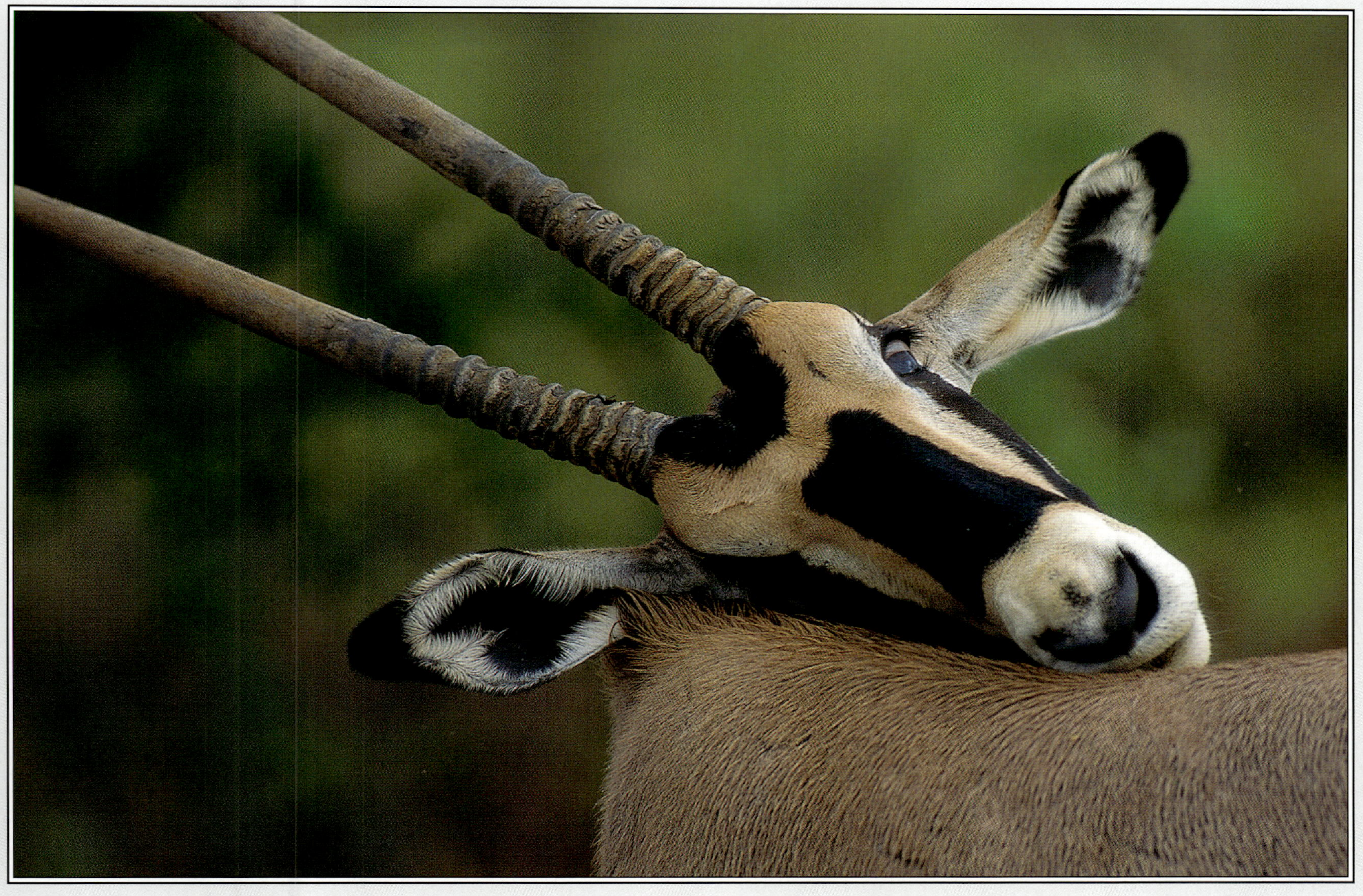

Mary Ann McDonald
United States of America
HIGHLY COMMENDED

Gemsbok scratching

"I was watching a large herd of gemsbok at Buffalo Springs National Reserve, Kenya, trying to capture the interesting patterns they formed. This individual reached back to bite at an itch. It was a case of being in the right place at the right time."

Nikon N90s with 500mm lens; beanbag; 1/500 sec at f4; Fujichrome Sensia 100

Manfred Danegger
Germany
HIGHLY COMMENDED

Roebuck

"I was in Bregenzer-Wald, Austria, in August when the deer were in rut. This picture of a male roe deer was taken from my car."

Nikon F5 with 600mm lens and converter; 1/500 sec at f5.6; Fujichrome Sensia 100

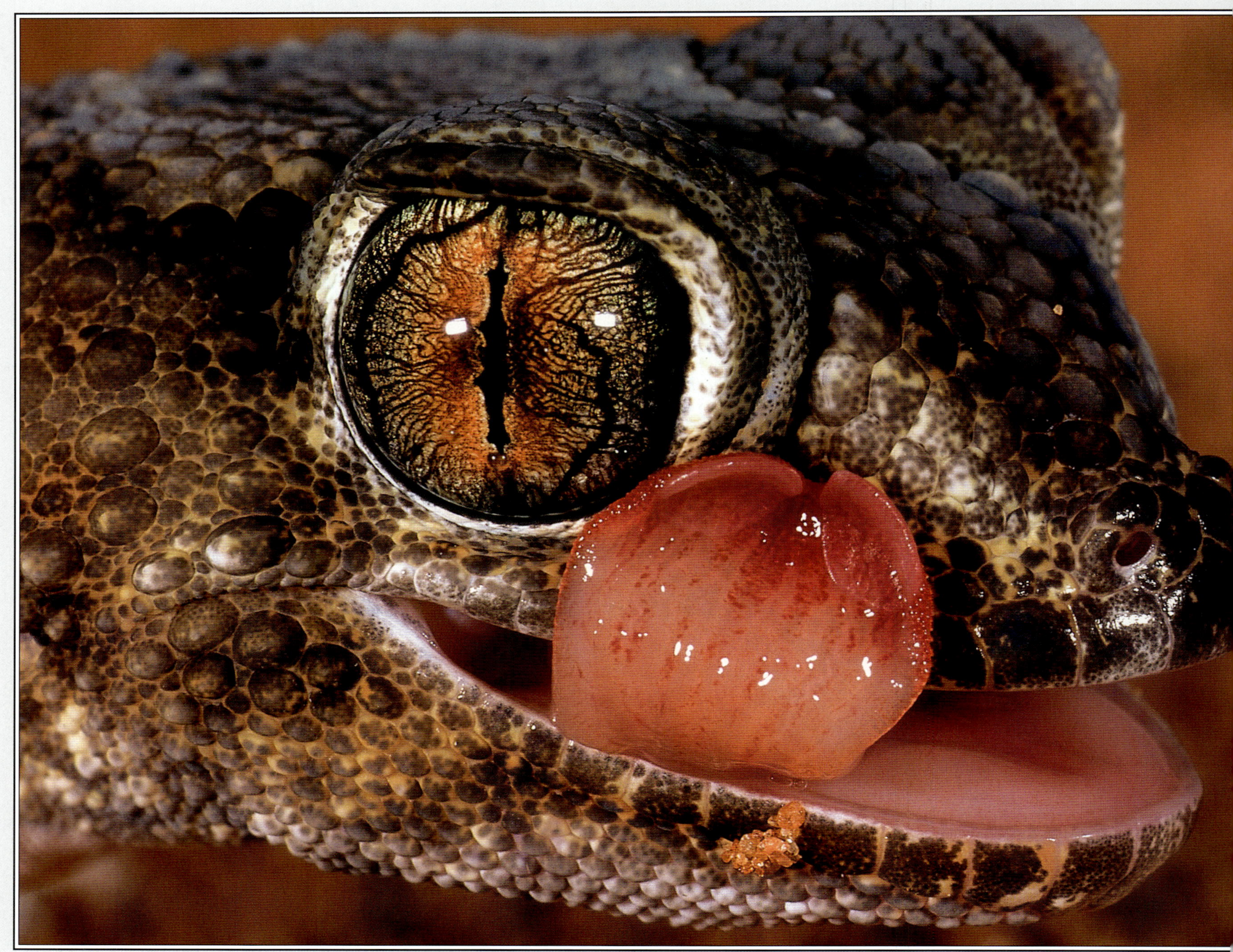

Martin Harvey

South Africa

HIGHLY COMMENDED

Giant ground gecko

"This 'grooming behaviour' seems to be characteristic of the desert-dwelling geckos which use their tongues to clean dust and moisture off their eyes. The giant ground gecko is nocturnal, and found in the Kalahari and Namib deserts."

Canon EOS A2 with 1[illegible]0 macro lens; two flashes; 1/125 sec at f32; Fujichrome Velvia

Michael Cufer

Australia

HIGHLY COMMENDED

Scorpion fish

"This scorpion fish was sheltered in among the kelp and other seaweeds in the protected area at Poor Knights Islands, New Zealand. Despite their sinister appearance, these fish are harmless and very approachable. But they taste disgusting."

Nikon F801 with 60mm macro lens; underwater housing; 1/125 sec at f16; Fujichrome Velvia

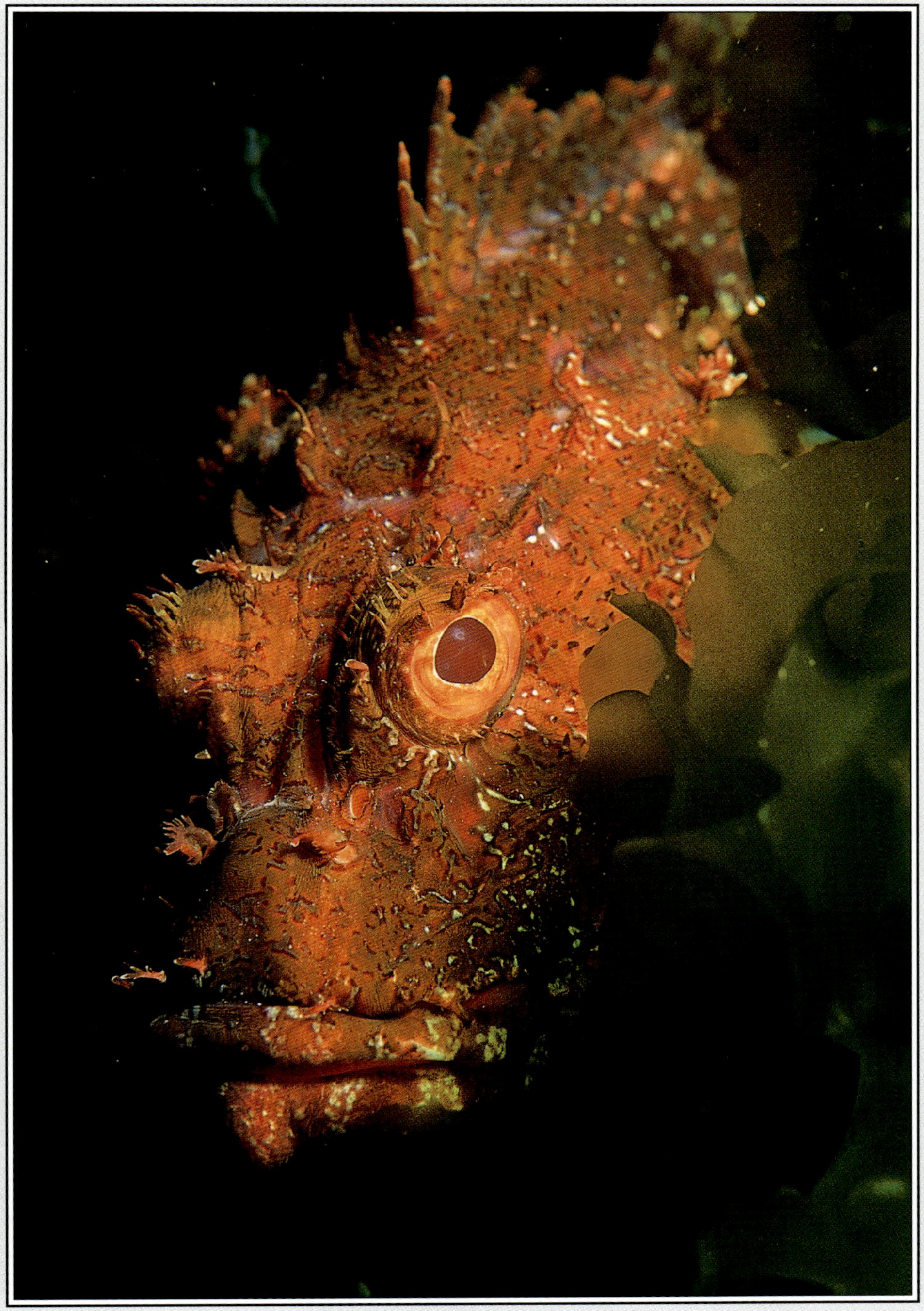

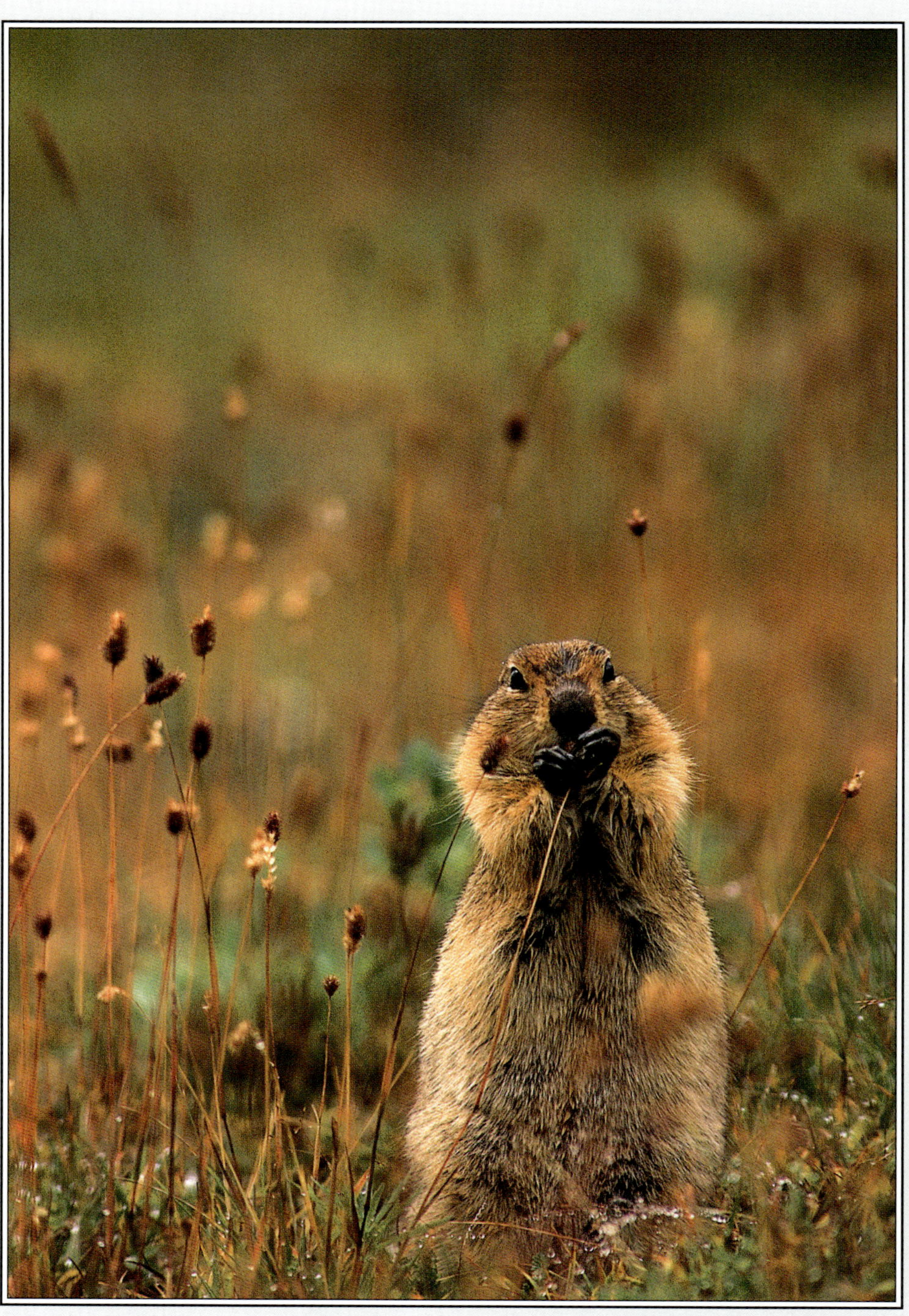

Barbara A Brundege
United States of America
HIGHLY COMMENDED

Arctic ground squirrel

"I spotted this Arctic ground squirrel eating the seedhead of a grass in Denali National Park, Alaska."

Nikon F4 with 300mm lens; 1/125 sec at f5.6; Fujichrome 100

Tim Neal
United Kingdom
HIGHLY COMMENDED

Red fox

"I had been watching this vixen in my orchard in the Blackmore Vale, Dorset, even before I owned a camera. She had become used to my presence, and would even appear when signalled. I always had this particular photograph in mind as it captures the true beauty of the fox. Being able to watch her at such close quarters was absolutely brilliant."

Nikon F90 with 70-210mm lens; 1/80 sec at f5.6; Fujichrome Sensia 100

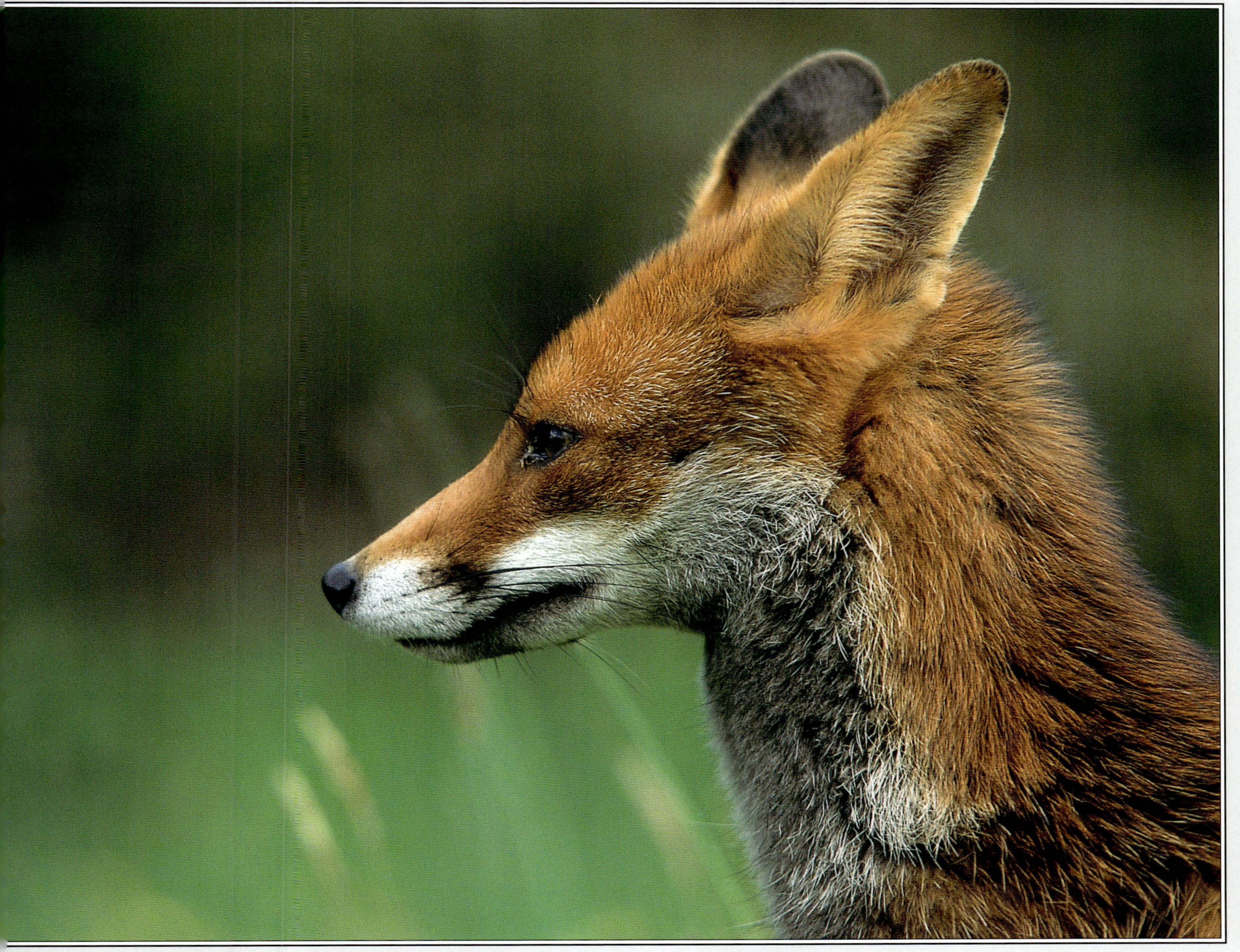

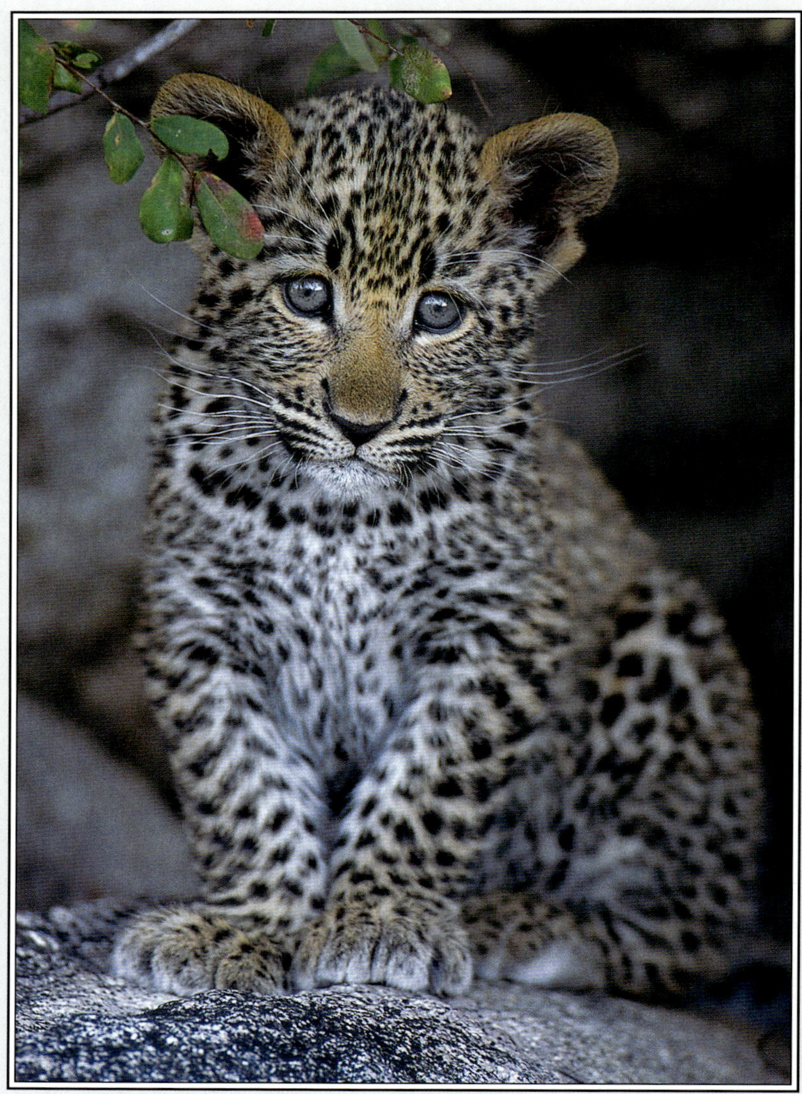

Peter Chadwick
South Africa
HIGHLY COMMENDED

Leopard cub

"This cub was the only one of the litter and was very bold. I often watched it at the entrance to its lair, in Mala Mala Game Reserve, amusing itself by chasing its tail or tumbling in the leaves."

Nikon FX90 with 300mm lens; flash; 1/60 sec at f4; Fujichrome Provia 100

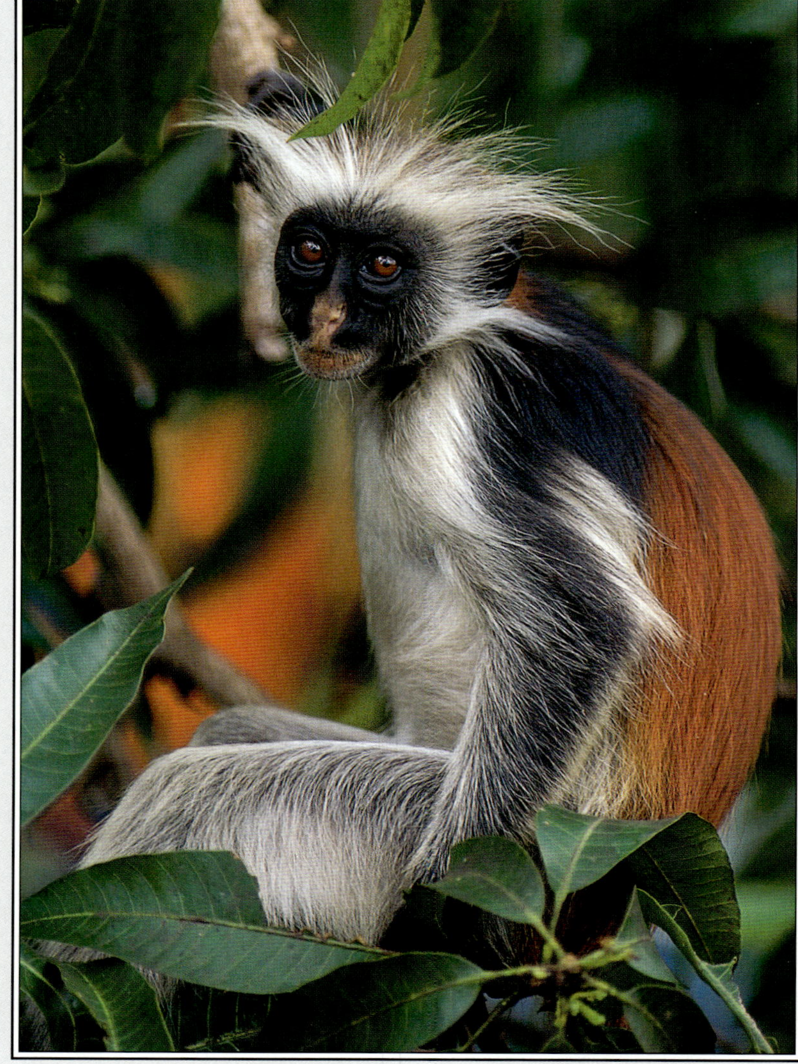

Raoul Slater
Australia
HIGHLY COMMENDED

Red colobus

"Many monkeys can be aggressive when they become familiar with people, but the wild colobuses of Jozani Forest Reserve, on Zanzibar Island, are gentle and amiable. One young monkey did cause me some grief. Fascinated by my tripod, he gave it a good shake each time I took a photograph. Only this shot was sharp."

Canon EOS A2 with 300mm lens; tripod; 1/30 sec at f4; Ektachrome Elite 100

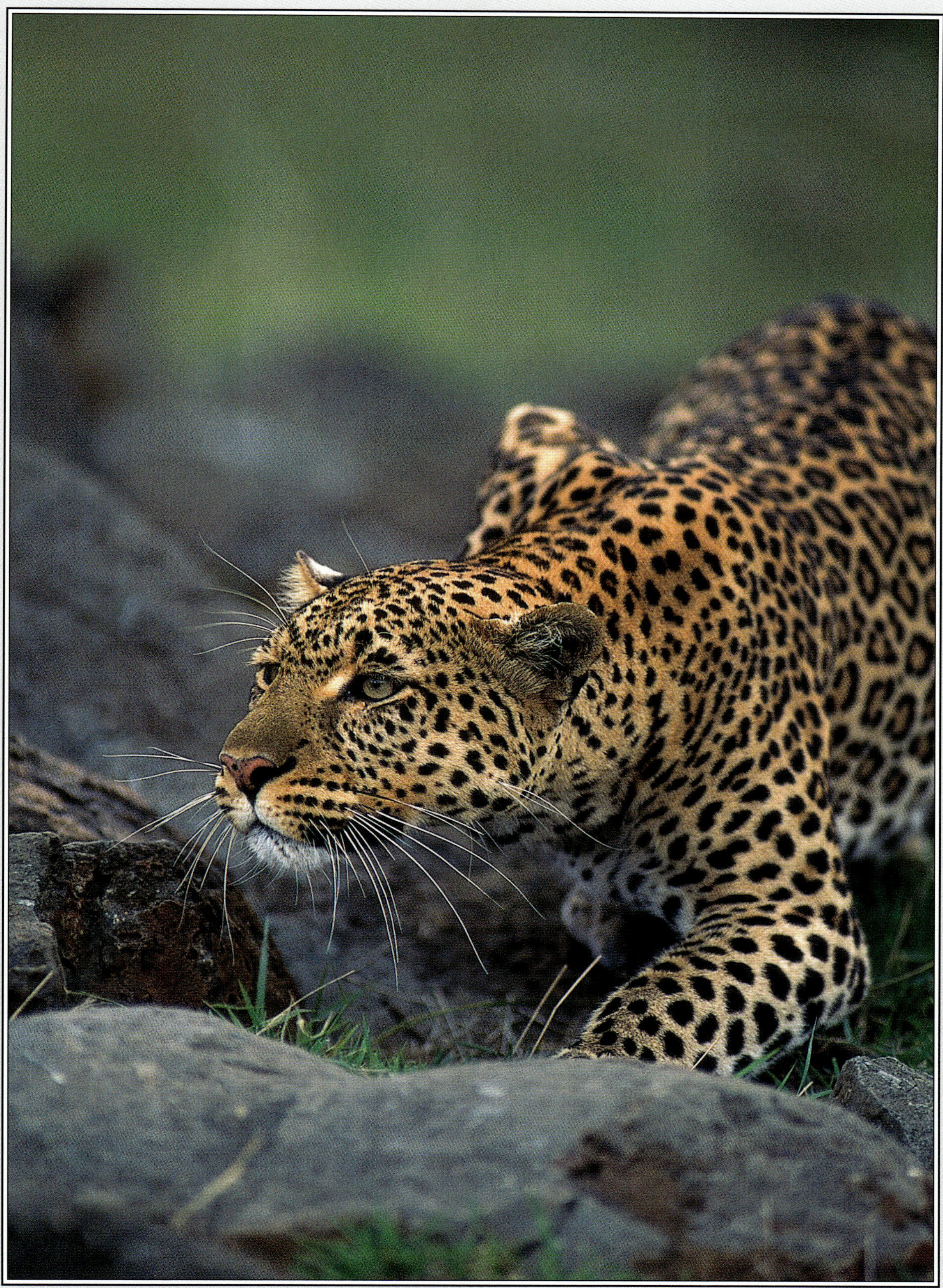

Anup Shah
United Kingdom
HIGHLY COMMENDED

Stalking leopard

"With total concentration on her prey, this female leopard stalked an unwary impala browsing in the Maasai Mara. Despite her stealth, the impala became aware of her presence. The leopard gave up and began to groom herself vigorously – a reaction typical of her kind."

Canon EOS 600 with 600mm lens; 1/125 sec at f5.6; Fujichrome

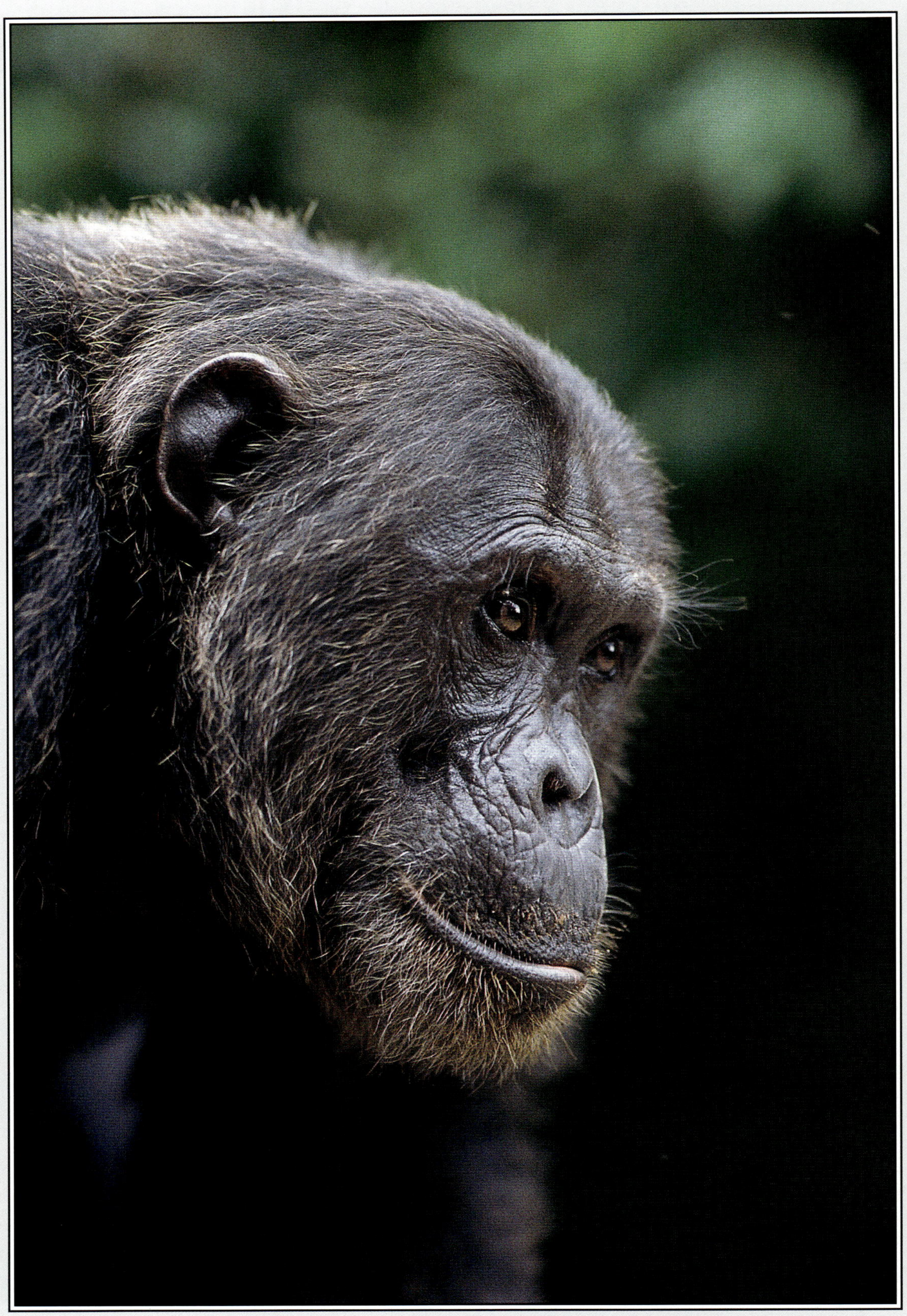

Jonathan Scott
United Kingdom
HIGHLY COMMENDED

Male chimpanzee

"Frodo, in his early twenties, is the top male of the Kasakela chimpanzee community in Gombe National Park, Tanzania. He is one of Fifi's sons, the oldest female at 36, and is exceptionally large, standing 1.5 metres tall. He delights in throwing his weight around, but I caught him in a pensive mood and got down low to emphasise his powerful presence."

Canon T90 with 85mm lens; 1/125 sec at f1.8; Fujichrome Velvia at 40

Melanie Krebs
Germany
HIGHLY COMMENDED

Olive colobus

"I was studying the behaviour of the male olive colobus monkey in the Taï National Park in the Ivory Coast. The male seems to be the main protector of the group but also helps care for the young. This male sat for a moment in a shaft of sunlight in the normally dark forest. He looked up to his group and then joined a female with her baby."

Canon EOS 500 with 75-300mm lens; 1/50 sec at f5.6; Fujichrome 100 rated at 200

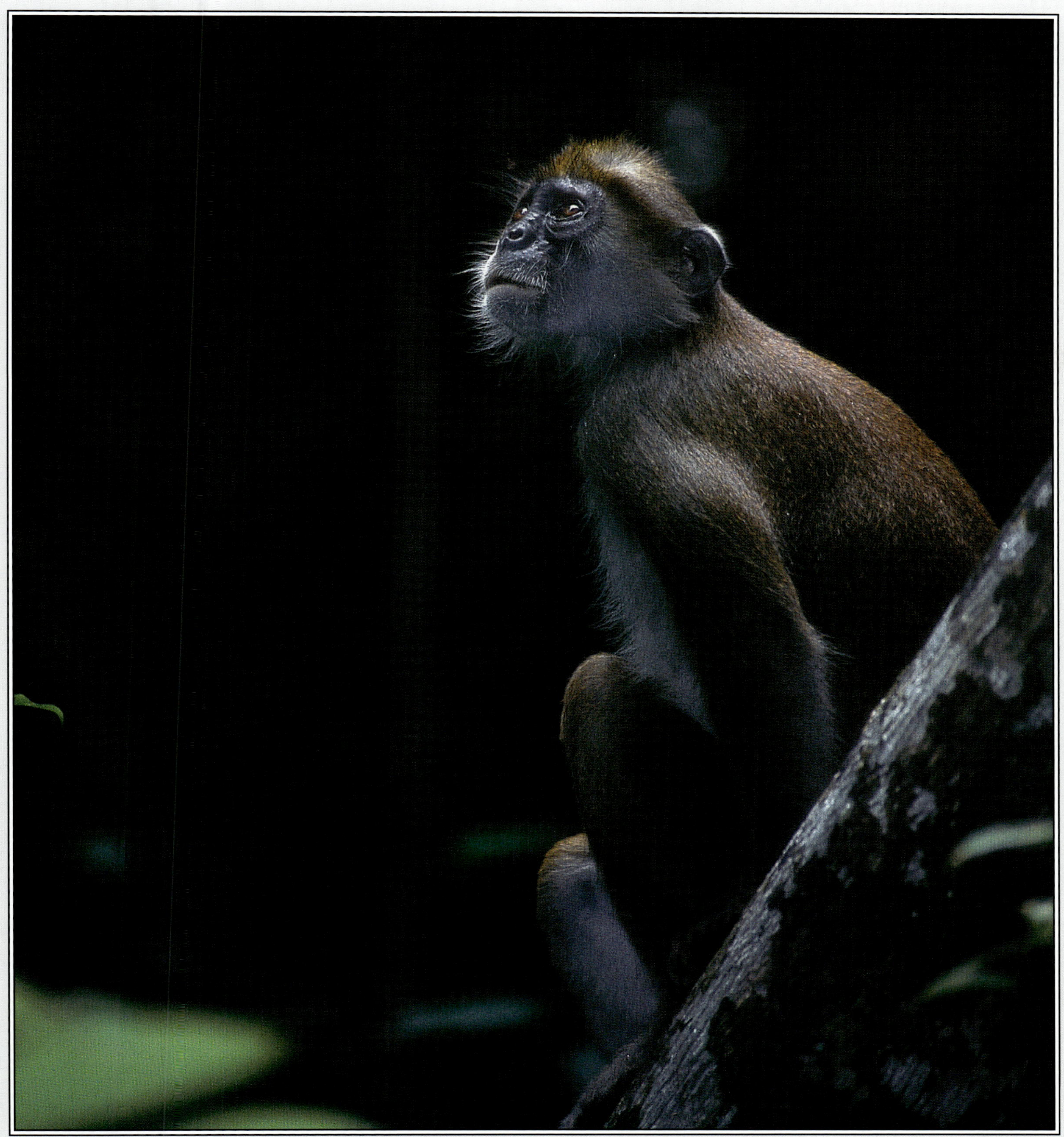

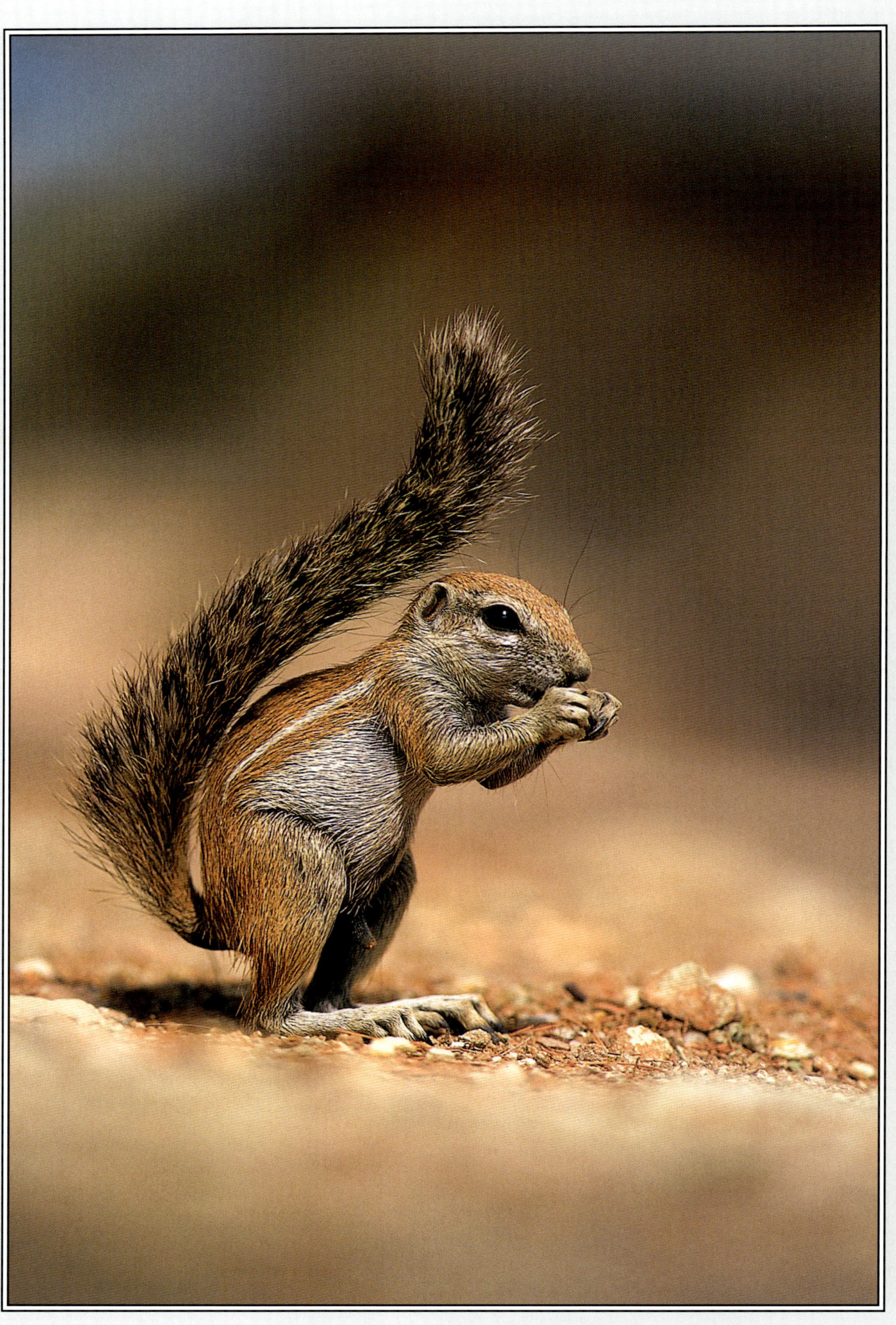

Heinrich van den Berg
South Africa
HIGHLY COMMENDED

Ground squirrel feeding

"Summer temperatures in the Kalahari Gemsbok National Park often soar above 40°C, and the animals have to be equipped to live in this intense heat. There's very little shade so the ground squirrel uses its tail as a sunshade while feeding."

Canon EOS 5 with 300mm lens; 1/30 sec at f11

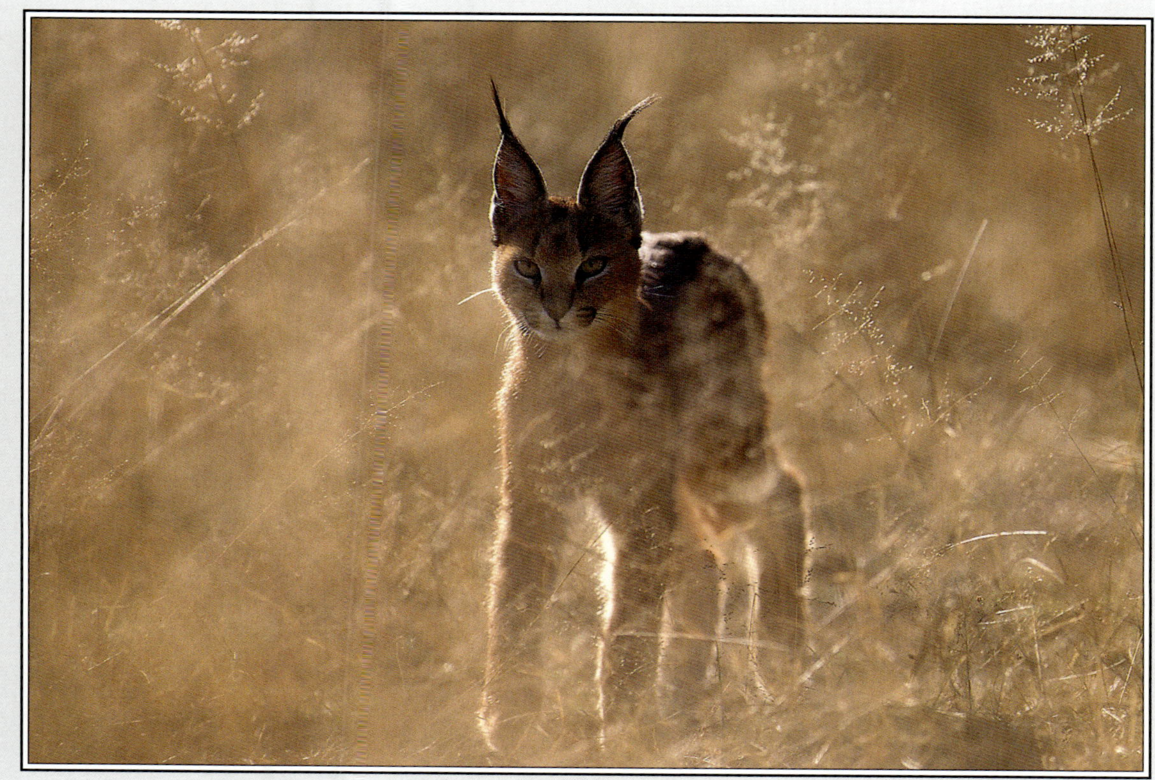

Kotaro Sano
Japan
HIGHLY COMMENDED

Caracal

"When the caracal disappeared into the bush, I guessed where it was likely to come out. I positioned the car so I was at my favourite angle and waited. The beautiful cat reappeared, just where I had hoped, and walked towards me looking for prey. All I had to do was stay calm and release the shutter."

Canon F1 with 500mm lens; 1/250 sec at f5.6; Fujichrome Provia 100

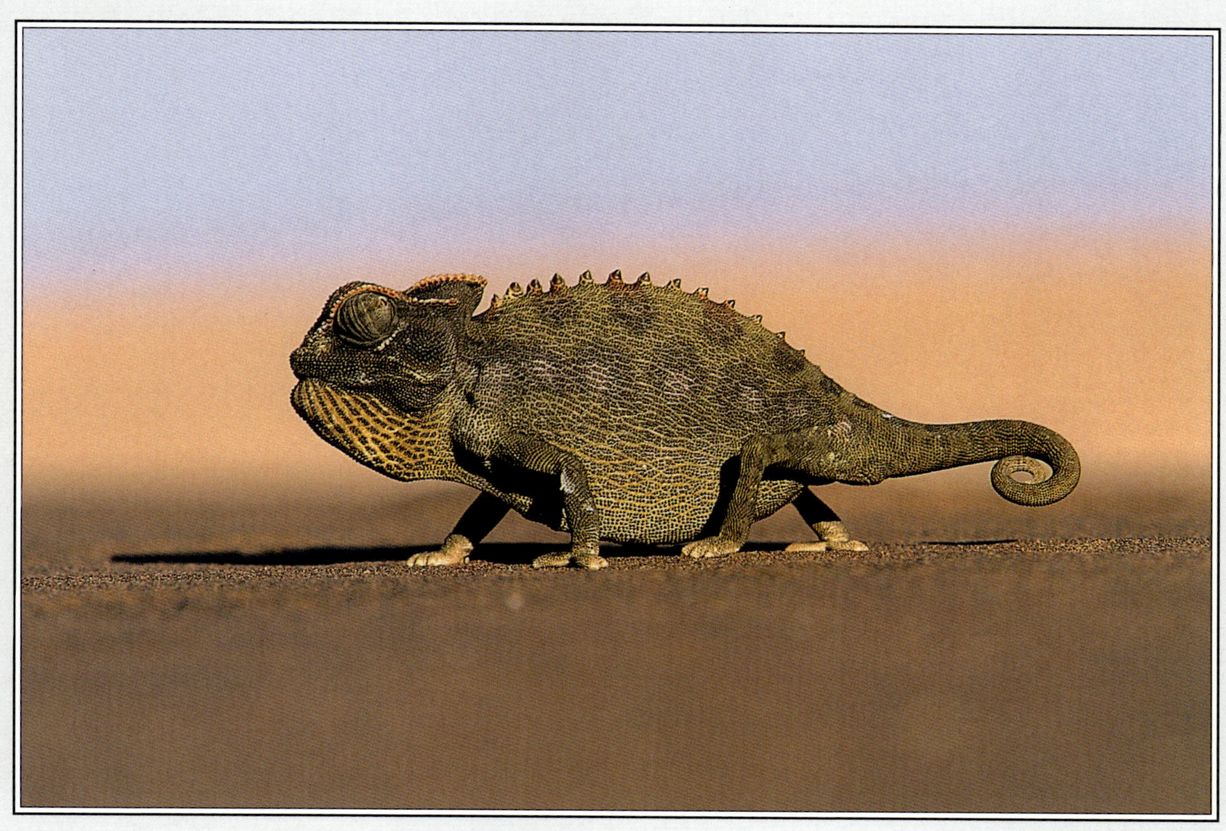

Philip van den Berg
South Africa
HIGHLY COMMENDED

Namaqua chameleon

"I spotted this remarkable inhabitant of the Namib desert crossing a desolate dune landscape in search of food. I went down low to photograph it from an unusual angle."

Canon EOS 5 with 70-200mm lens and x1.4 converter; 1/200 sec at f5.6; Fujichrome Velvia

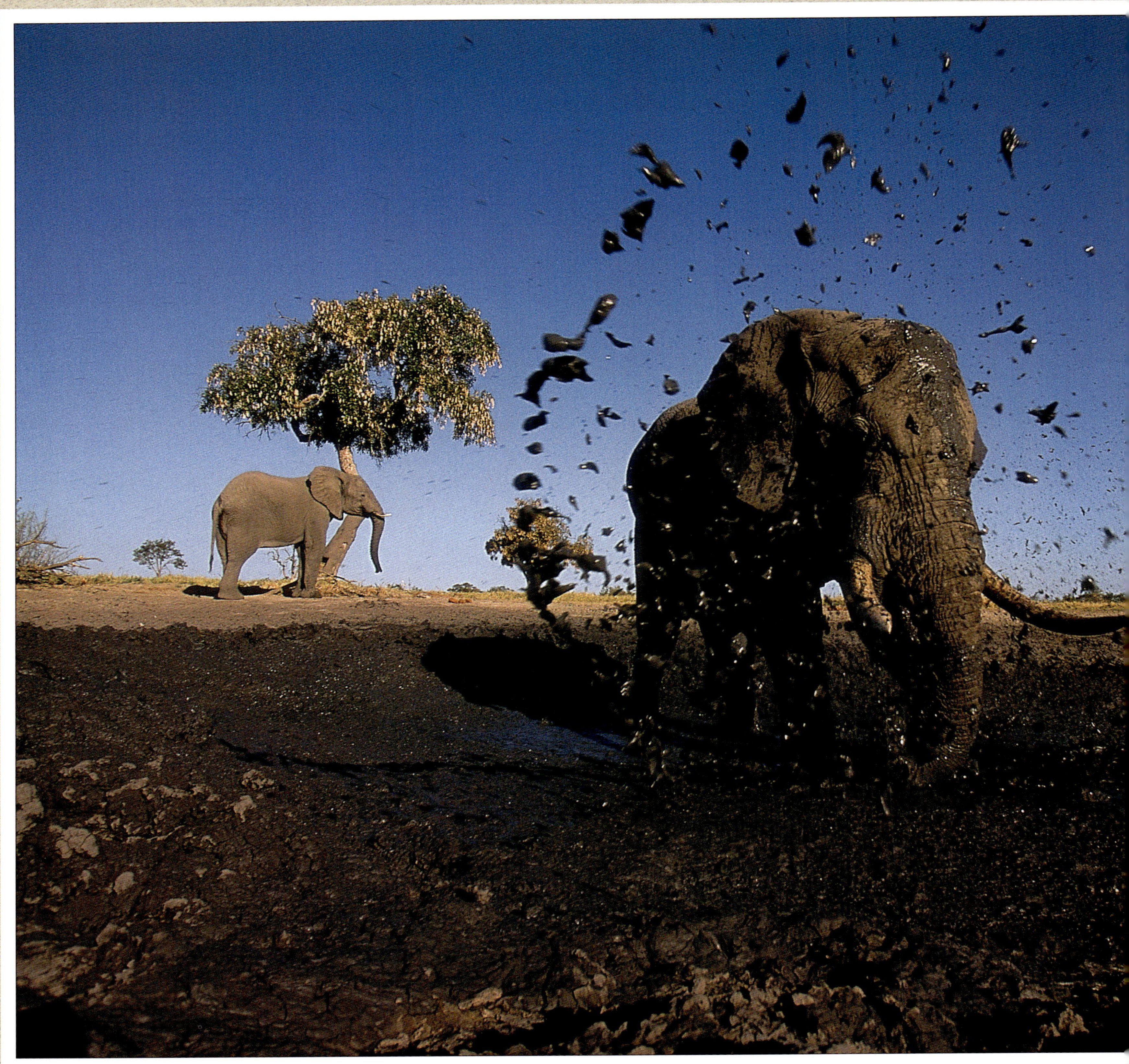

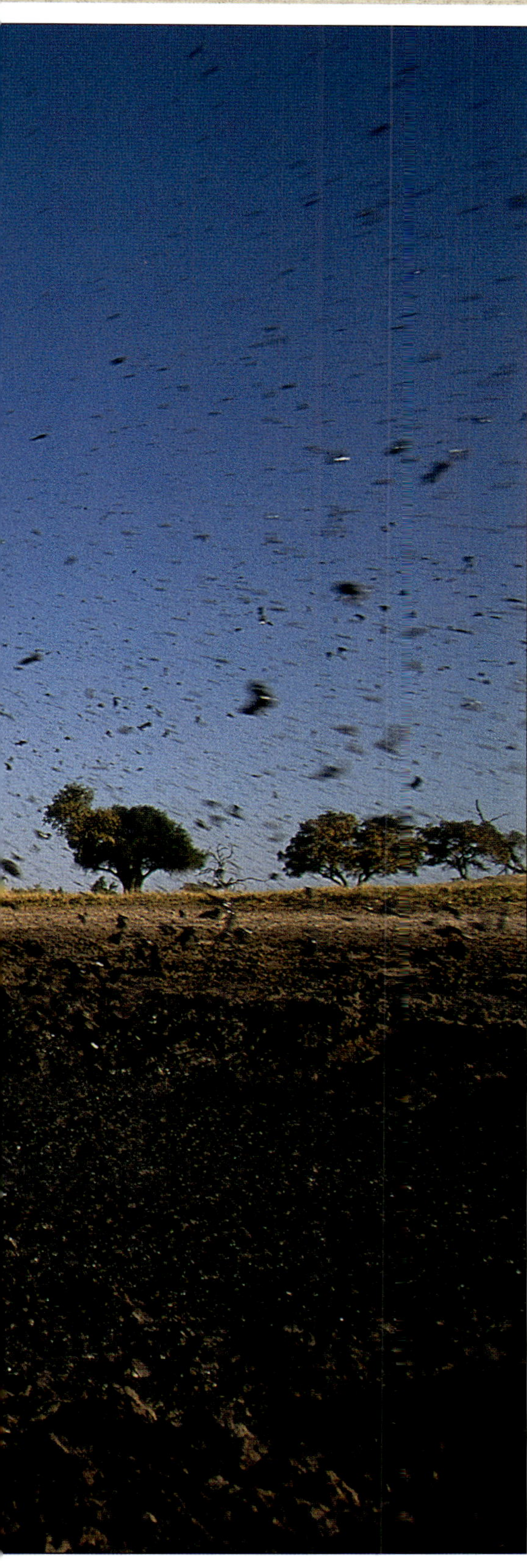

Animal Behaviour

- MAMMALS -

The subjects should be actively doing something. Pictures are judged on their interest value as well as their aesthetic appeal.

Andy Rouse
United Kingdom
WINNER

Elephant spraying mud

"I wanted to get an unusual shot of an elephant in this mud wallow in Botswana, so I buried my camera at the edge and retreated to a safe distance. The elephant stared at my camera for several minutes, then raised its trunk and deliberately sprayed it with mud. Hurriedly I pressed the trigger."

Canon EOS 5 with 17-35mm fisheye lens; 1/125 sec at f11; Fujichrome Velvia rated at 40.

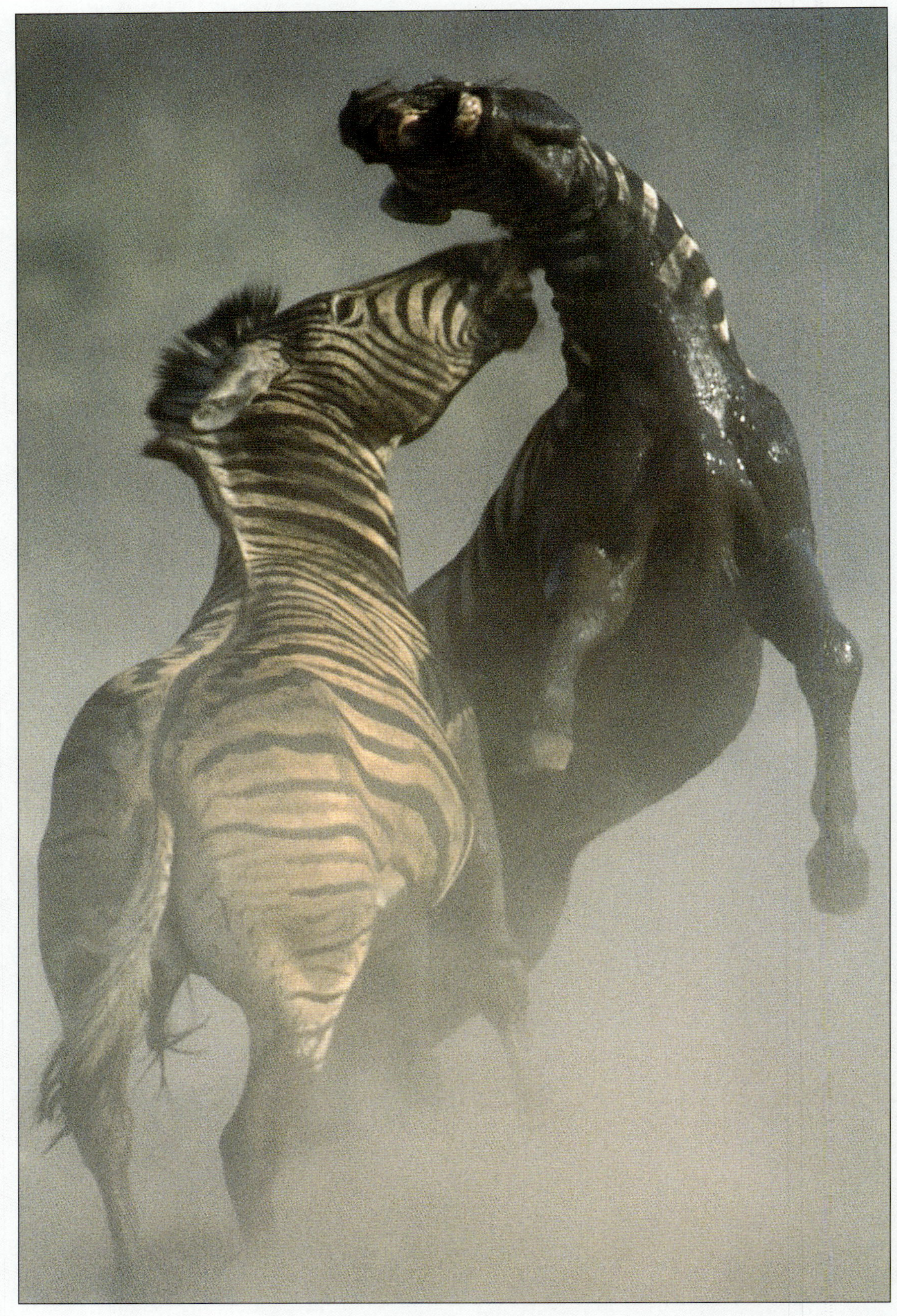

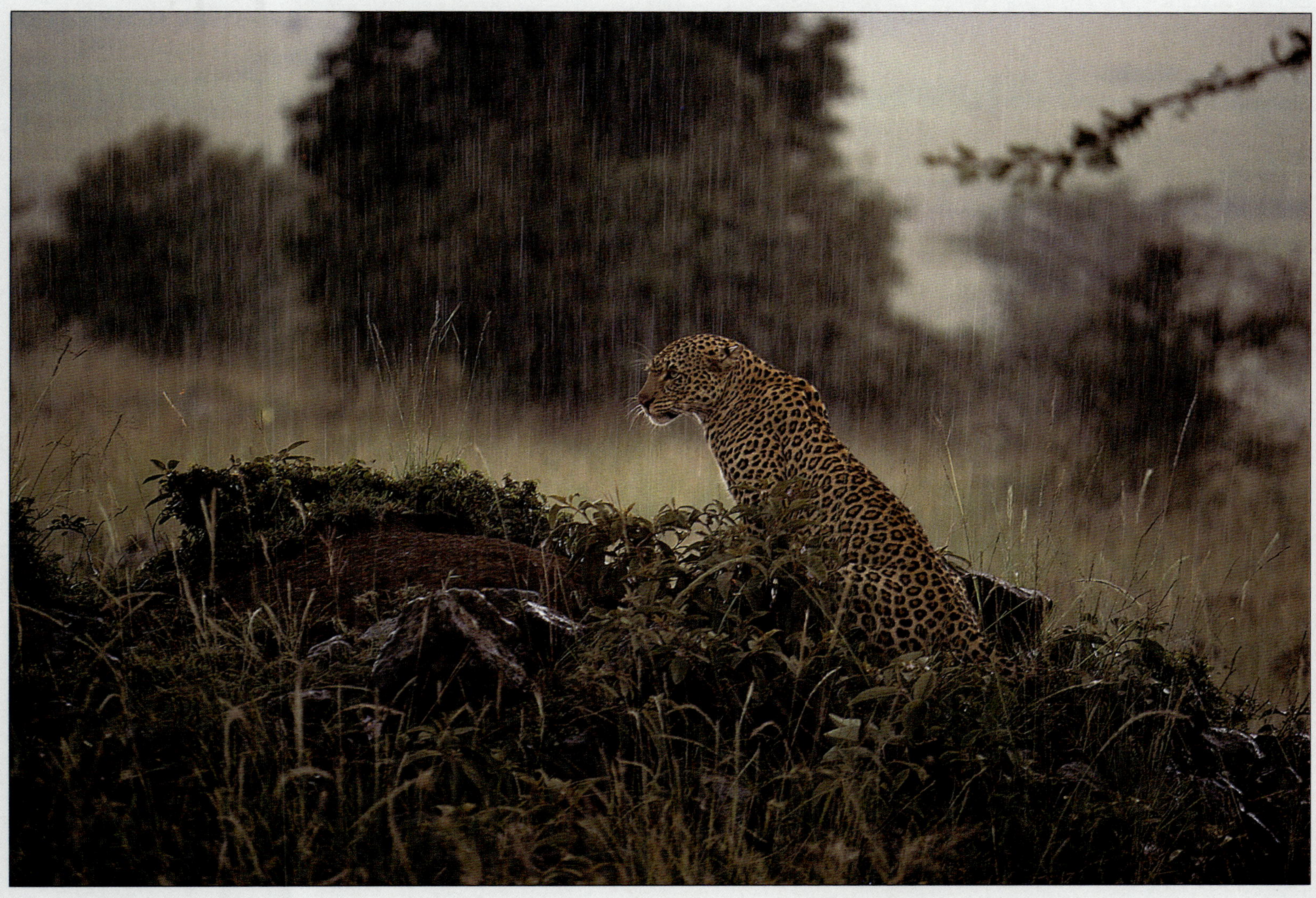

Robert Wong
United States of America
RUNNER-UP

Plains zebras fighting

"I watched a zebra herd, in Namibia's Etosha National Park, which drank regularly from the same waterhole. One individual was always trying to pick a fight. This time he had met his match."

Canon EOS 1N with 600mm lens and x1.4 converter; 1/500 sec at f5.6; Fujichrome Provia

Erwin & Peggy Bauer
United States of America
HIGHLY COMMENDED

Leopard in rainstorm

"The female leopard, whose cub was hidden nearby, was stalking a herd of impala when a sudden, torrential downpour struck. The impala fled and the photograph reflects the leopard's dejection."

Canon EOS1 with 300mm lens

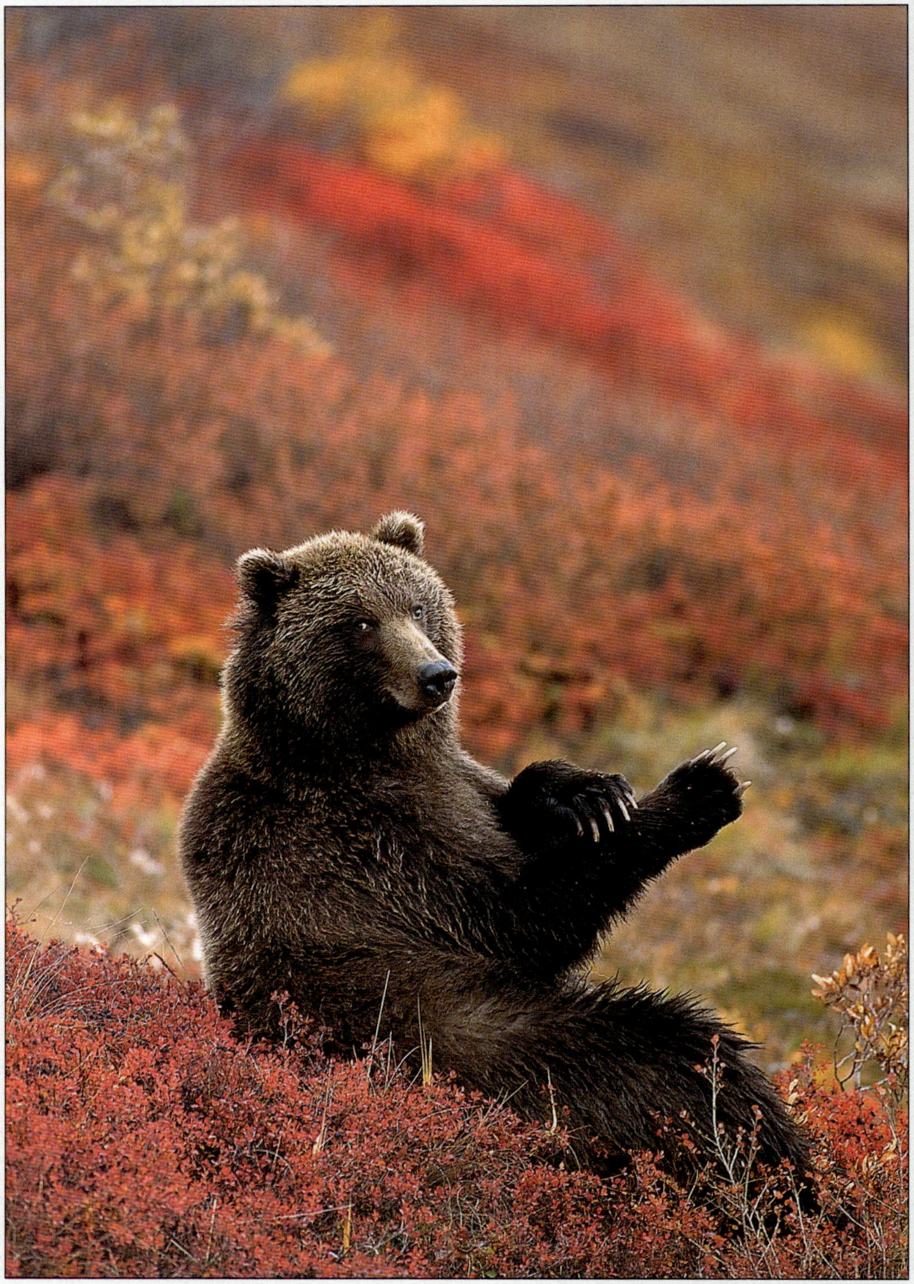

Hugh Rose
United States of America
HIGHLY COMMENDED

Grizzly bear scratching

"After a swim in the creek in Denali National Park, Alaska, this female grizzly sat in a patch of alpine blueberries, which were turning red in the autumn, and had a good scratch. She has only four claws on her right paw, so was easy to identify. I called her Four-Claw Paw."

Canon EOS A2 with 300mm lens; tripod; 1/125 sec at f5.6; Fujichrome 100

Staffan Widstrand
Sweden
HIGHLY COMMENDED

Polar bears by ice crack

"It was an overcast, rainy day in North Baffin National Park, Canada, when a mother polar bear and cub came along and peered down an ice crack looking for seals. It was my first sighting of this splendid animal, and she came so close that I feared for my safety. However, when I changed the film the noise of the automatic rewind frightened them both away."

Nikon F90 with 300mm lens; tripod; 1/125 sec at f4; Fujichrome Velvia

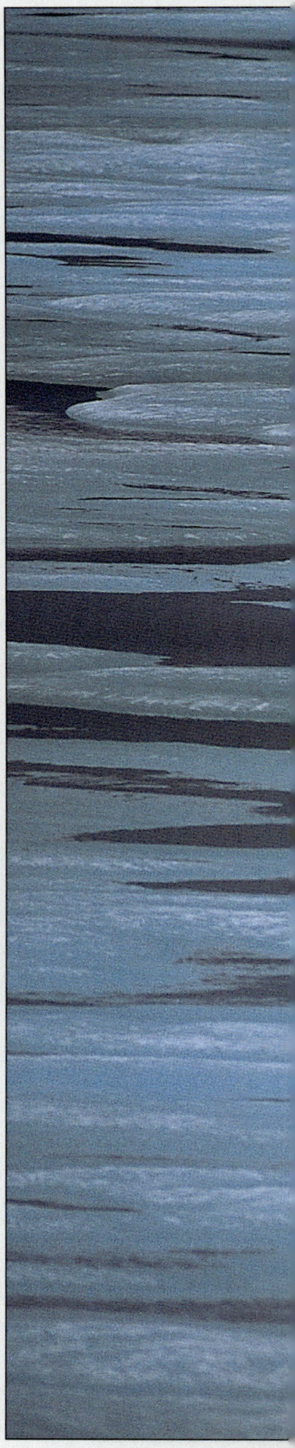

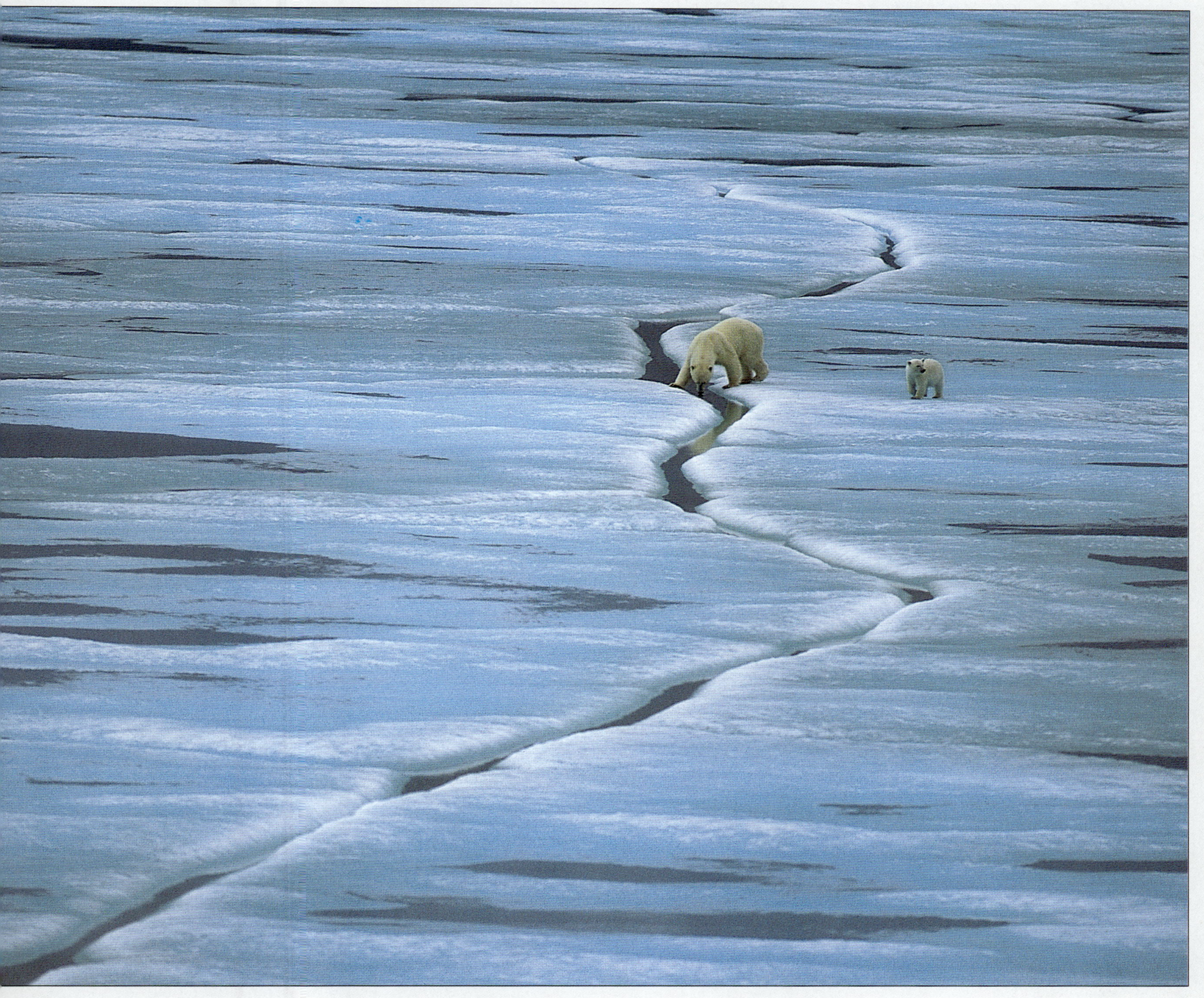

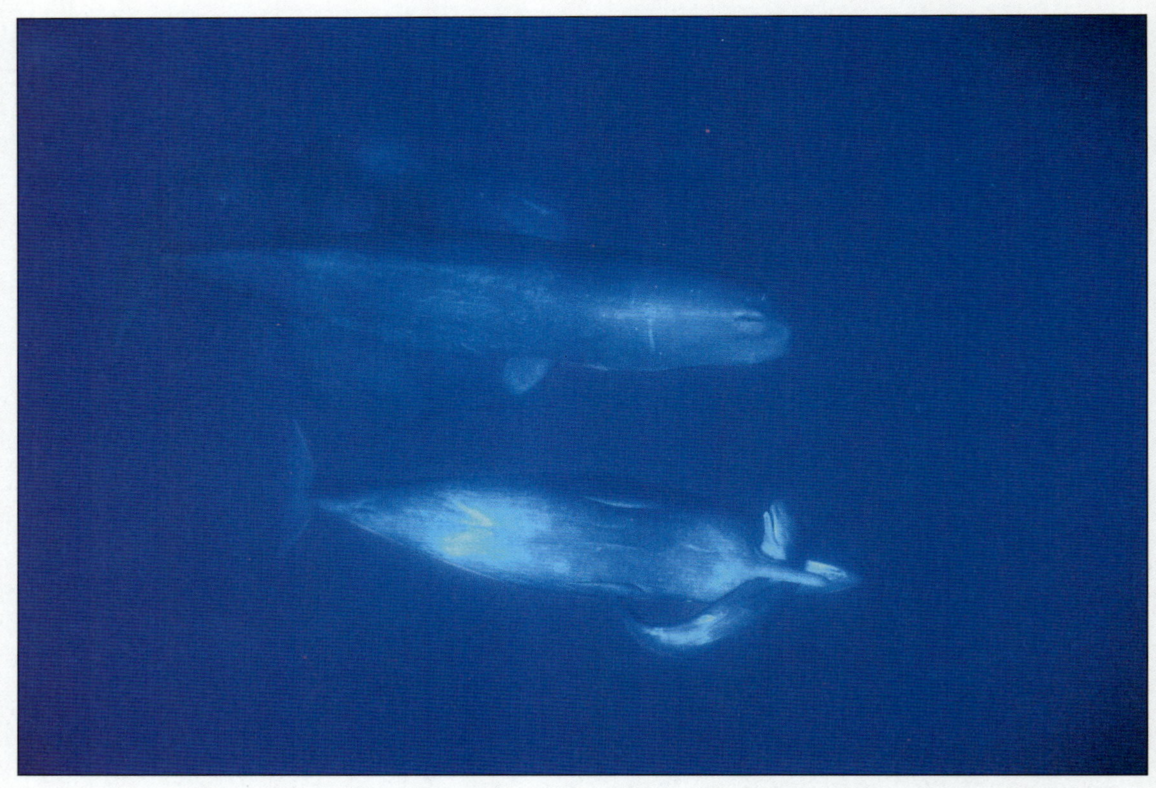

Roland Seitre

France

HIGHLY COMMENDED

Sperm whale carrying calf

"I was photographing these sperm whales off the Azores island of Pico. To my astonishment one individual, probably the mother, was swimming on her back and carrying a very young calf in her mouth. When they surfaced ahead, the calf was nowhere to be seen. The small body was found the next day floating on the surface, and biologists concluded that it had been stillborn."

Nikon F90 with 20mm lens; underwater housing; f5 6; Fujichrome Sensia 100

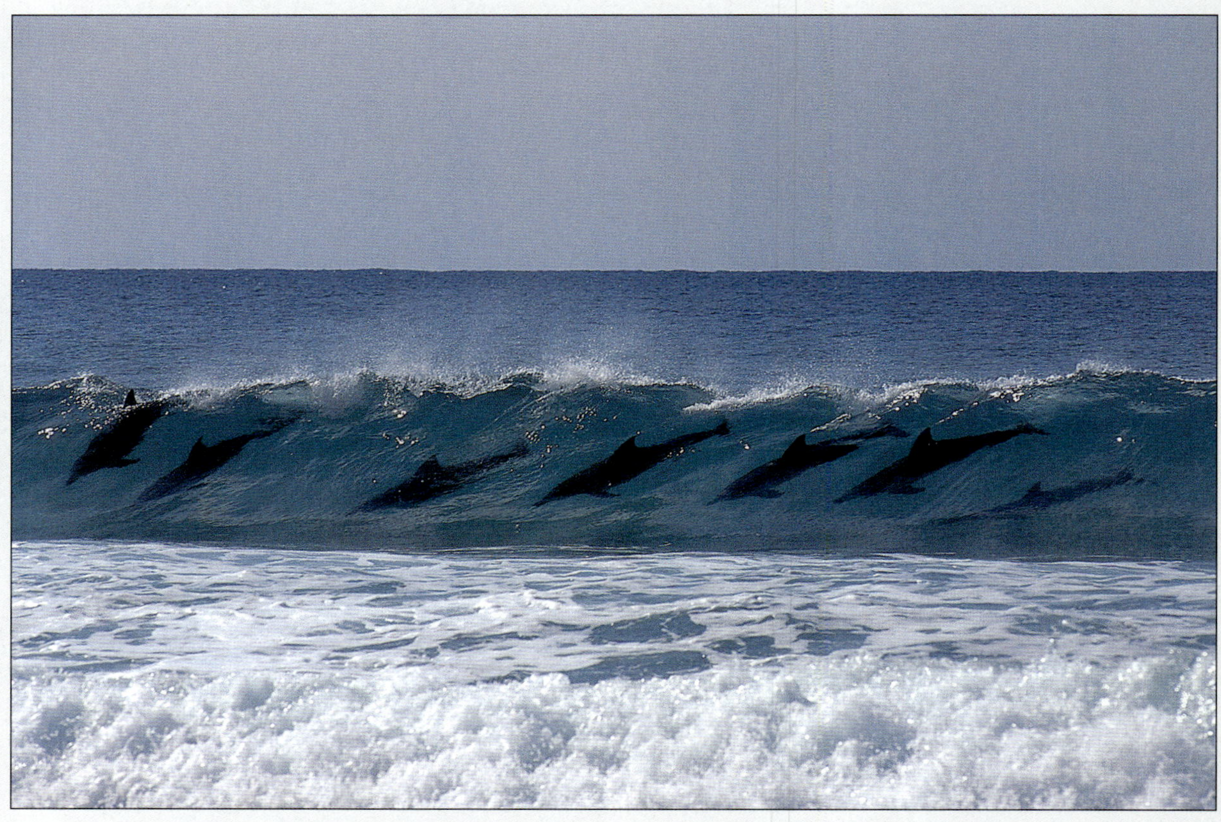

Tony Karacsonyi

Australia

HIGHLY COMMENDED

Surfing bottle-nosed dolphins

"I was so euphoric when I saw these seven bottle-nosed dolphins surf the wave that I almost forgot to take the shot. Another couple were walking along Mollymook Beach, New South Wales, and we turned to each other and said: 'Wow!' There were no other words to describe it."

Nikon 801 with 300mm lens; 1/1000 sec at f8; Fujichrome 100 rated at 200

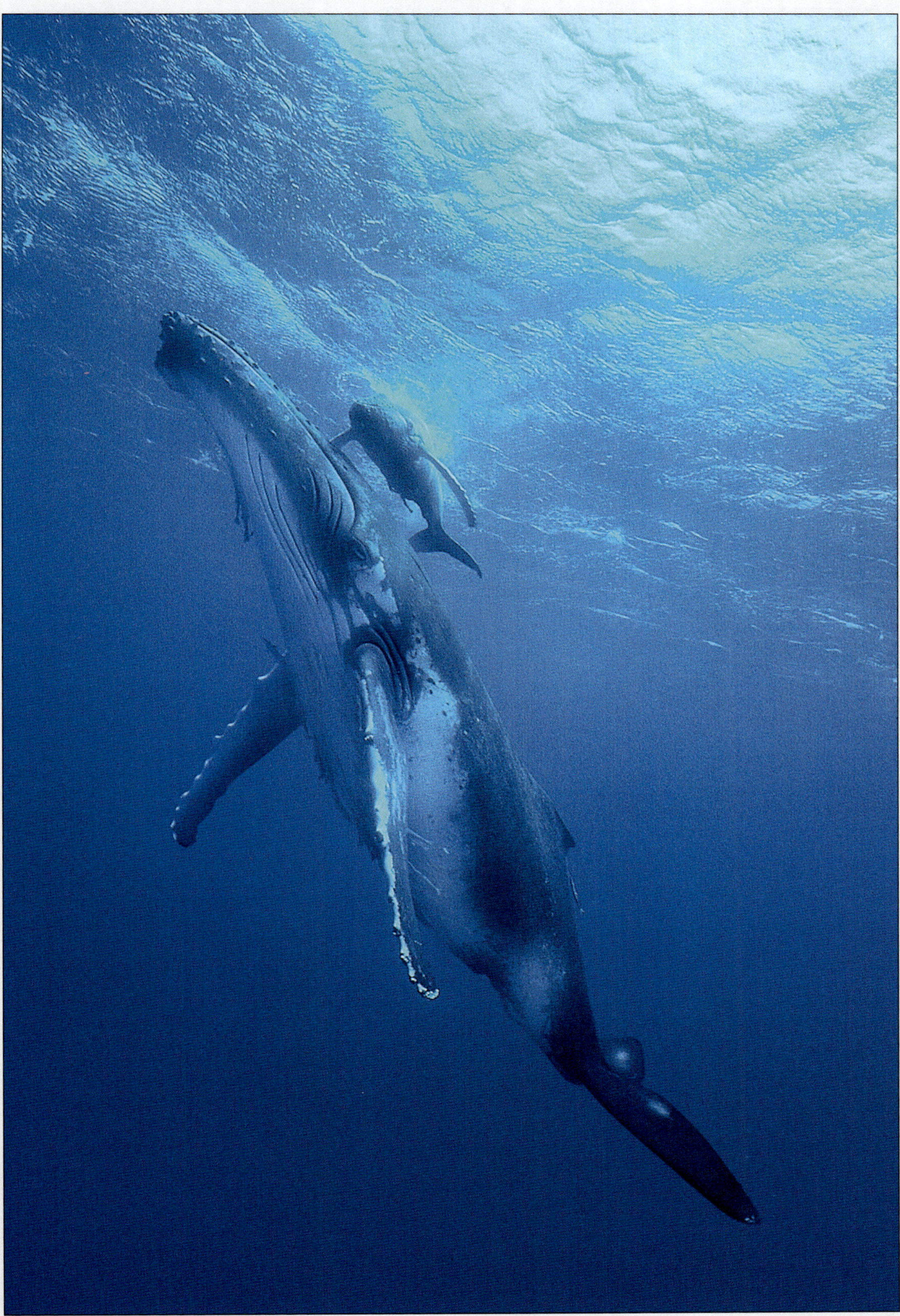

Amos Nachoum
United States of America
HIGHLY COMMENDED

Humpback whale with calf

"Some southern humpback whales migrate annually from Antarctica to the warm waters off Tonga to give birth and mate again. I had snorkelled down to about 40 feet, and when I looked up, there she was, towering over my head. The whale was gently pushing her young calf to the surface to take a breath of air."

Nikonos III with 15mm lens; 1/125 sec at f5.6; Kodachrome 64 rated at 80

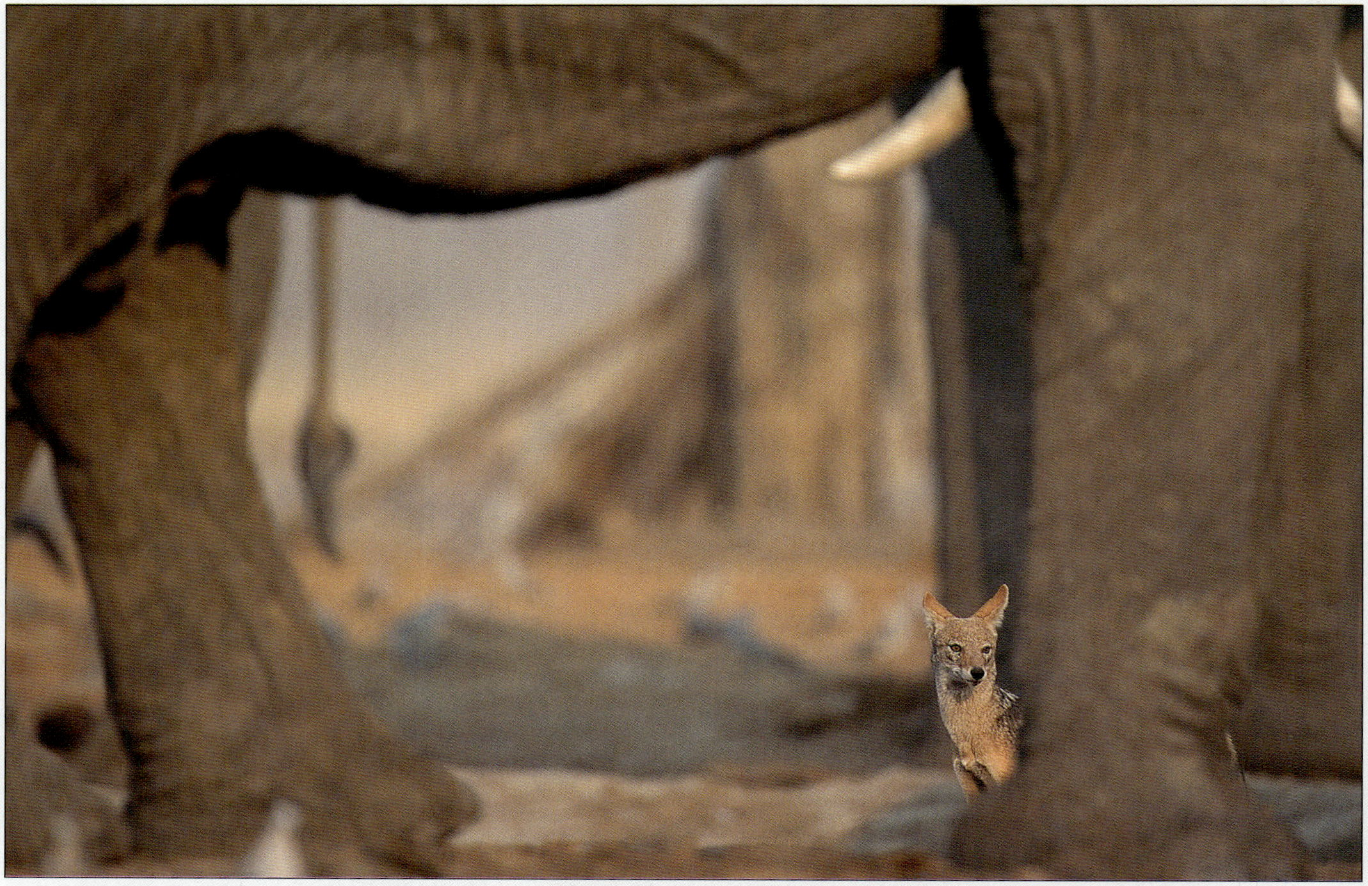

Theo Allofs
Germany
HIGHLY COMMENDED

Jackal among elephants

"It was early morning in Botswana's Chobe National Park and thirsty animals were coming to the waterhole. Huge flocks of doves were flying in to drink among the elephants' feet. This black-backed jackal peered out from behind an elephant's leg, watching and waiting for the right moment to pounce. It reminded me of an animal version of David and Goliath."

Nikon F5 with 600mm lens; bean bag; 1/500 sec at f4; Fujichrome Sensia 100

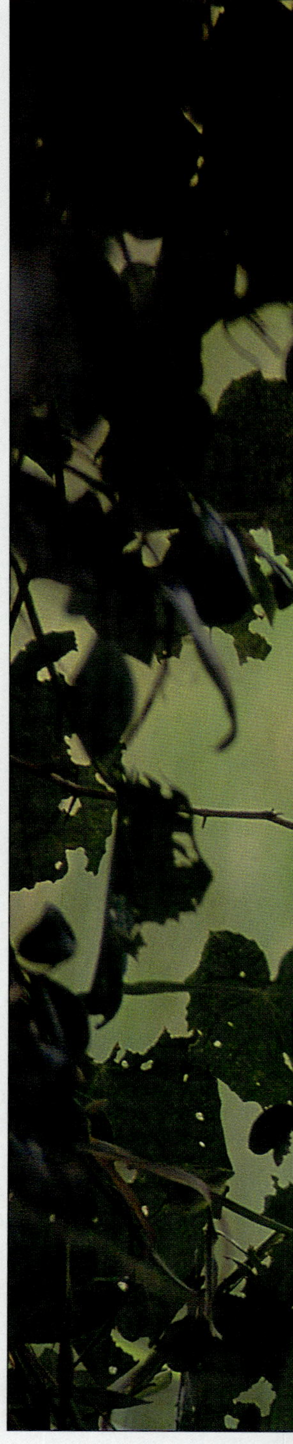

Brent Hedges
Australia
HIGHLY COMMENDED

Leopard pawing at foliage

"I followed this young female leopard for most of the day in the Maasai Mara, Kenya. She walked past the vehicle almost within touching distance, stopped, and stood on her hind legs using her front paw to pull down the leaves to smell them. I pressed the button and hoped for the best."

Nikon F5 with 80-200mm lens; 1/250 at f2.8; Fujichrome Velvia

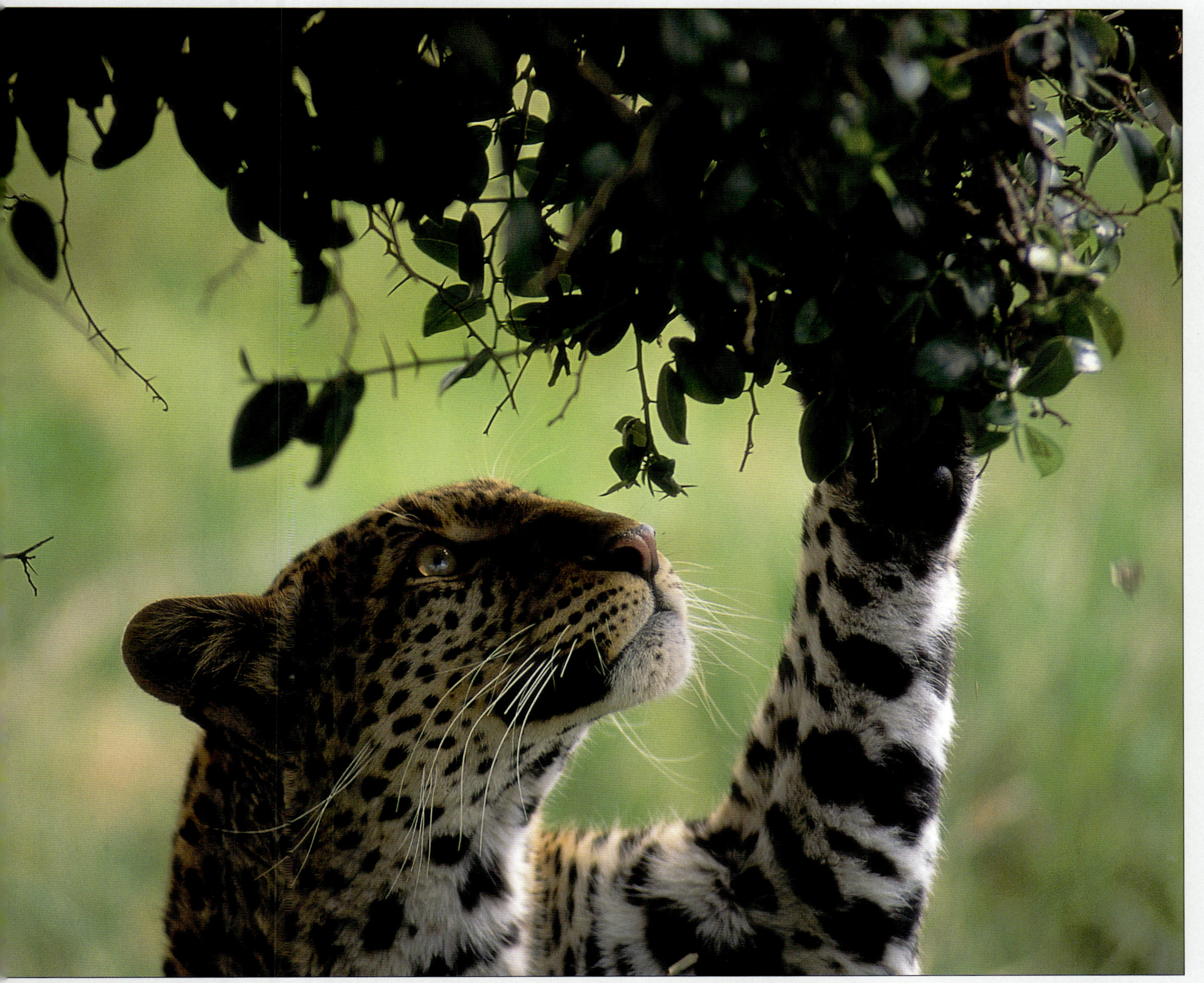

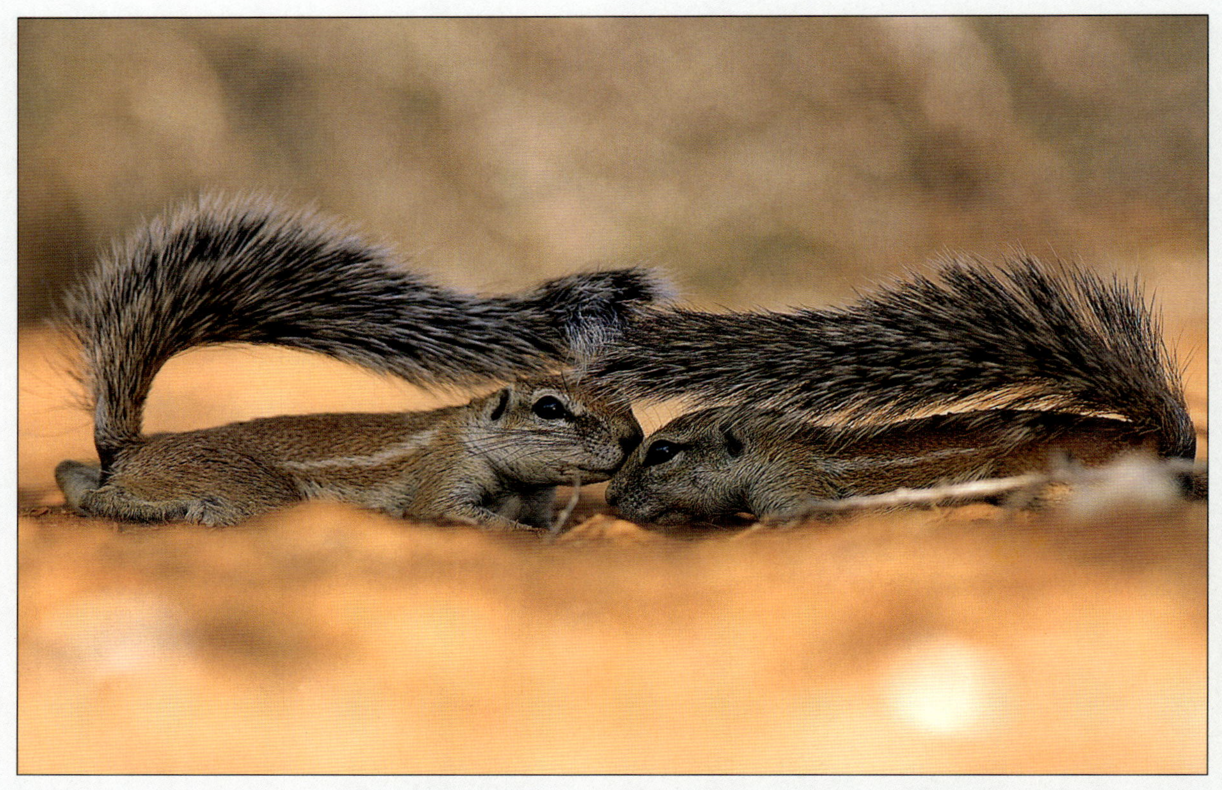

Heinrich van den Berg
South Africa
HIGHLY COMMENDED

Ground squirrels in shade

"The ground squirrels were playing around the campsite in Kalahari Gemsbok National Park, South Africa. It was so hot that every now and then they would run to the shade of a tree, dig down to expose the cooler sand and lie flat on their stomachs to cool off. After a few seconds, they would start playing again."

Canon EOS 5 with 300mm lens; flash; 1/60 sec at f8; Fujichrome Velvia

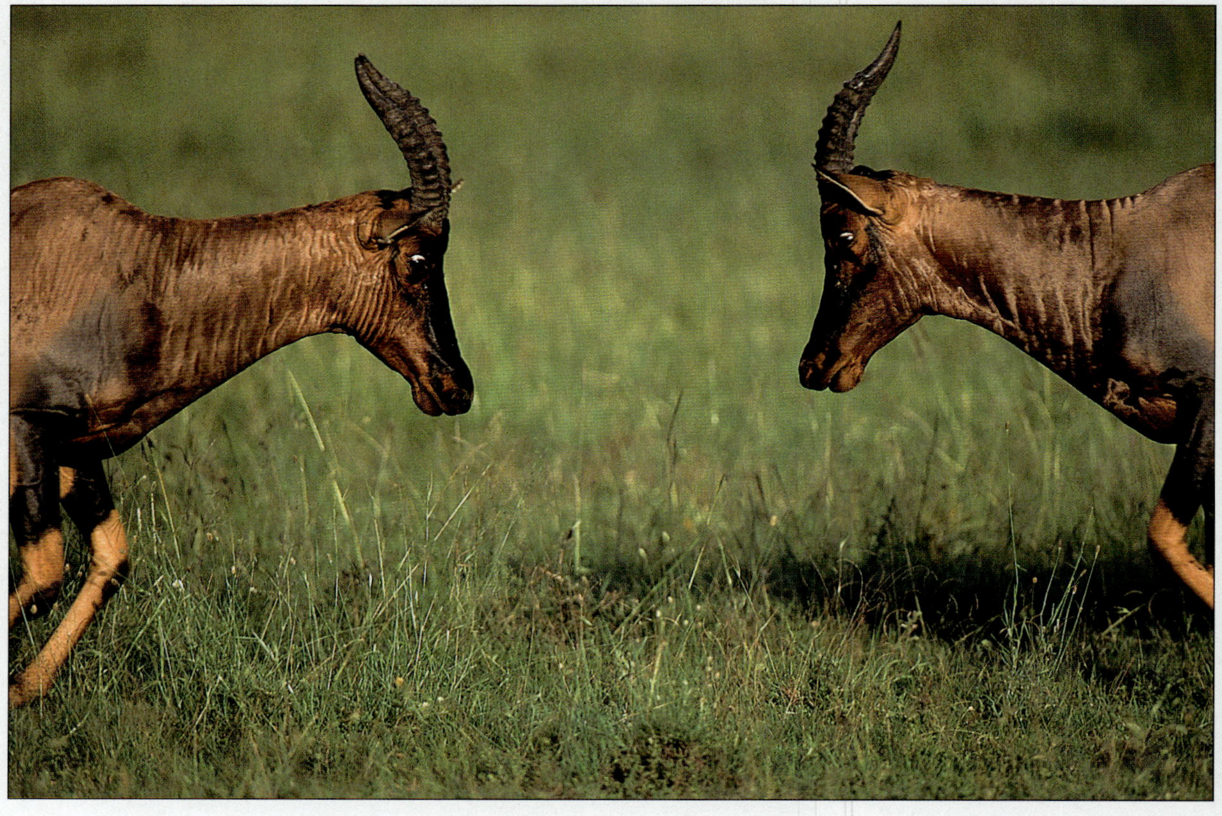

Fritz Pölking
Germany
HIGHLY COMMENDED

Topi square-up

"Working for a year in the Maasai Mara, Kenya, I had the chance to photograph many of the animals. Close to the leopard and cubs I was photographing regularly, was a large herd of topi. They would sometimes spar with each other, but it was only play-fighting."

Nikon F4 with 300mm lens; car-mount; Fujichrome 100

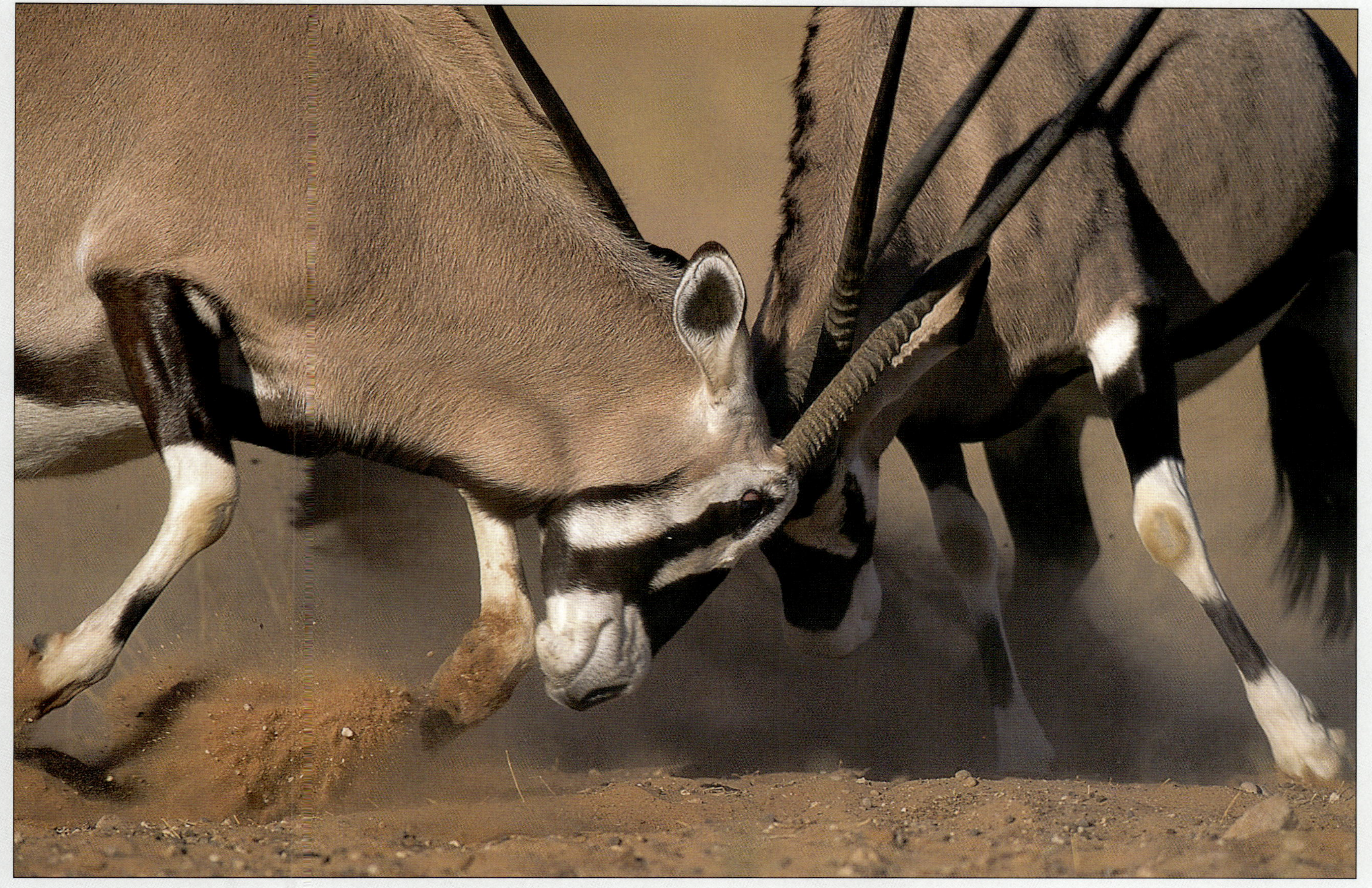

Richard du Toit
South Africa
HIGHLY COMMENDED

Gemsbok fighting

"Several groups of gemsbok came out from the dunes as I waited at a waterhole in the Auob river valley in the Kalahari. Some of the males were very wary of each other, squaring up as they approached the water to drink. These two males suddenly dropped their heads and clashed horns in a brief but furious fight."

Canon EOS 1N with 500mm lens; 1/640 sec at f4.5; Fujichrome Velvia

Animal Behaviour

- BIRDS -

The birds should be actively doing something. Pictures are judged on their interest value as well as their aesthetic appeal.

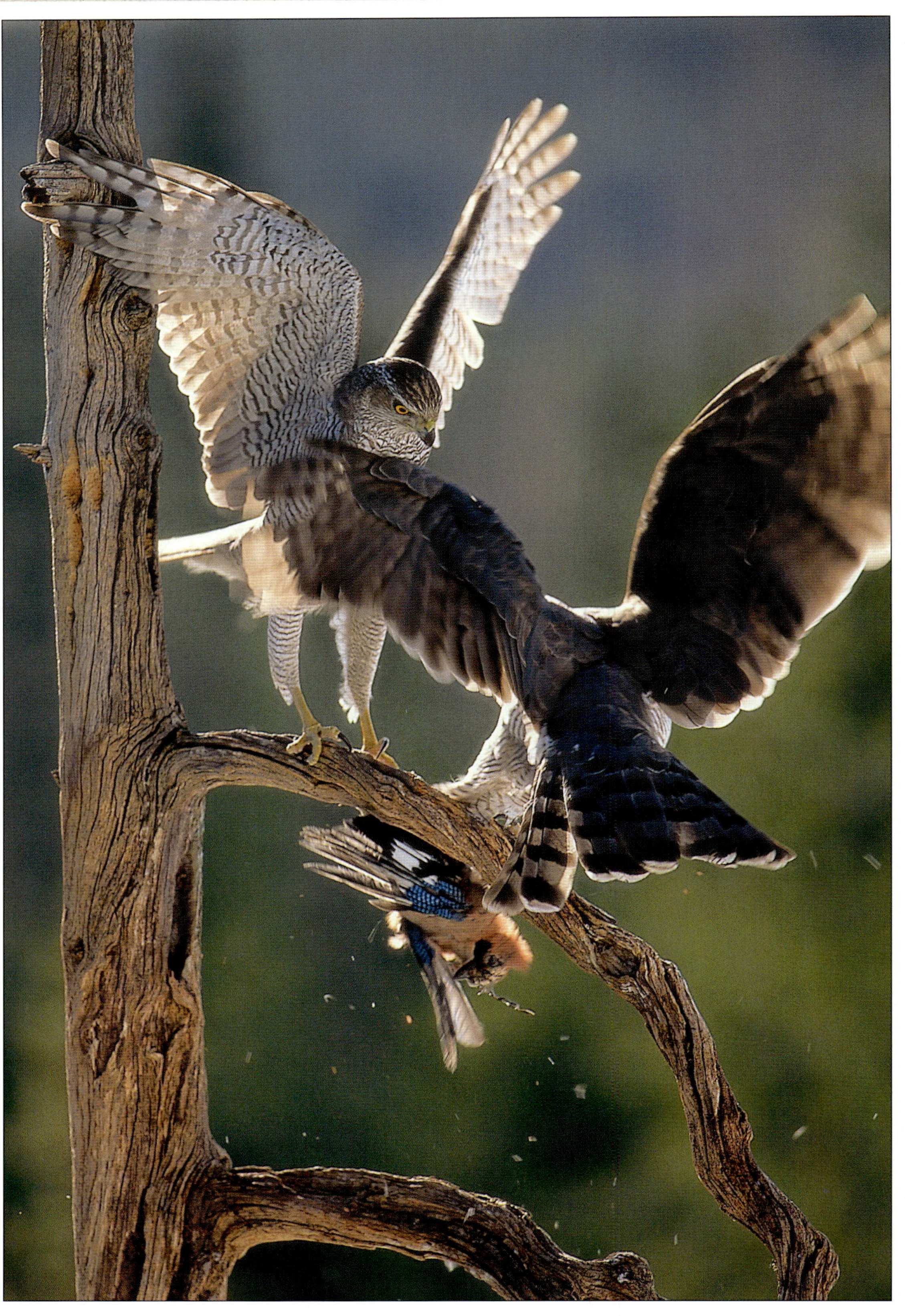

Kari Reponen
Finland
WINNER

Goshawks courtship feeding

"It was a very cold March morning in Anttola, south-east Finland. The male goshawk was giving the prey, a jay, to the female, and they were calling loudly. The atmosphere of the picture is unique, with the strong morning light being reflected off the snow and illuminating the birds from below."

Nikon F4 with 300mm lens; tripod; 1/500 sec; Fujichrome Velvia

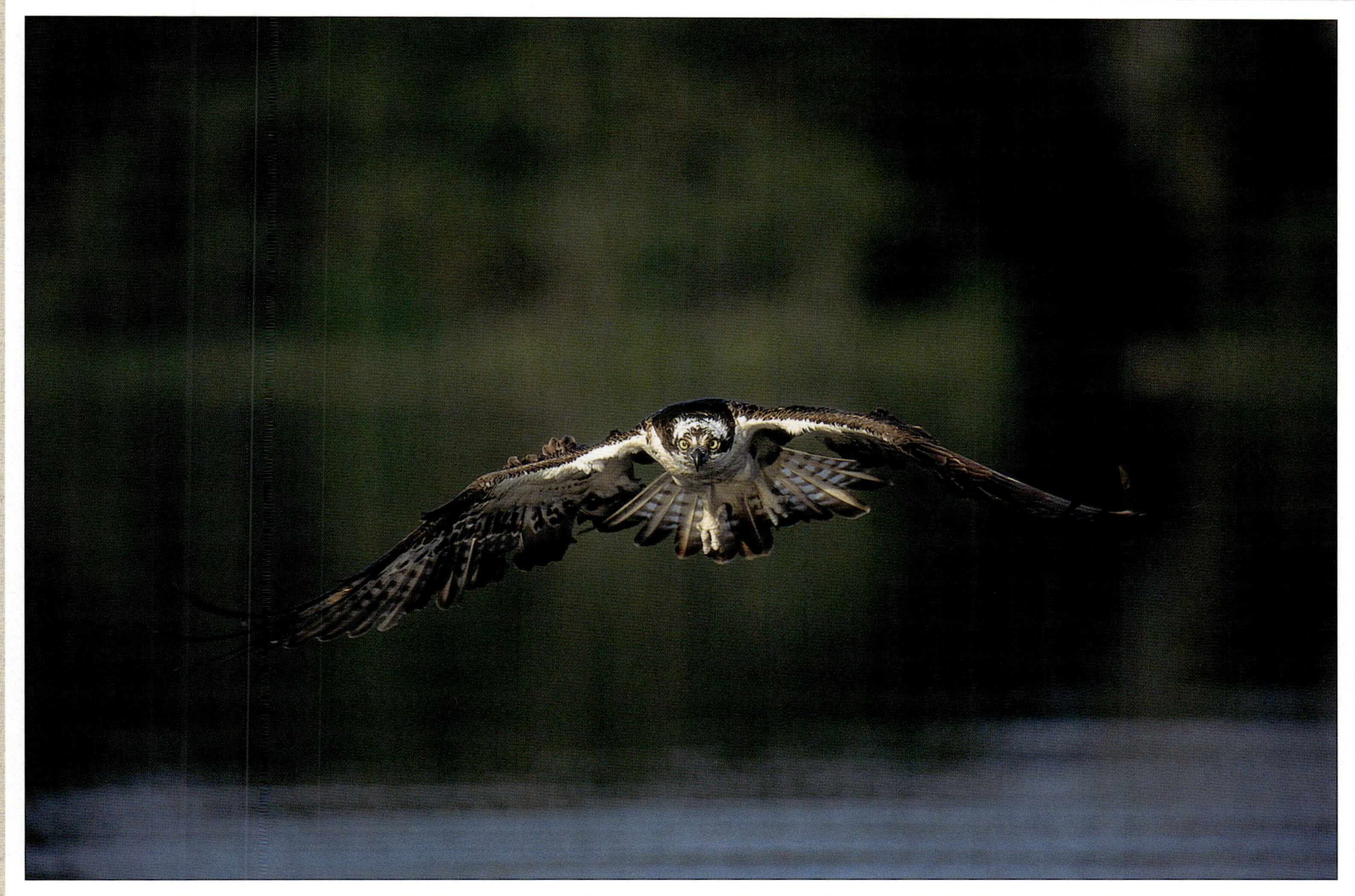

Bernhard Volmer
Germany
RUNNER-UP

Osprey in flight

"I love travelling in Scandinavia because of the opportunities to photograph interesting animals and impressive landscapes in a fantastic variety of light. On this occasion, the osprey flew quite close to me over the lake so I had the chance to take this shot."

Nikon F5 with 300mm lens and x1.4 converter; 1/1000 sec at f4; Fujichrome Sensia

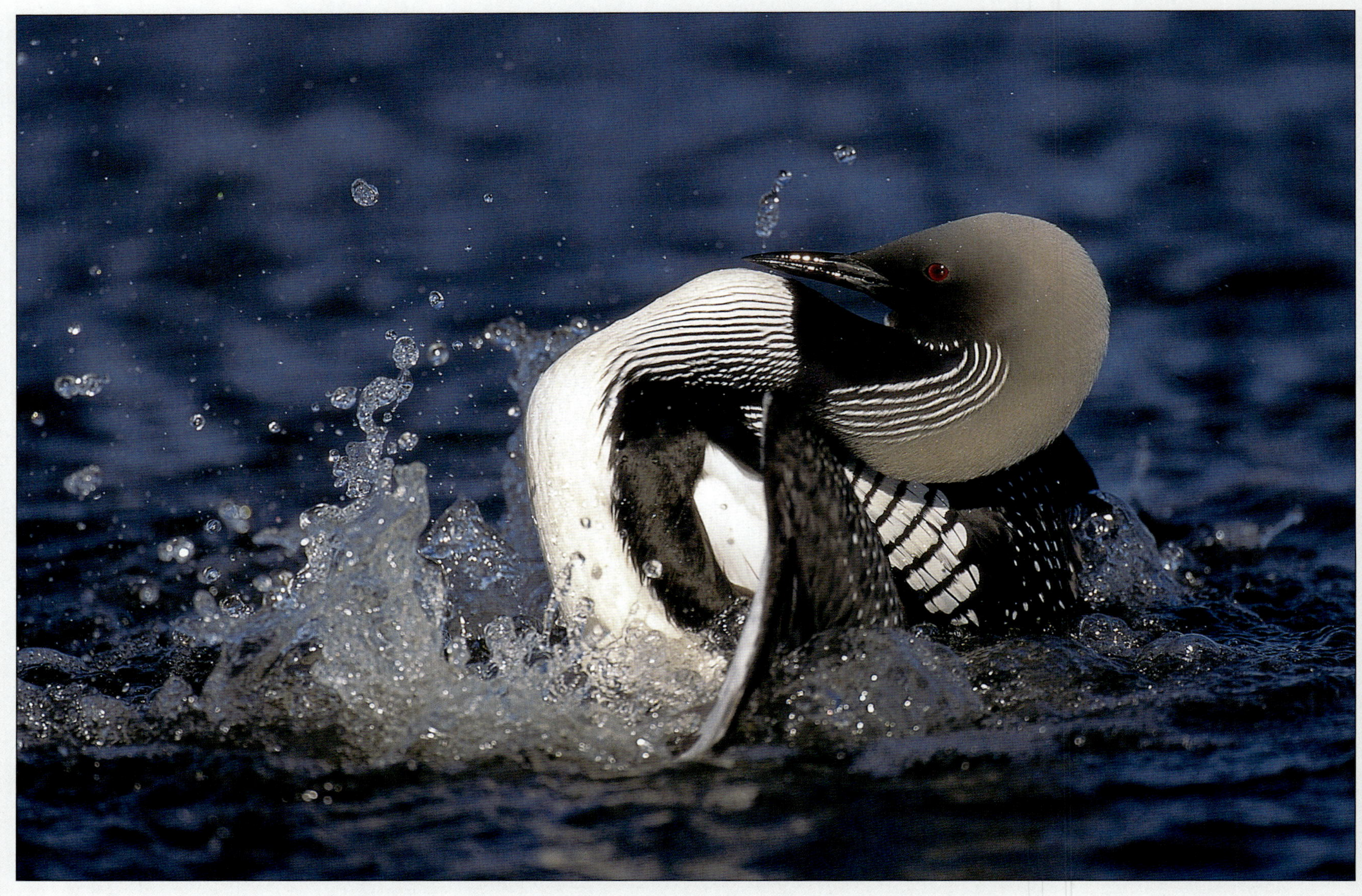

Timothy Gallagher
United Kingdom
SPECIALLY COMMENDED

Pacific Loon bathing

"I photographed this Pacific Loon in northern Manitoba, near Hudson Bay. The bird suddenly plunged into the pond and began splashing its wings and rearing up in the water. The rich bright light from the low, morning sun enhanced the colour of the plumage. As I took the picture I thought it looked like an oriental painting."

Nikon F4 with 500mm lens; 1/1500 sec at f4; Fujichrome 100

Rolando Gil

Spain

HIGHLY COMMENDED

Silver gull

"It was my first trip to Australia, and I had been taking photographs of silver gulls for several days when I spotted this particular pose – a bored yawn at my constant presence?"

Nikon F4 with 180mm lens; 1/250 sec at f8; Fujichrome Velvia

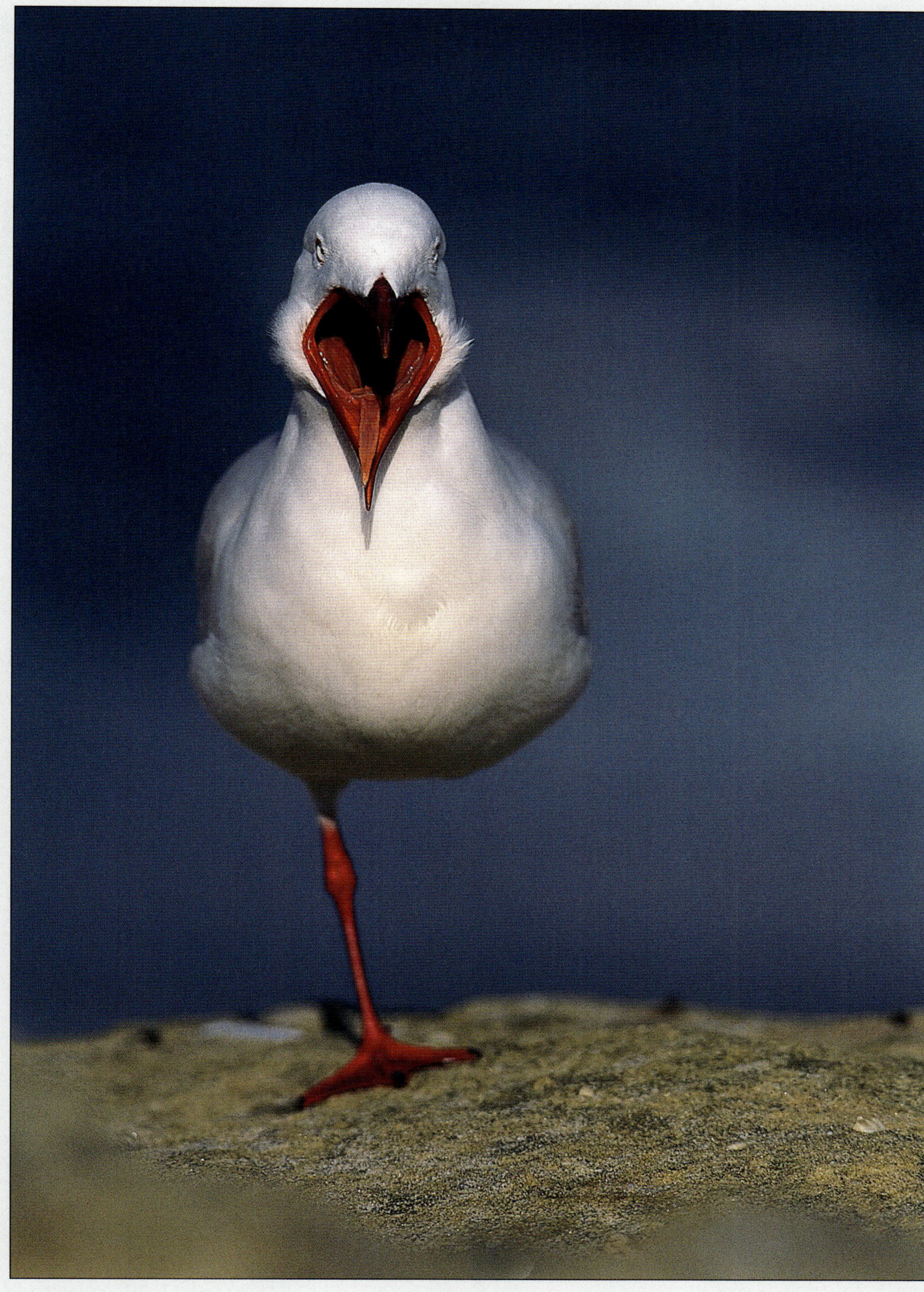

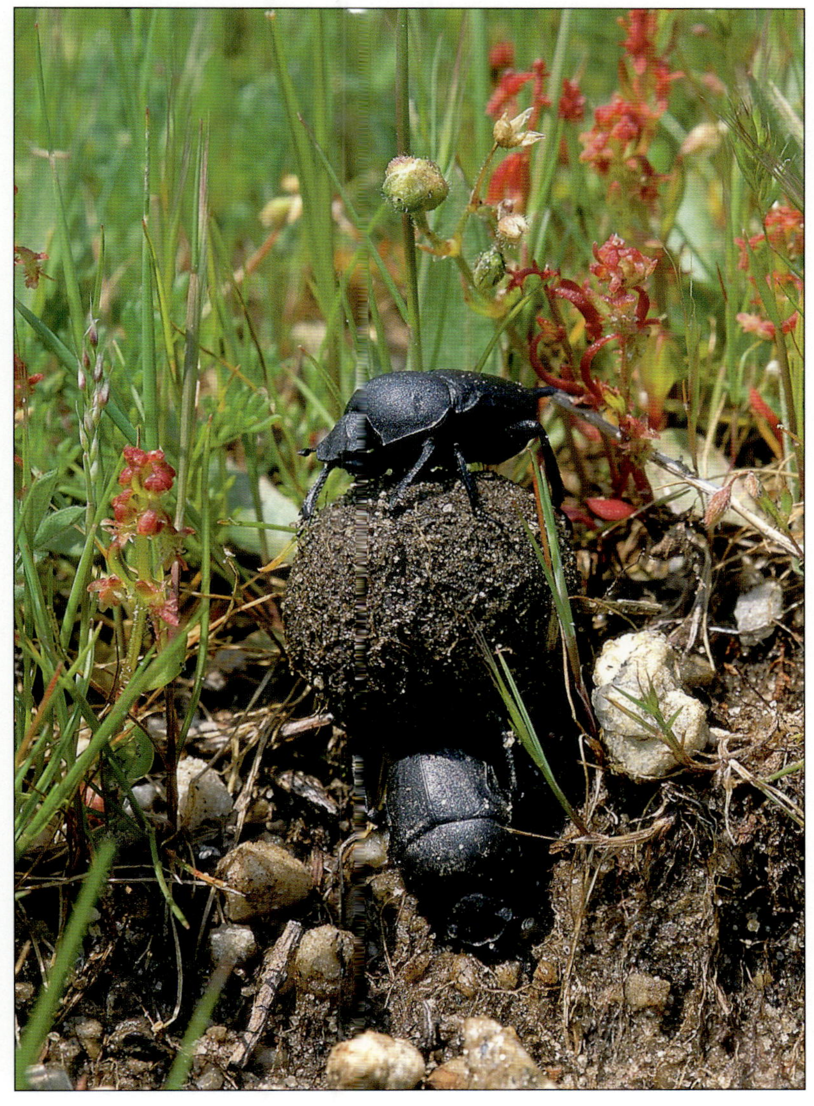

Carola Huhn
Germany
HIGHLY COMMENDED

Dung beetles

"I spotted these two dung beetles rolling their dung-ball through the grass in J[illegible]ze Baja, Turkey. They were very fast on the flat, but when it fell into a cow's hoofprint, I had time to set up my tripod. To get the ball out, the male anchored himself to some plant stems with his rear legs and pulled, while the female pushed from behind."

Nikon F5 with 105mm lens; tripod; Fujichrome Velvia

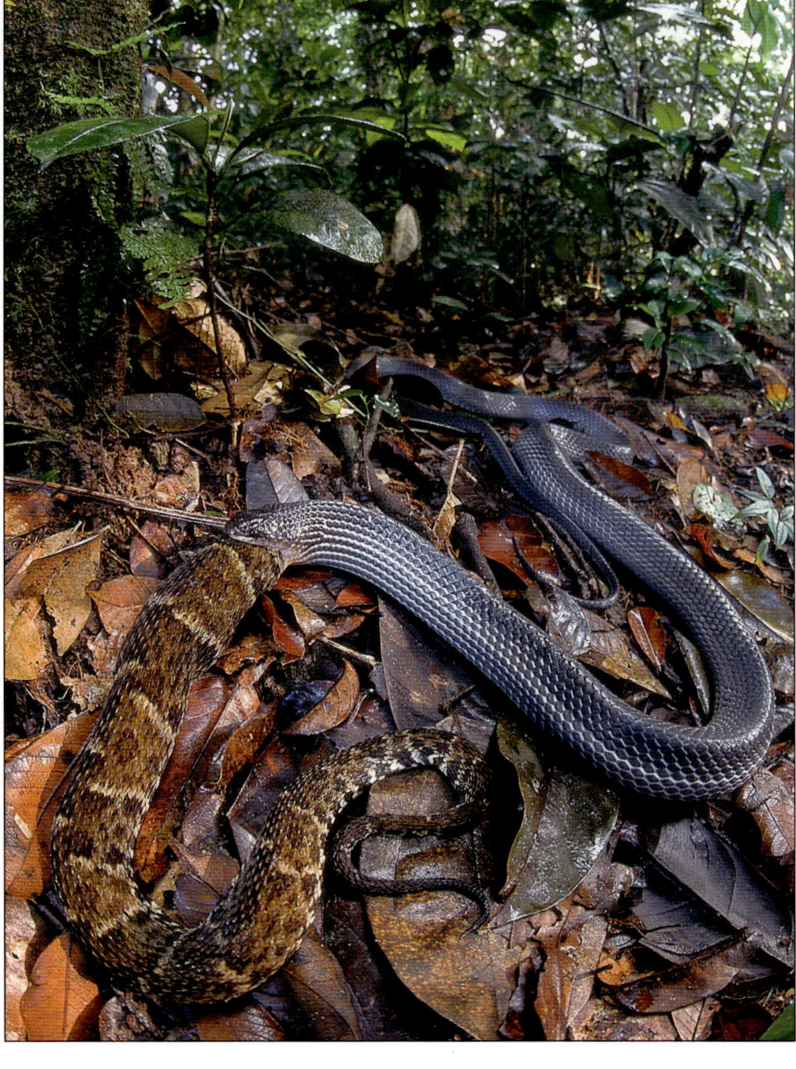

Ian Stephen
United Kingdom
HIGHLY COMMENDED

Snake eats snake

"Despite being poisonous, the common lancehead, one of the most abundant snakes in the Amazonian forest of Columbia, frequently falls prey to the mussurana. Snakes make up a large proportion of the diet of this powerful constrictor, which is immune to their venom."

Canon EOS 1 with 15mm lens; 1/8 sec at f8; Fujichrome Provia 100

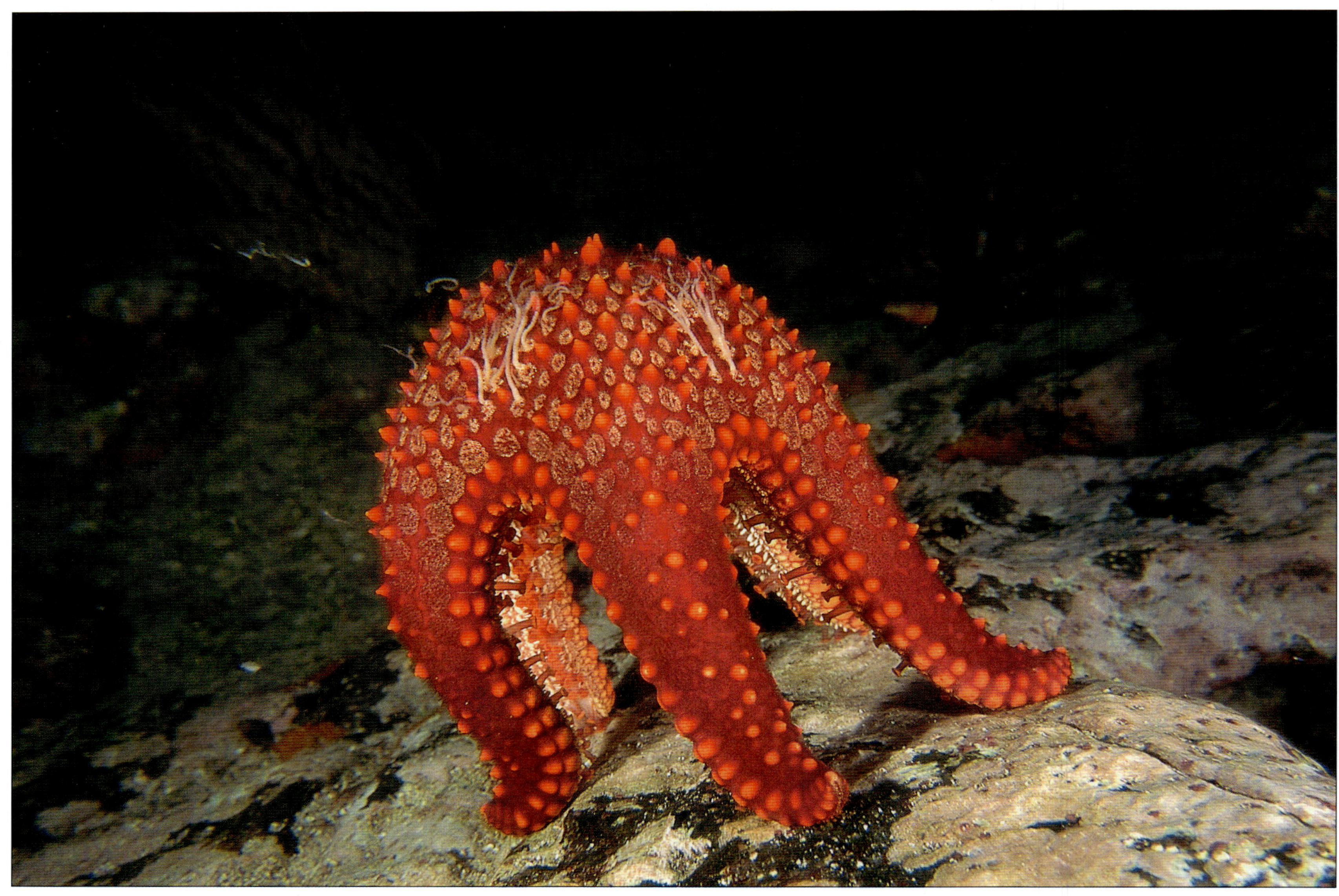

John Liddiard
United Kingdom
HIGHLY COMMENDED

Starfish spawning

"The bright red colour first attracted my attention to this starfish in the Galapagos, but I could not work out why it was in such an unusual, bridged position. I then realised it was lifting itself up into the current to release streams of spores."

Nikon F801 with 28-70mm lens; underwater housing; strobe; Fujichrome Sensia 100

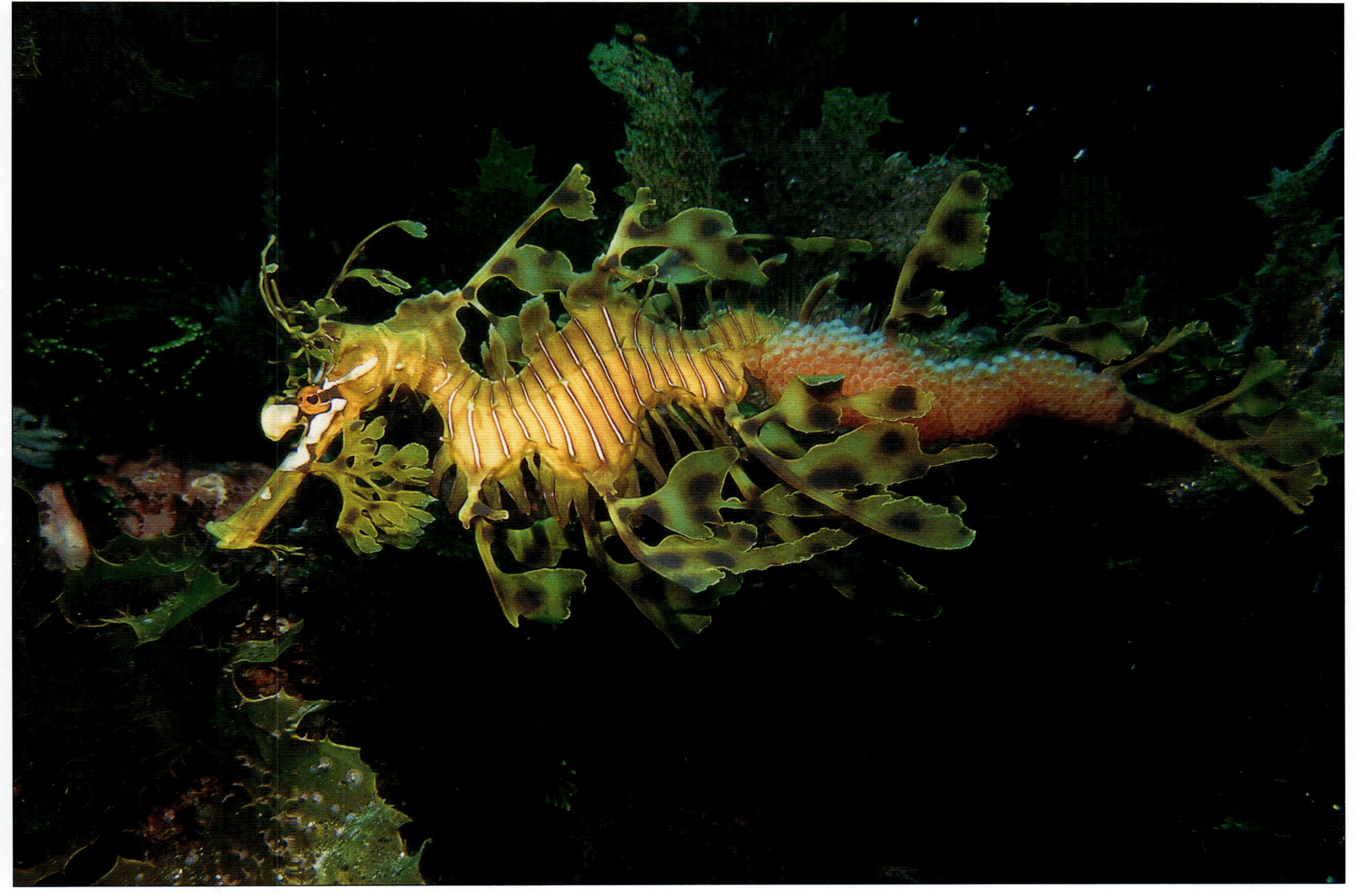

George Gornacz
Australia
HIGHLY COMMENDED

Leafy sea dragon carrying eggs

"This spectacular leafy sea dragon was so well camouflaged that it was almost impossible to find in its weedy home off Kangaroo Island, South Australia. *The male takes full parental responsibility, carrying the eggs around attached to his tail until they hatch."*

Nikon F90x with 60mm lens; underwater housing; twin flashes; 1/60 sec at f16; Fujichrome Sensia 100

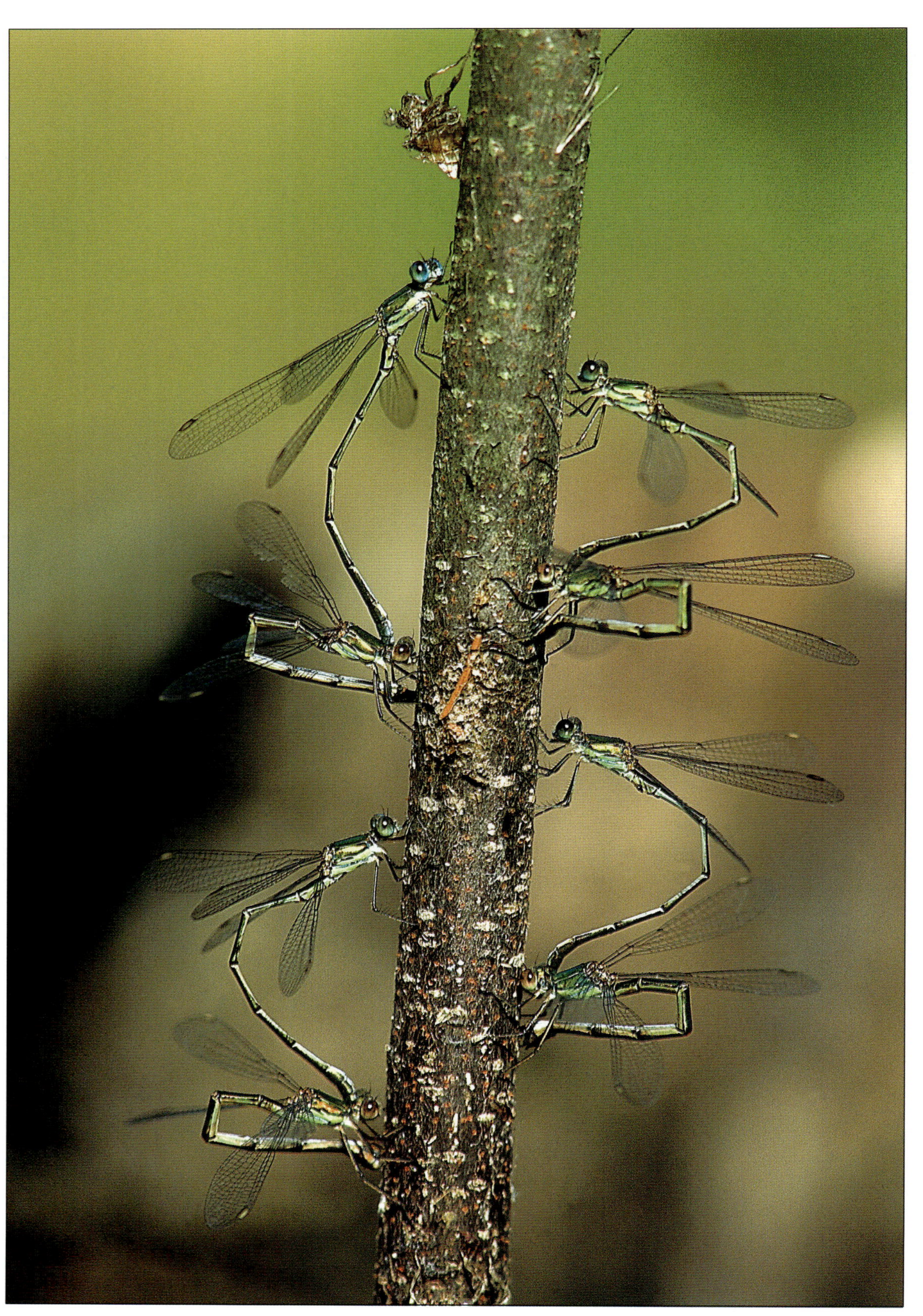

Dr Hermann Brehm

Germany

HIGHLY COMMENDED

Damselflies egg-laying

"A new pond was built in a wood near my home, and soon began to attract different species of dragonflies and damselflies. One day I found a large number of emerald damselflies, all trying to lay their eggs under the bark of small branches. Getting the pairs in perfect parallel was difficult."

Canon T 90 with 200mm lens; monopod; 1/125 sec at f4; Fujichrome Velvia

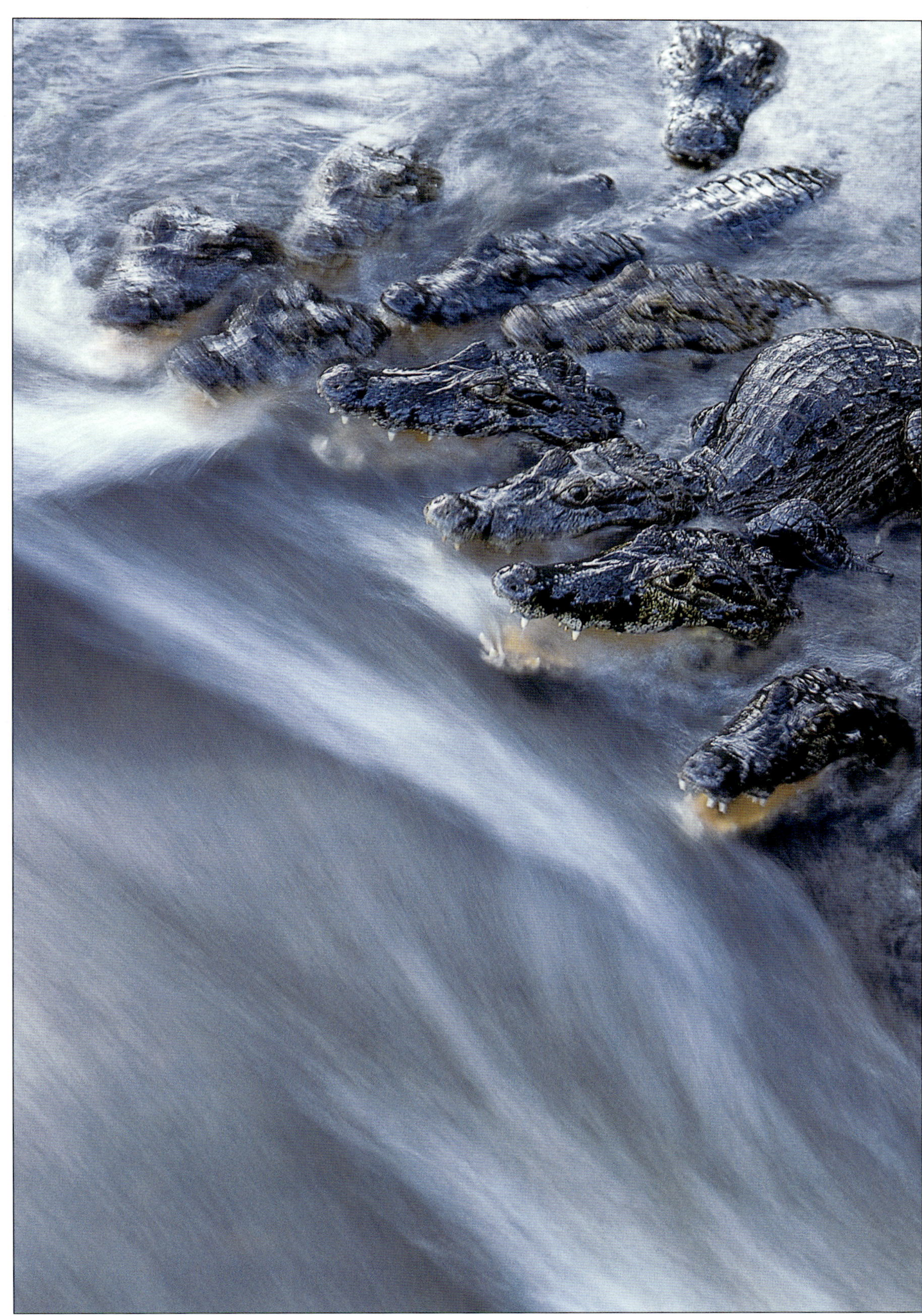

Fritz Pölking
Germany
HIGHLY COMMENDED

Caimans in river

"As twilight approached in Brazil's Pantanal, the largest wetland in the world, these caimans lined up with wide-open mouths to catch passing fish. I have never seen this behaviour before, and it took three evenings before I captured the right light and image."

Nikon F5 with 105mm lens; tripod
Fujichrome Sensia 100

British Wildlife

Entries must feature wild plants or animals, which can be in wild or urban settings.

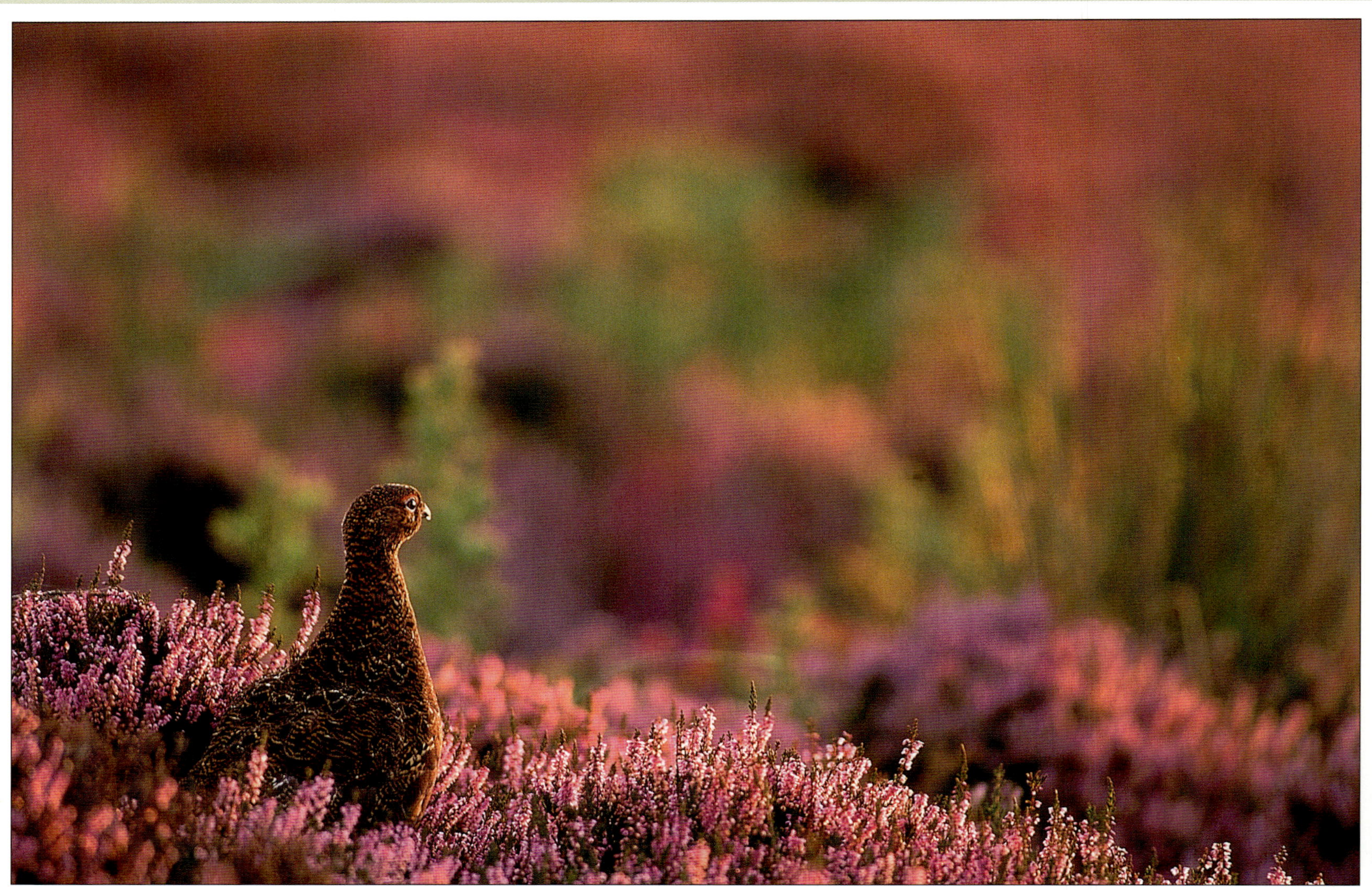

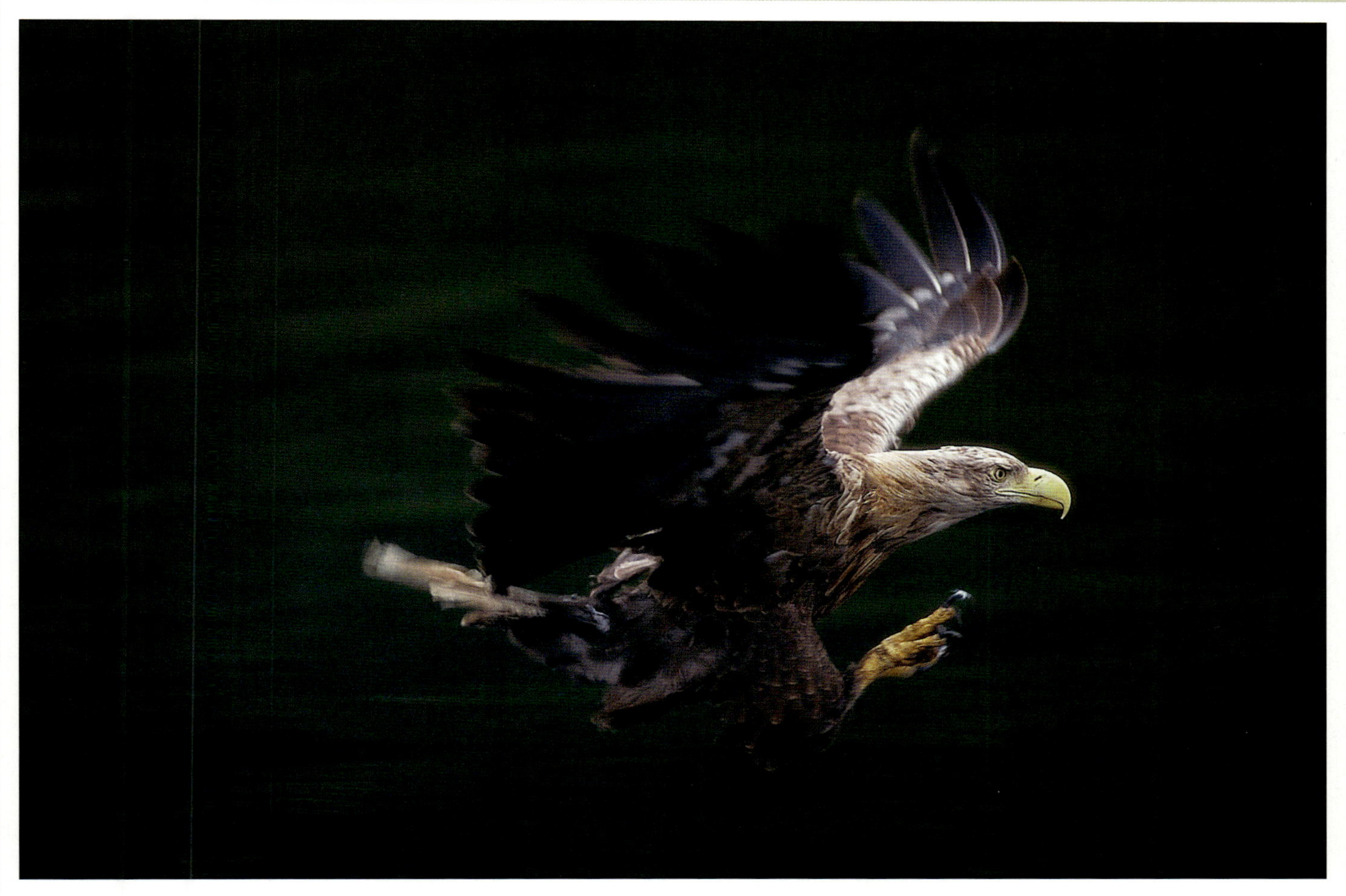

Roy Glen
United Kingdom
WINNER

Red grouse in heather

"It was sunrise on the North Yorkshire Moors in August, and the heather was in flower covering the ground with a deep pink carpet. In places the grouse are accustomed to roadside vehicles, so I was able to manoeuvre quite close to this bird."

Nikon F4E with 500mm lens; beanbag; 1/60 sec at f4; Fujichrome Velvia

Laurie Campbell
United Kingdom
RUNNER-UP

Sea eagle fishing

"I photographed this sea eagle fishing in July 1997, off the west coast of Scotland. I was working on a contract for Scottish Natural Heritage to illustrate the re-introduction of this species from Scandinavia, and there were only 12 pairs nesting in Scotland."

Nikon F5 with 500mm lens; 1/250 sec at f4; Fujichrome Provia 100 rated at 200

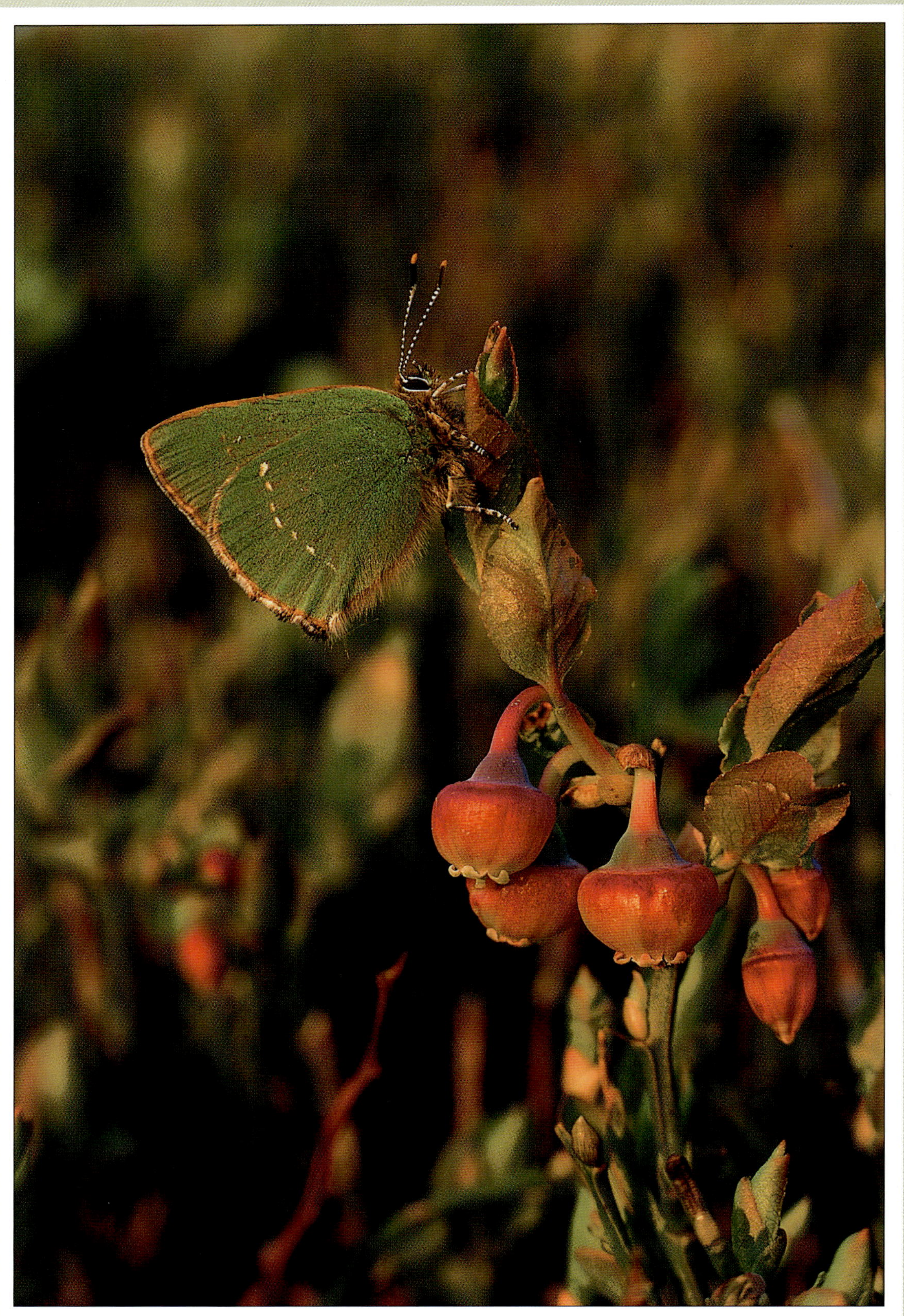

Simon Booth
United Kingdom
SPECIALLY COMMENDED

Green hairstreak on bilberry

"Spotting a green hairstreak at rest is difficult as it is only the size of a thumbnail and can be very flighty. This female was feeding on bilberry on a moorland in Lancashire. Sheep are also very fond of this plant, so finding both the flowers intact and the butterfly is a real challenge."

Canon EOS 100 with 50mm lens and 13mm extension tube; 1/30 sec at f8; Fujichrome Velvia

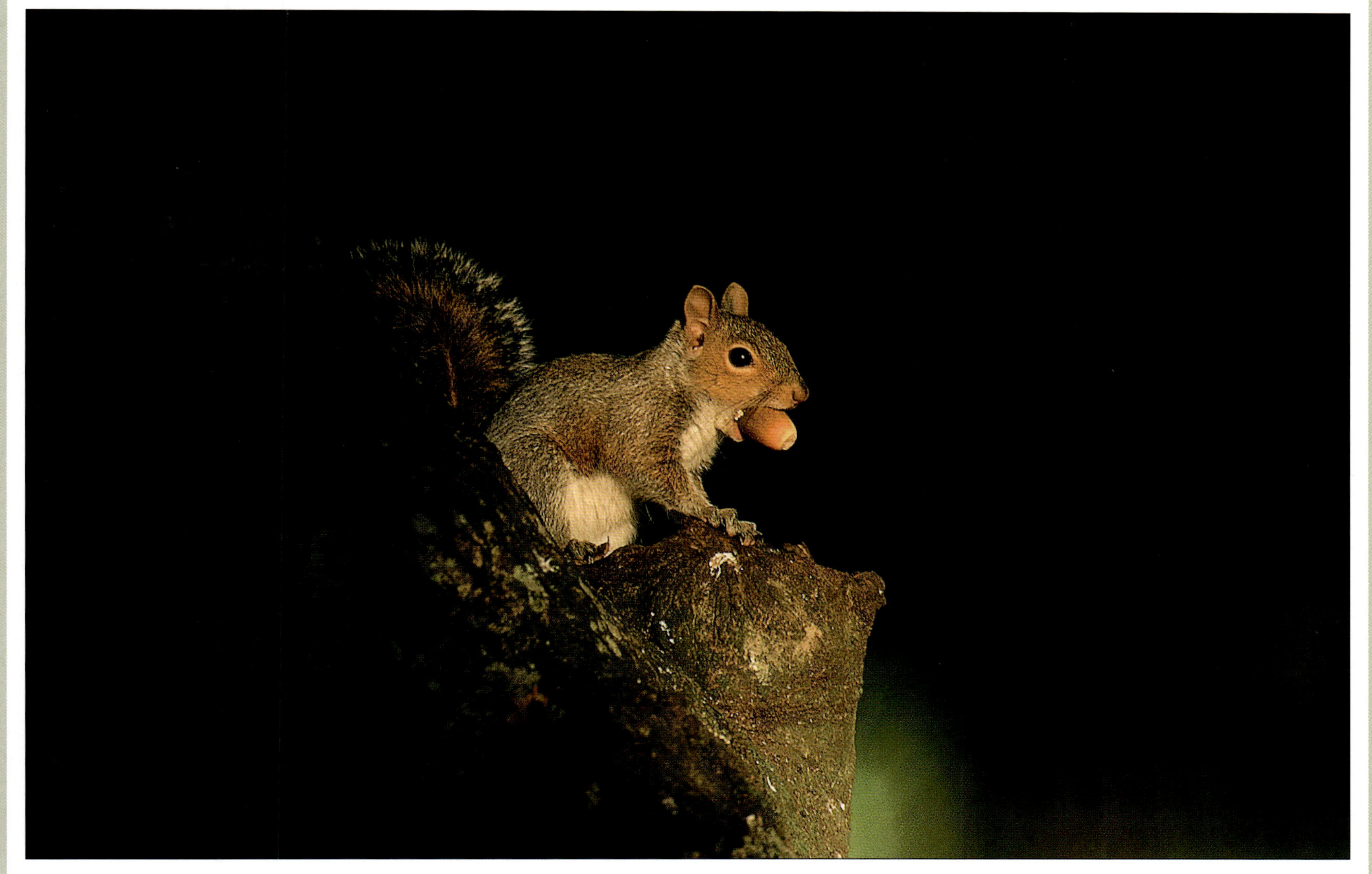

Andy Rouse
United Kingdom
HIGHLY COMMENDED

Grey squirrel with acorn

"The squirrel had been hiding nuts in a tree in the New Forest for several minutes before he stopped to watch me. The animal is lit by a single shaft of autumn sunlight."

Canon EOS 1N with 600mm lens; 1/125th at f5.6; Fujichrome Velvia rated at 40

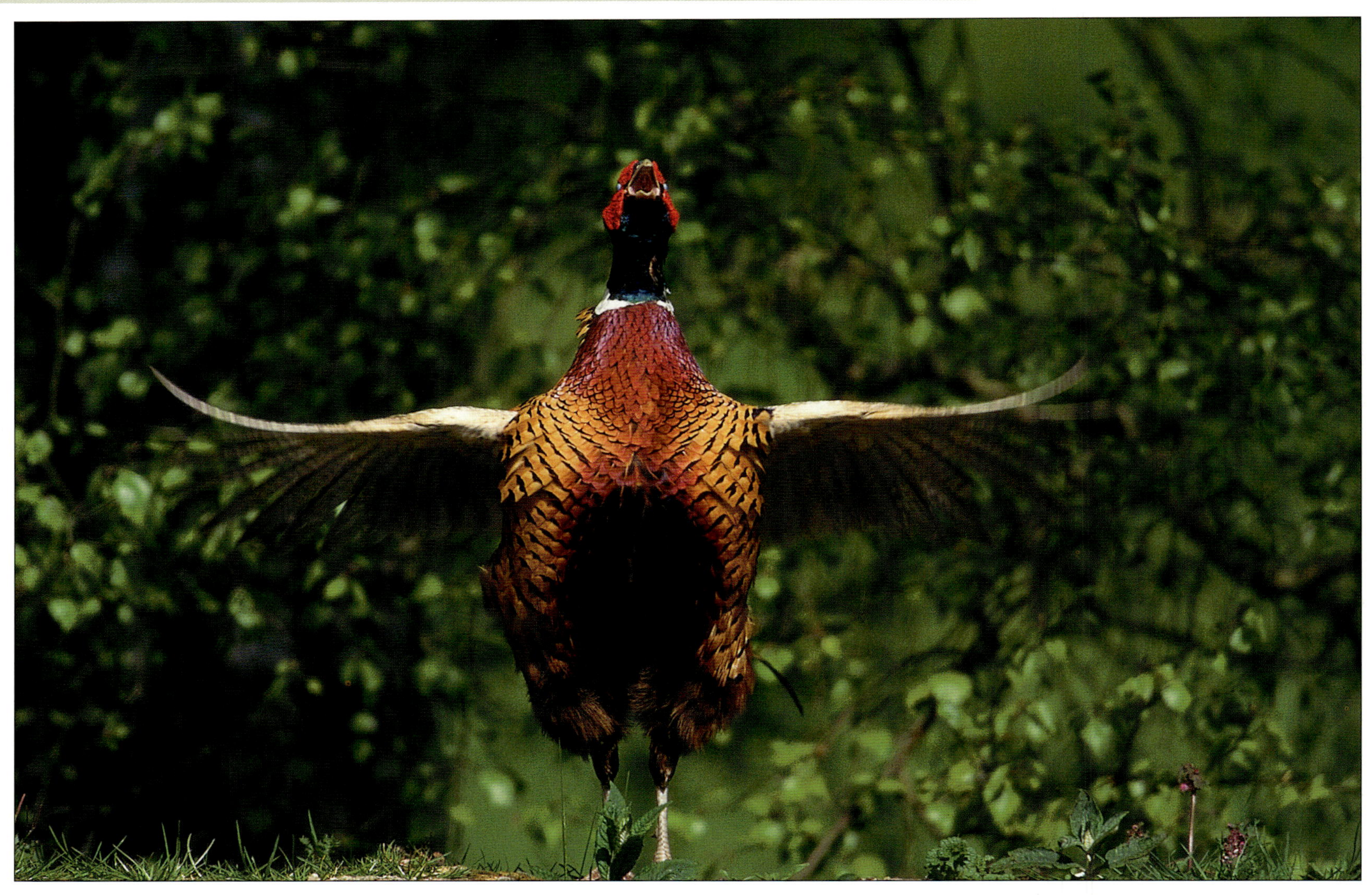

Terry Andrewartha
United Kingdom
HIGHLY COMMENDED

Pheasant displaying

"I had watched this cock pheasant come to the same area every day and display. It chased off other cocks and appeared to be defending its territory, although I never saw any hen birds. I photographed it at six frames per second, using five rolls of film."

Canon EOS 1N with 600mm lens and x1.4 converter; tripod; 1/1000 sec at f6.3; Fujichrome 100 rated at 200

John Cancalosi
United States of America
HIGHLY COMMENDED

Red deer stag

"I saw this stag during the rut in Surrey. After thrashing its antlers around in the bracken, it raised its head to roar."

Nikon F5 with 500mm lens; 1/250 sec at f4; Fujichrome Velvia

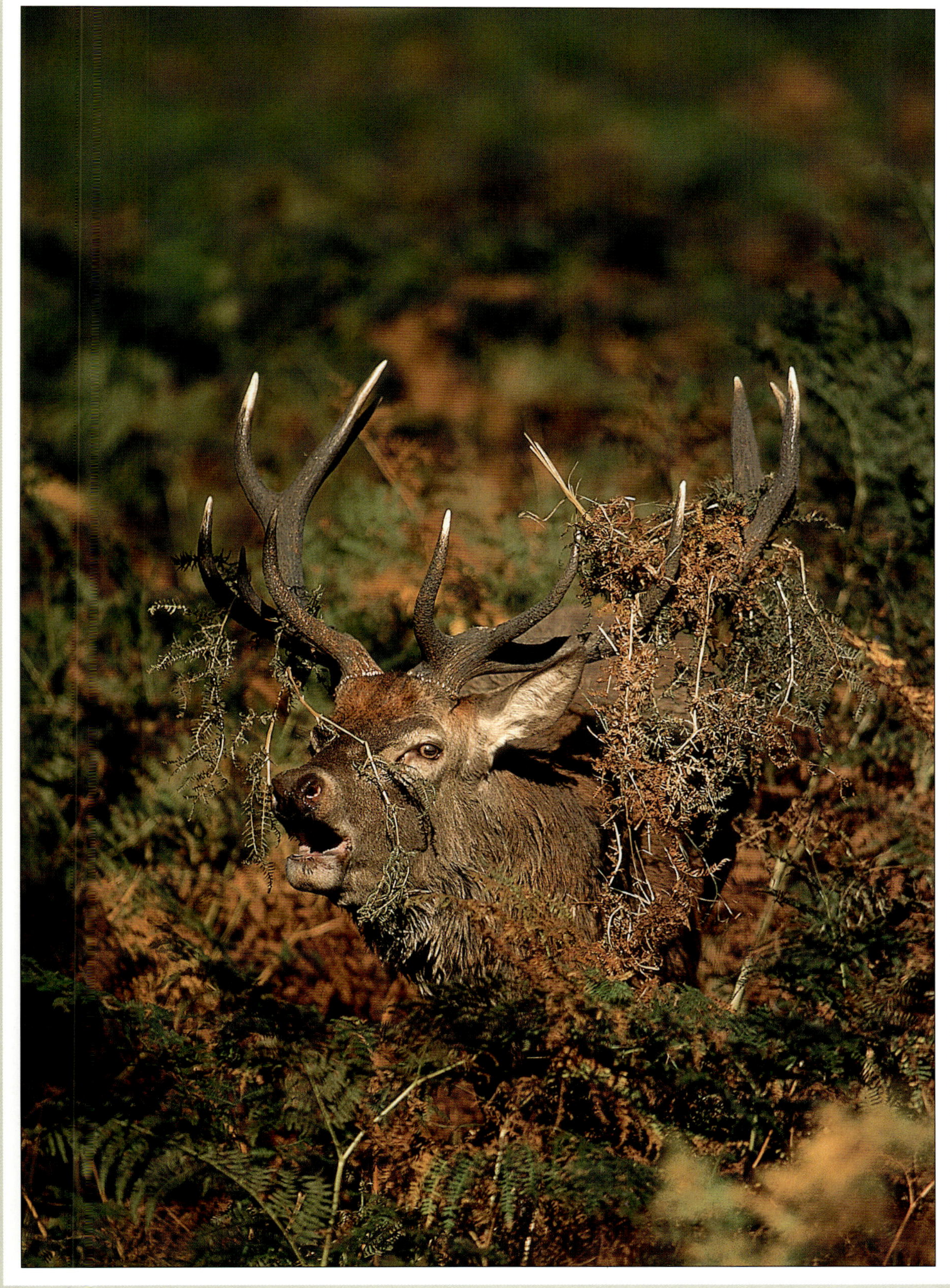

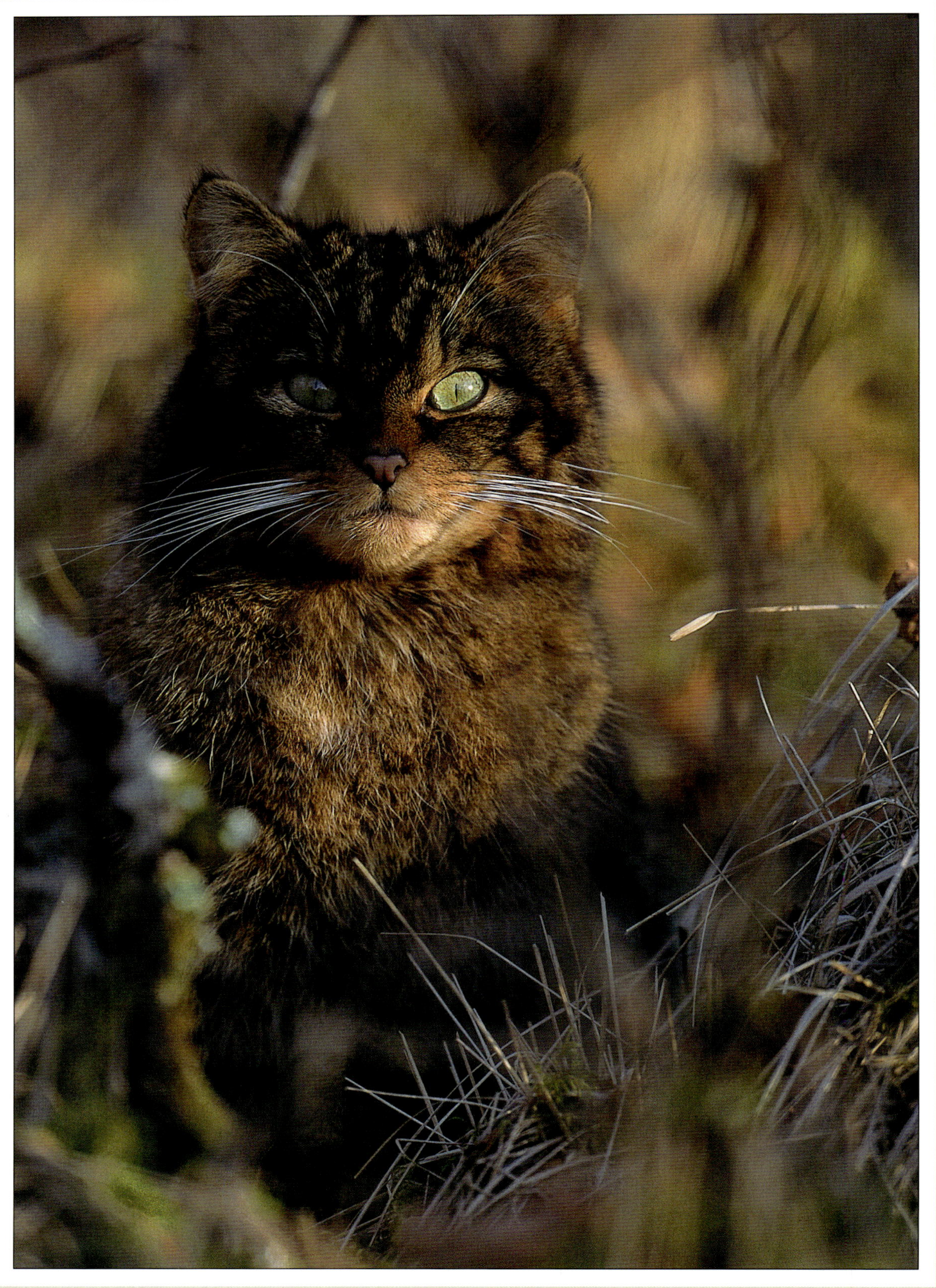

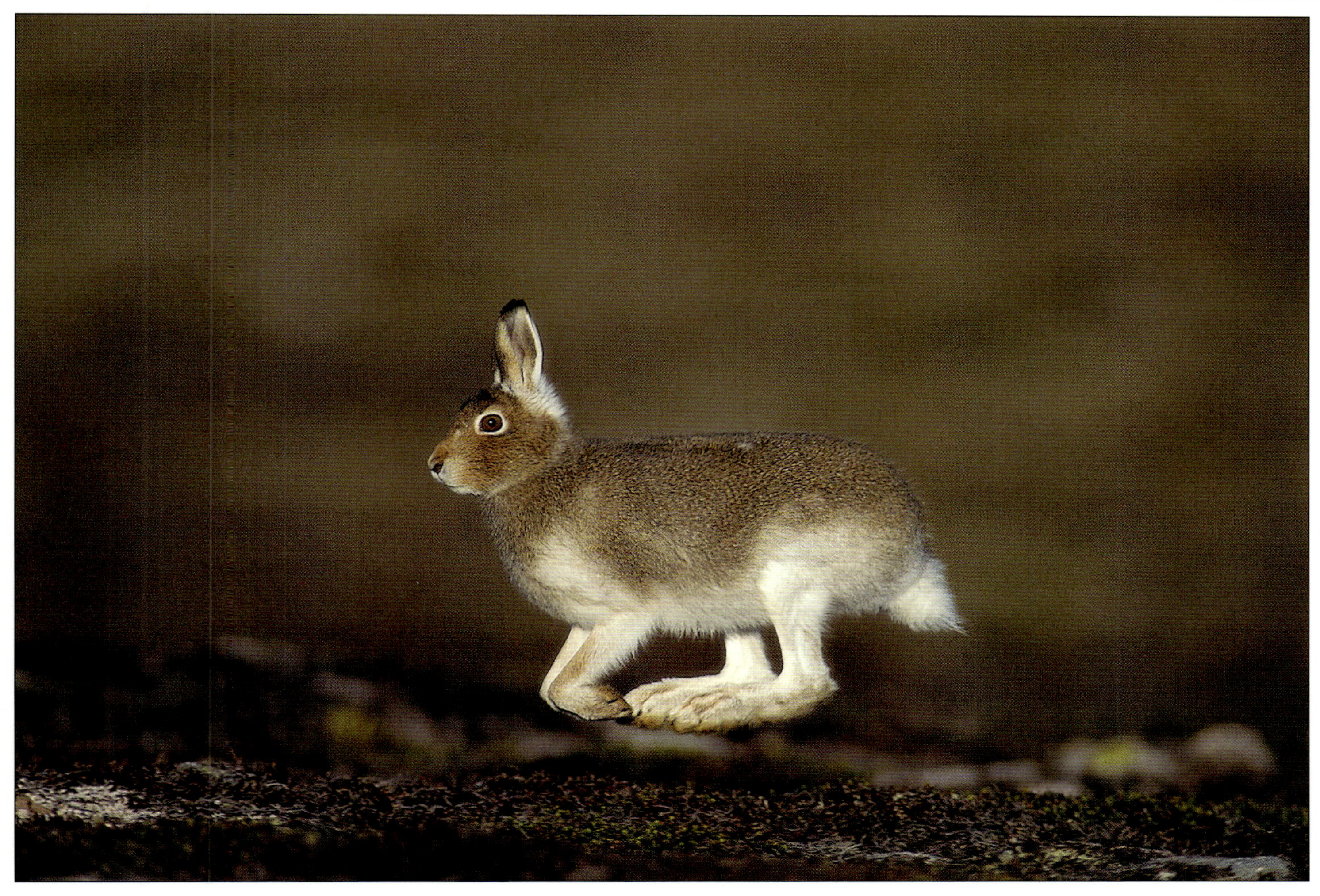

Laurie Campbell
United Kingdom
HIGHLY COMMENDED

Scottish wildcat

"This young female wildcat, still with much of her thick winter coat, was one of two kittens hand-reared and released back into the wild. I photographed them over a two-year period in a remote part of the Highlands. They were very wary, and I would not have got so close without the lady who reared them close by my side."

Nikon F5 with 200-400mm lens; 1/125 at f4; Fujichrome Provia 100

Neil McIntyre
United Kingdom
HIGHLY COMMENDED

Mountain hare

"I have photographed hares on the Monadhliath Mountains, in Scotland, for many years. This particular hare had a regular path, so I hid myself among some large rocks and waited for it to run by."

Canon EOS 1N with 400mm lens and x1 converter; 1/500 sec at f4; Fujichrome Sensia at 100

In Praise of Plants

Pictures should highlight the beauty and importance of flowering and non-flowering plants.

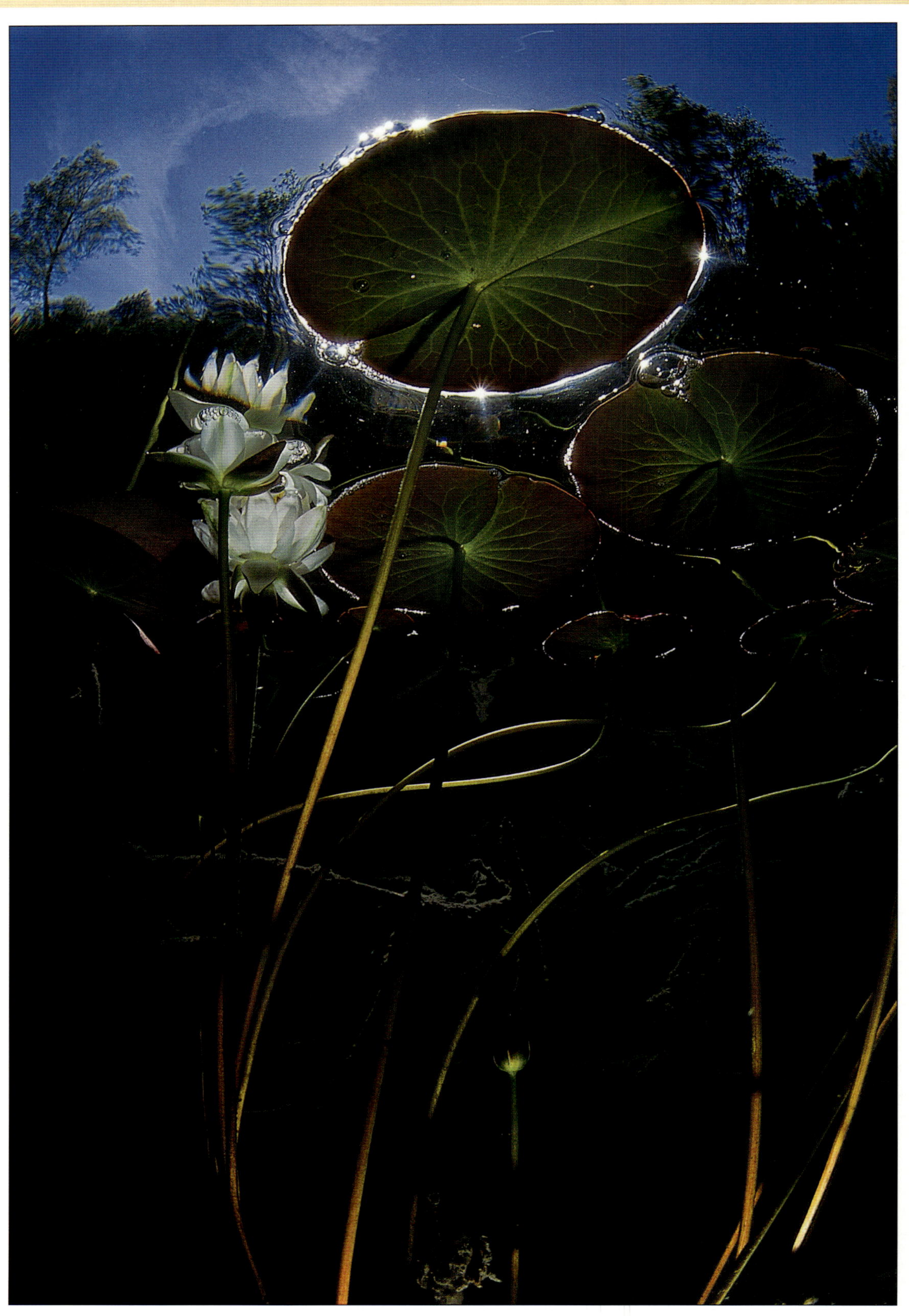

Fredrik Ehrenström
Sweden
WINNER

White water lilies

"Nearly a quarter of Sweden's lakes are seriously polluted by acid rain, and this small one, Great Horse Lake, near Göteborg, is no exception. Little survives in these very acidic waters, except for a few dragonfly nymphs, water-spiders and these beautiful white water lilies. The water is crystal clear due to the lack of plankton."

Nikon 801s with 16mm lens; underwater housing; two flashes; 1/30 sec at f11; Fujichrome Velvia

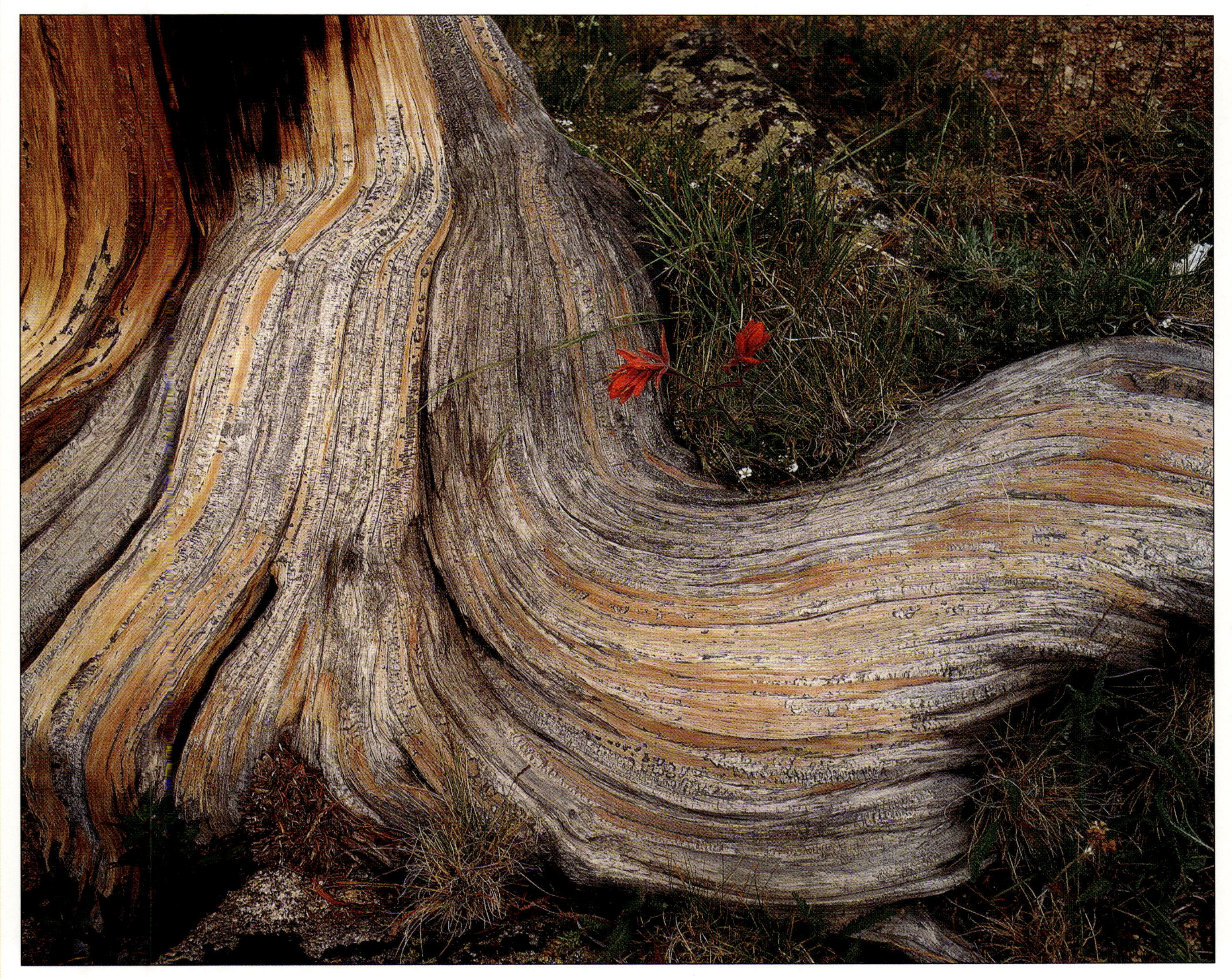

Robert McKemie
United States of America
RUNNER-UP

Bristlecone pine and Indian paintbrush

"To get this shot, I rose well before sunrise to be at Mount Goliath Natural Area, 11,000ft above sea level in the Rocky Mountains. When the light was good, I spent about an hour looking for just the right situation and was rewarded by this red Indian paintbrush growing near the beautifully-shaped trunk of the bristlecone pine."

Pentax 6x7 with 75mm lens; tripod; 1/30sec at f16; Kodak Lumiere

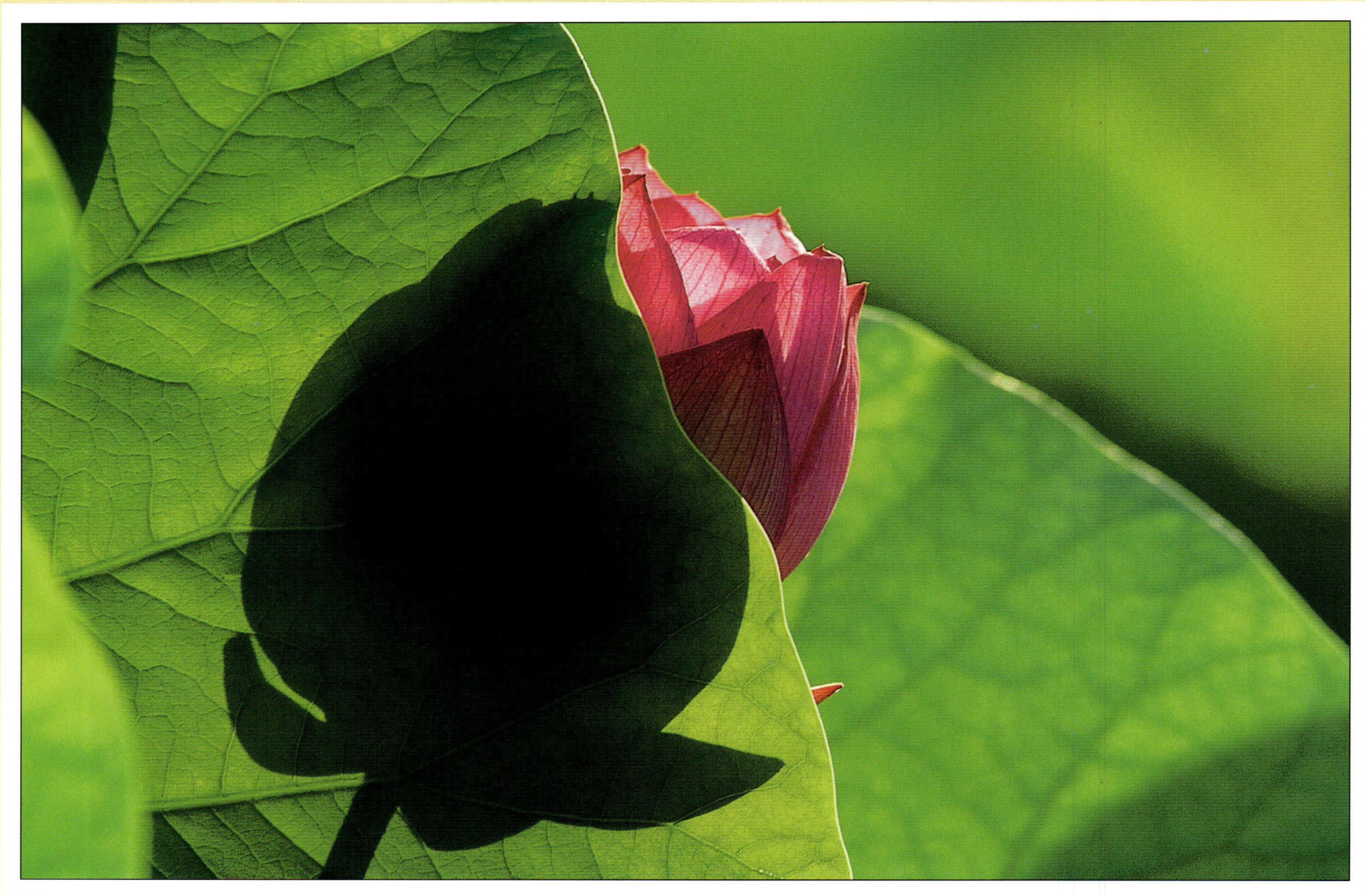

Jun Ogawa
Japan
HIGHLY COMMENDED

Sacred lotus

"Seeds from this species of lotus have been discovered in 2,000-year-old peat. It blooms every year and the buds open just after sunrise."

Nikon F3 with 400mm lens and x1.4 converter; tripod; 1/60 sec at f5.6; Fujichrome Velvia rated at 40

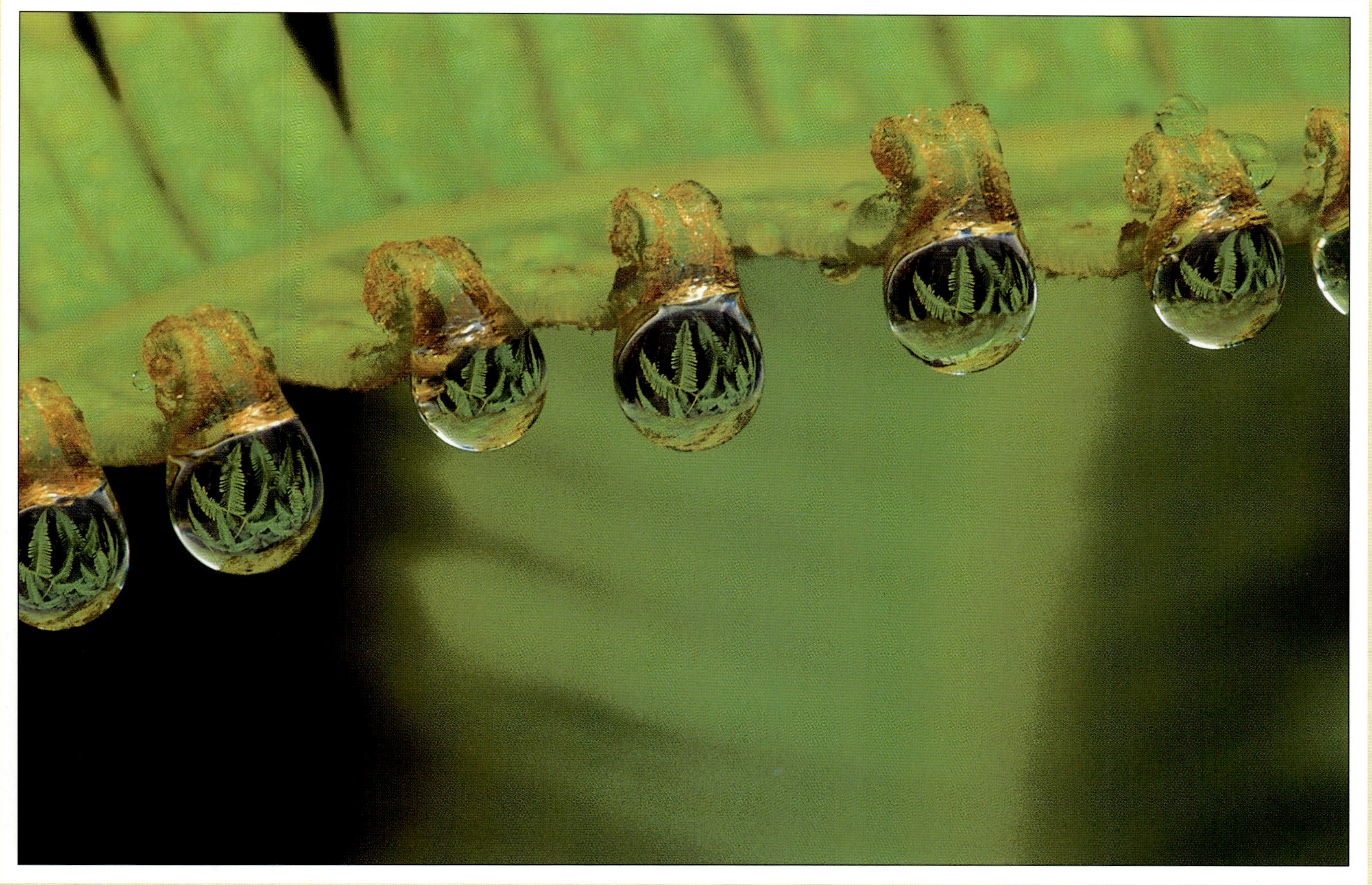

Whit Bronaugh
United States of America
HIGHLY COMMENDED

False staghorn fern

"A fine mist in Volcanoes National Park, Hawaii, had allowed the raindrops to accumulate evenly on the frond of this false staghorn fern. Each drop acted like a lens, creating images of the entire plant in the background. It is a refracted image, not a reflection, and is upside down – the fronds of this species hang downwards."

Nikon F3 with 200mm lens with close-up lens and extension tube; tripod; 4 sec at f32; Fujichrome Velvia 50

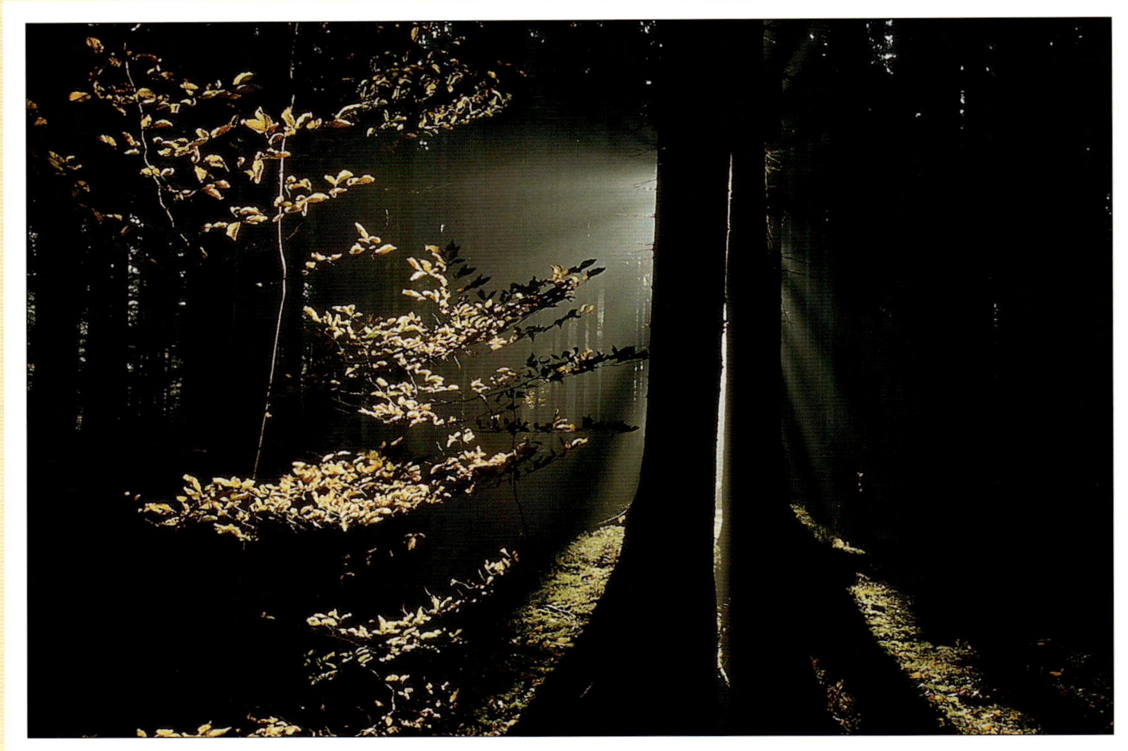

Frank Krahmer

Germany

HIGHLY COMMENDED

Sunrays through trees

"The forest south of Munich is a magical place for photography when the sun shines through the trees in the early morning. Especially fascinating, one misty October, was the way the sun lit up a small beech tree struggling for light in the woodland gloom."

Canon EOS 1RS with 20-35mm lens; 1/15 sec at f11; Fujichrome Velvia 50

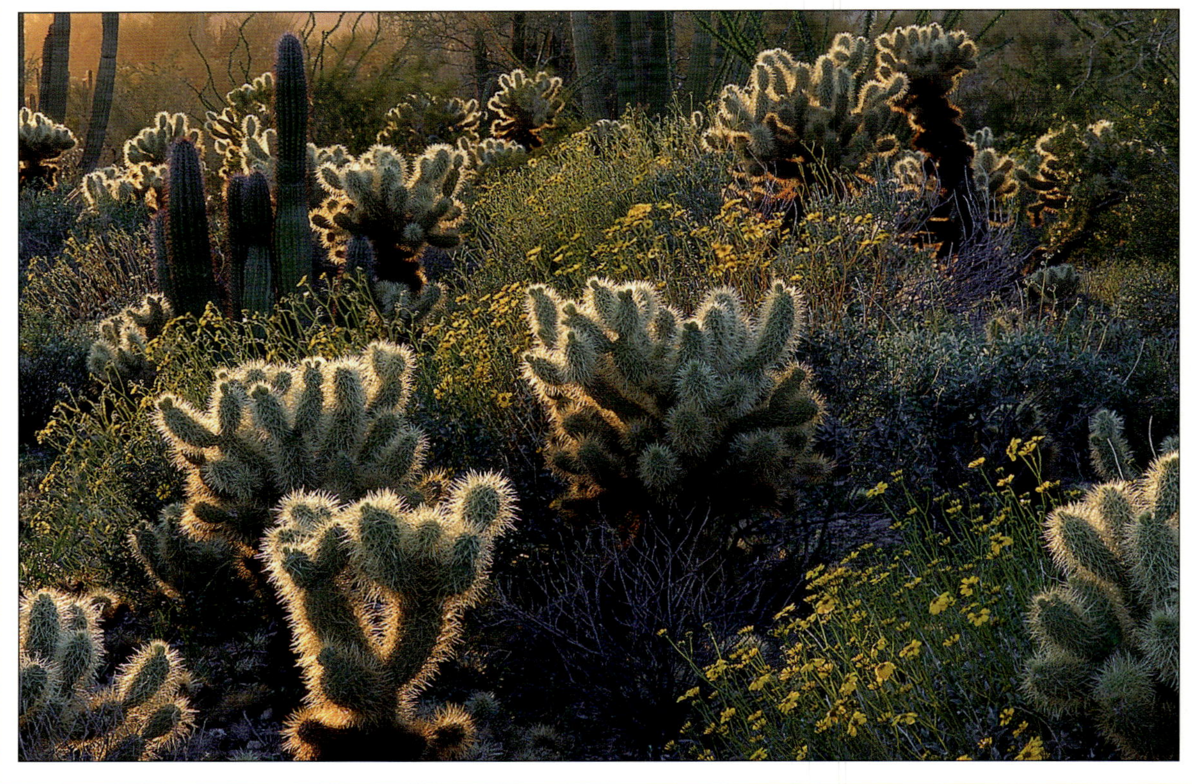

Theo Allofs

Germany

HIGHLY COMMENDED

Cactus field

"The flowers were bursting into bloom among the cacti after the prolific spring rains in Organpipe National Monument, Arizona. The sun was already low when I came across this field of chollas interspersed with bright yellow brittlebush. The backlight created a beautiful halo-like glow outlining the chollas giving them a deceptively soft, cuddly appearance."

Nikon F5 with 80-200mm lens; tripod; 1/4 sec at f22; Fujichrome Velvia

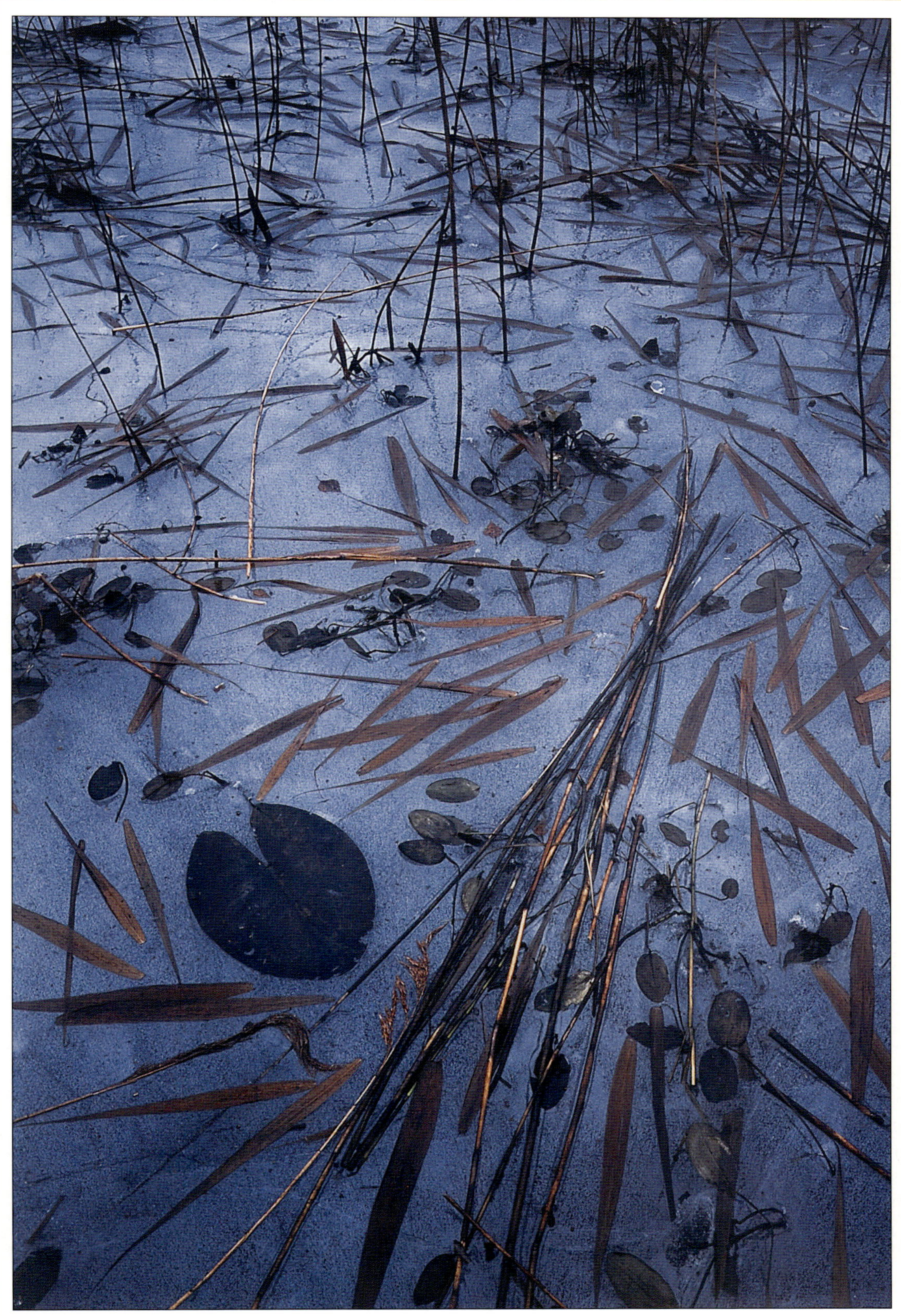

Pål Hermansen
Norway
HIGHLY COMMENDED

Leaves on ice

"This image was taken in March when the ice was melting on a lake close to my home. I was fascinated by the striking patterns of chaos and order that the scattered leaves and reeds made"

Nikon F4 with 35mm lens; 4 secs at f22

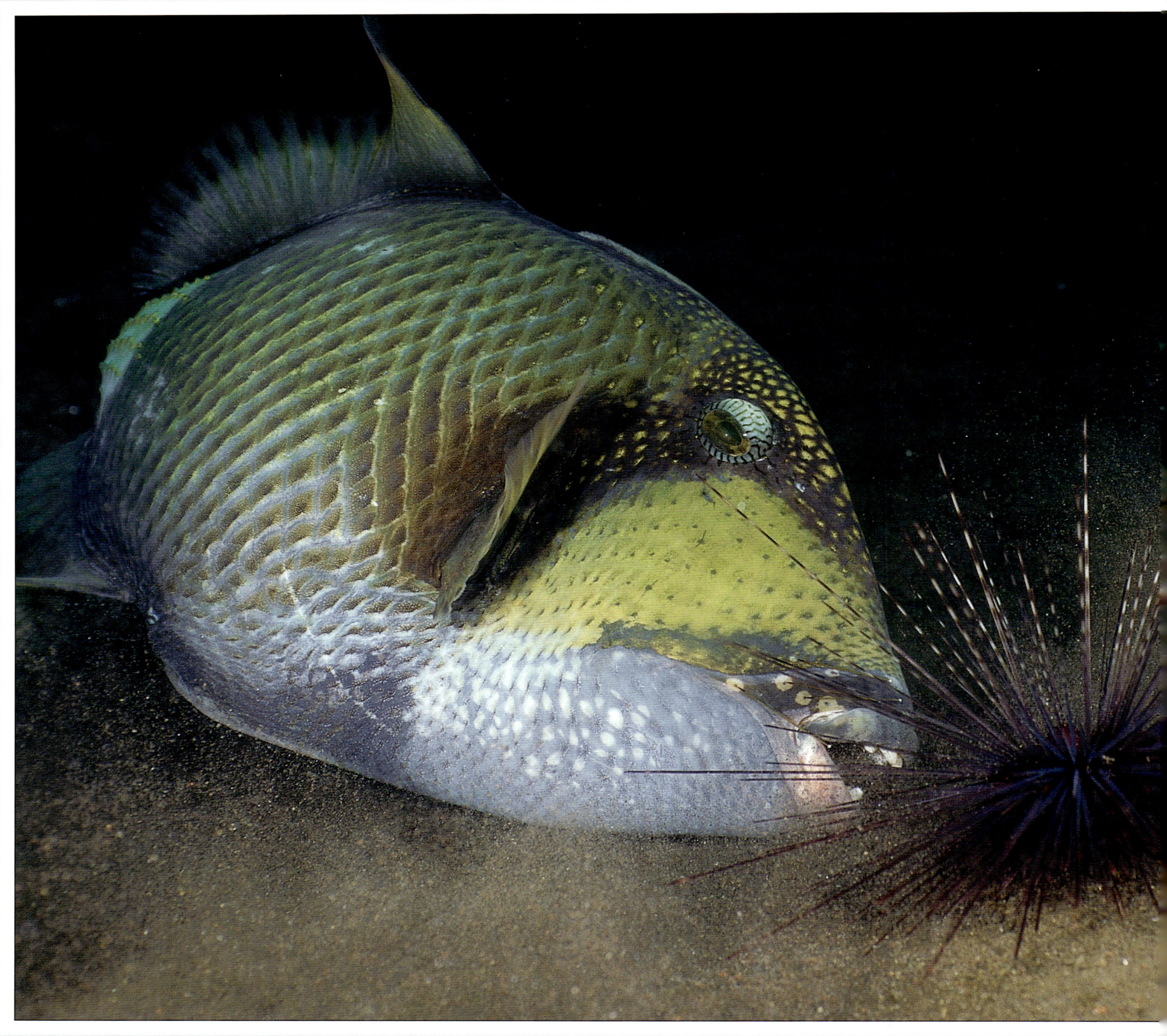

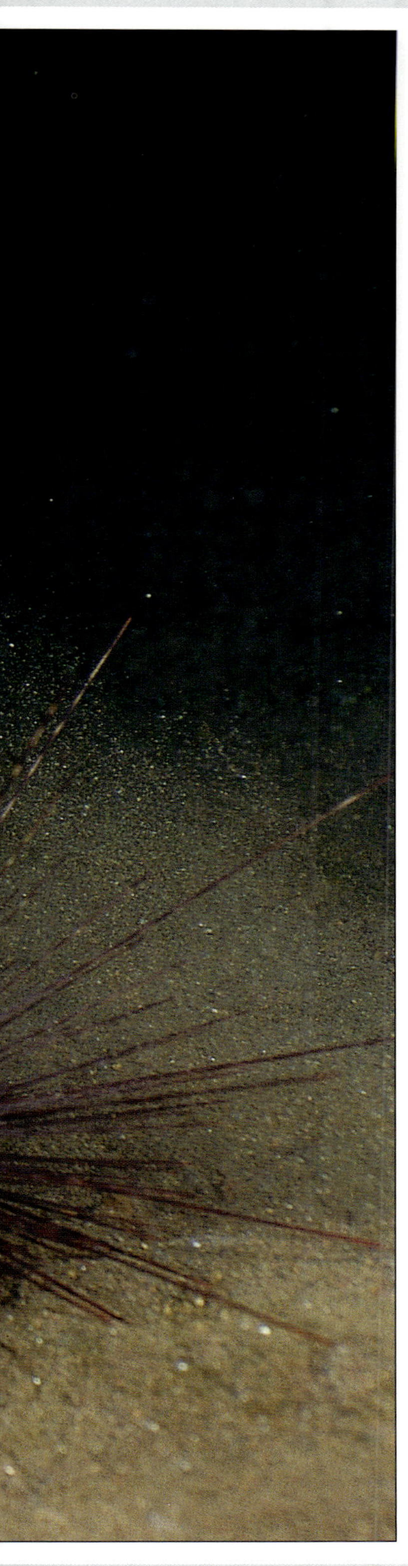

The Underwater World

Pictures, which must have been taken under water, can illustrate any marine or freshwater subject.

Fred Bavendam
United States of America
WINNER

Triggerfish attacking sea urchin

"This sea urchin had mistakenly left its hiding place, in the waters off Bali, before darkness fell. The titan triggerfish was very determined in its attack. Despite a number of spines penetrating or breaking off in its face, it eventually managed to turn the urchin over and bite off pieces until nothing but a pile of broken spines was left."

Nikon F4 with 20-35mm lens; underwater housing; two strobes; 1/60 at f8

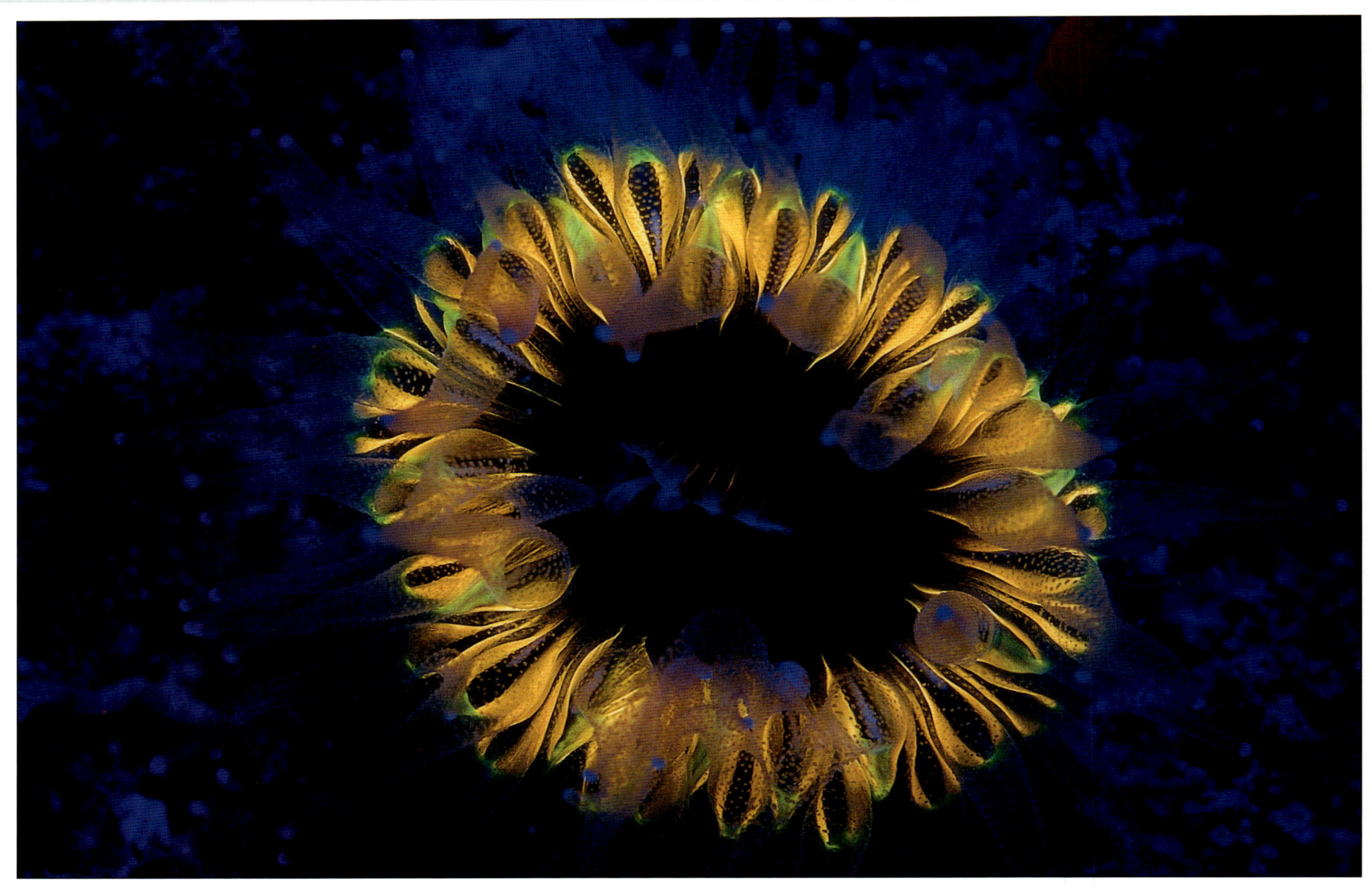

Dan Welsh-Bon
United States of America
RUNNER-UP

Fluorescent cup coral

"Many marine animals and plants fluoresce under certain conditions. By using my own special techniques, I managed to reveal this phenomenon in a solitary cup coral."

Nikonos III with 35mm lens and 1:1 extension tube; dual strobe; 1/60 sec at f11; Fujichrome 100

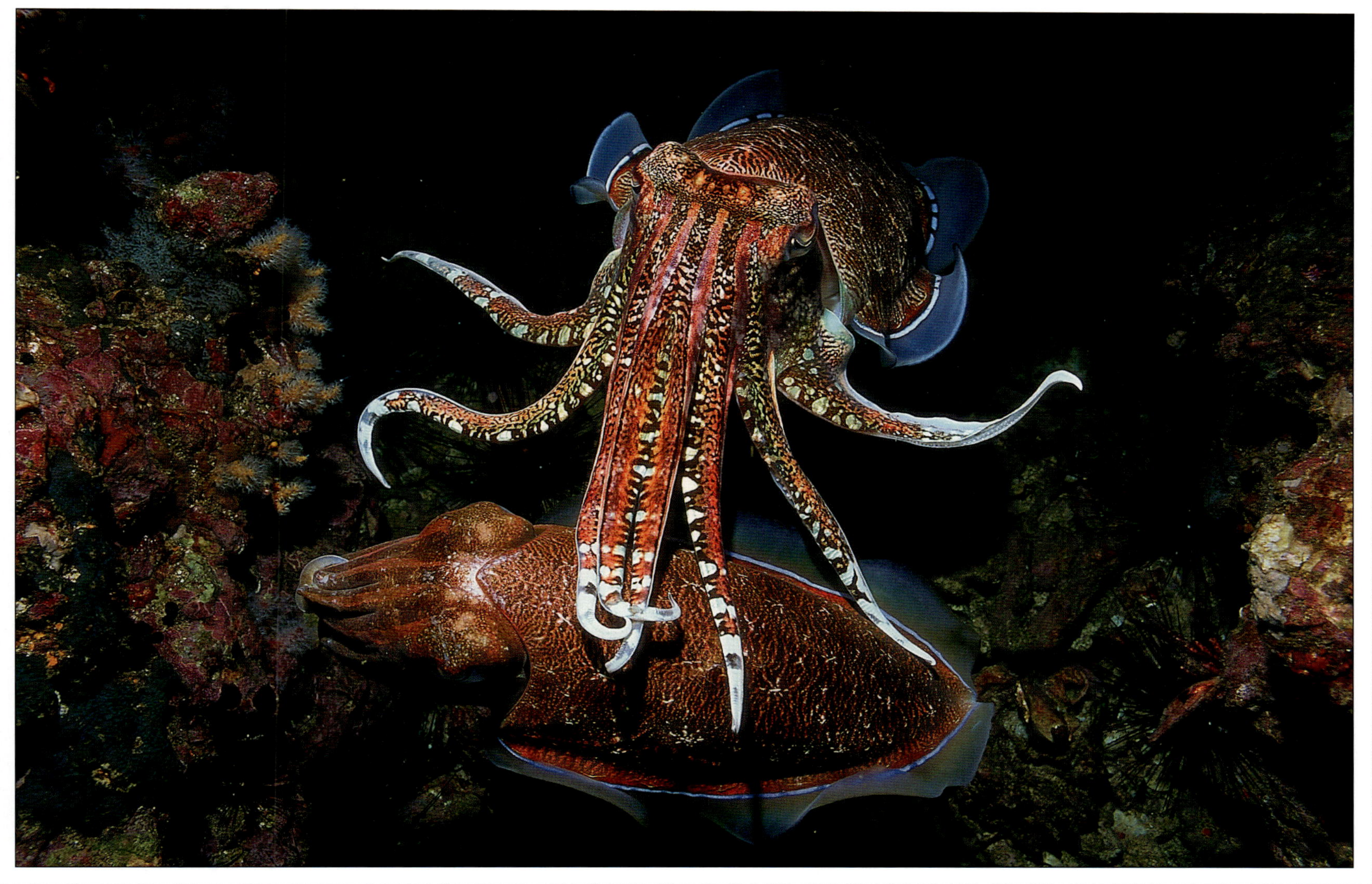

Georgette Douwma
Netherlands
HIGHLY COMMENDED

Cuttlefish

"This male cuttlefish, in the Andaman Sea, Thailand, was protecting the egg-laying female from rivals, as he had already passed a bag of his sperm to her. She will not use this until the final moment before she lays her eggs. Therefore, he is always on the look out for other males trying to get in on the act at the last minute."

Nikon F4 with 35mm lens; underwater housing; flash; 1/60 sec at f5.6

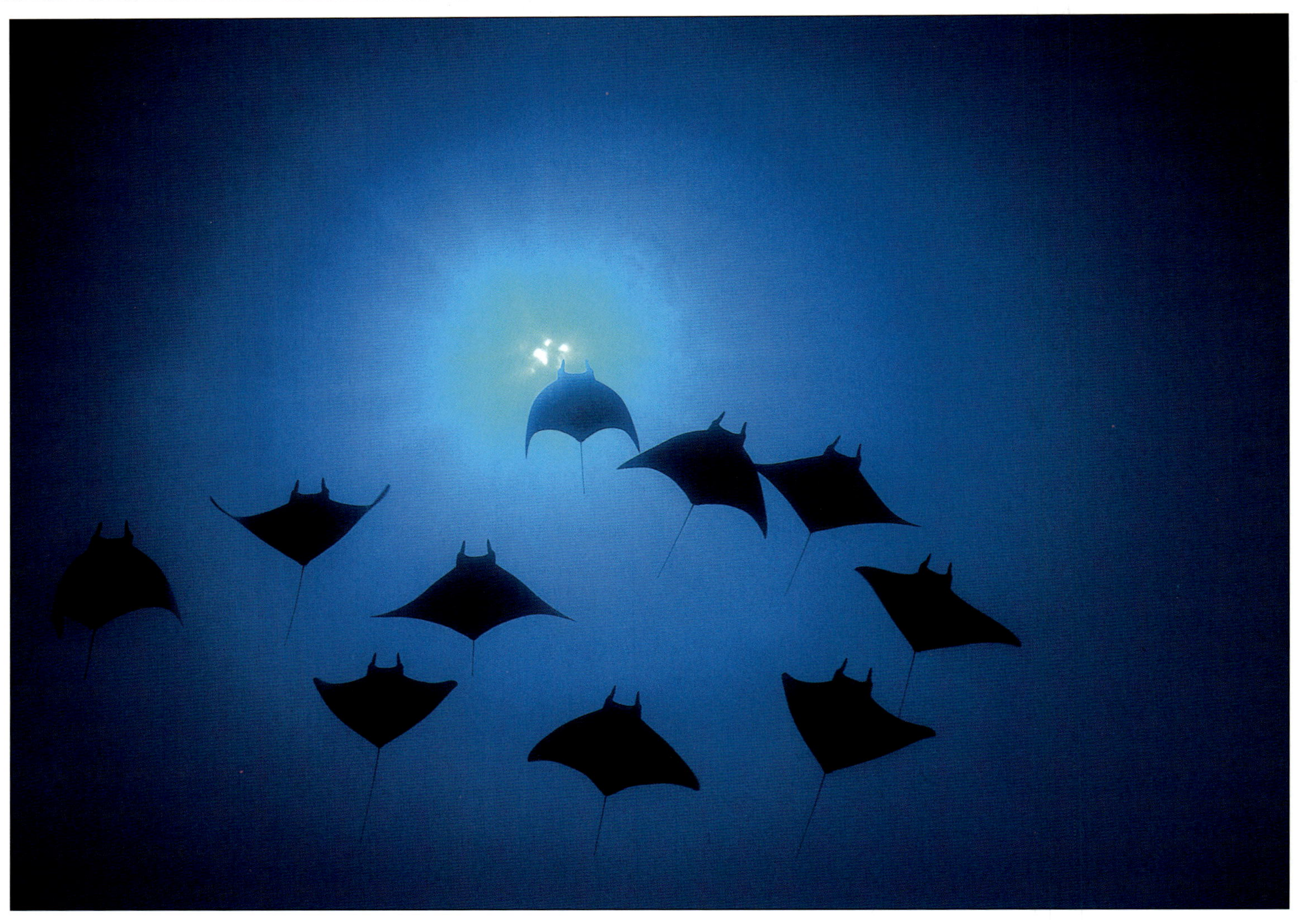

Michael Cufer
Australia
HIGHLY COMMENDED

School of devil rays

"I was more than 60 metres down off Gizo Island, in the Solomon Islands, searching for silvertip sharks, when I looked up and saw this school of devil rays near the surface. I made a quick and risky ascent to 25 metres and had only enough time to shoot two frames."

Nikonos 5 with 20mm lens; 1/250 sec at f5.6; Fujichrome Velvia

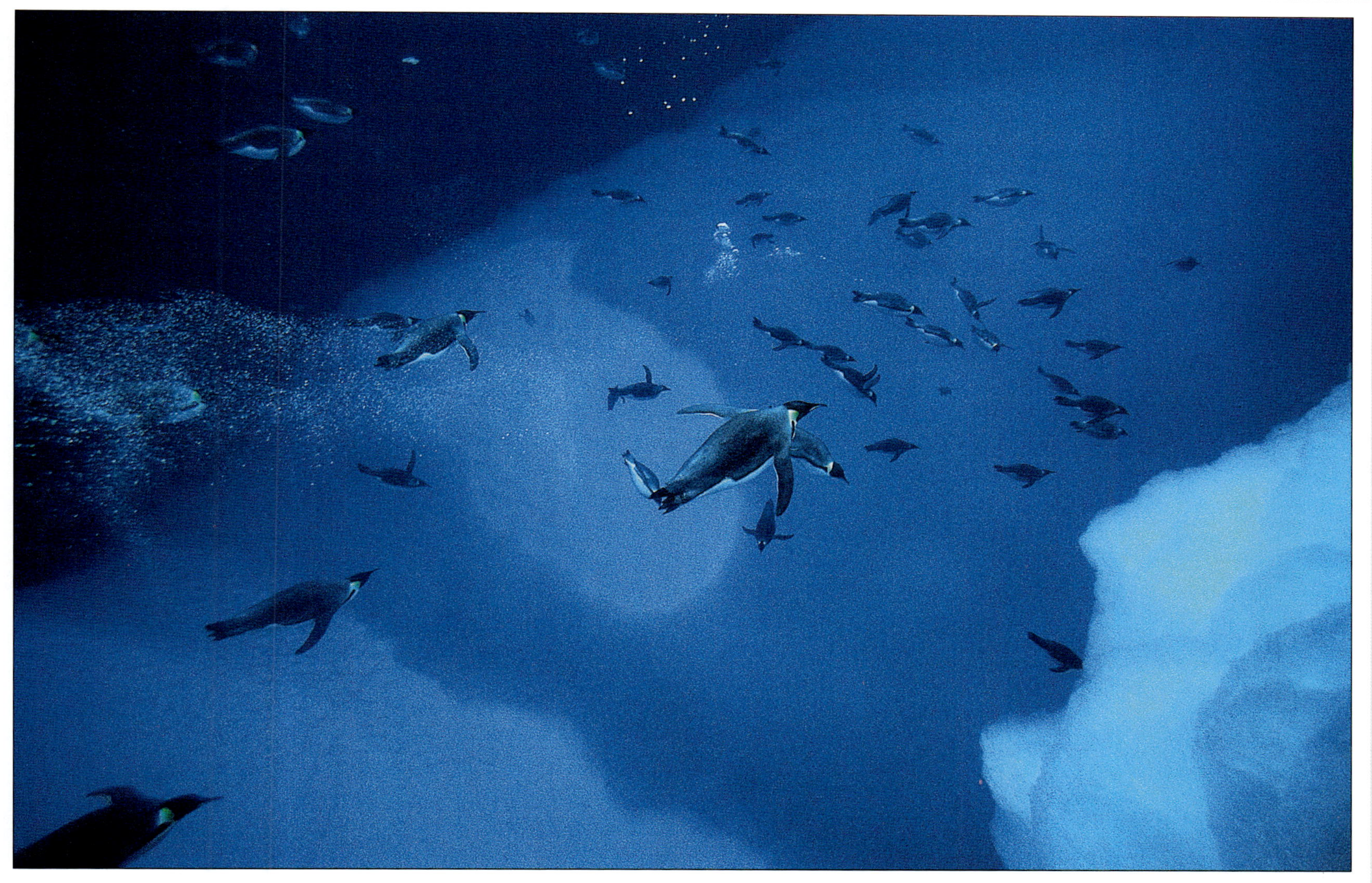

Erik Stavseth Lornie
United Kingdom
HIGHLY COMMENDED

Emperor penguins underwater

"I spent two years working as an engineer for the British Antarctic Survey at Halley Base by the Weddell Sea, where we were lucky to have a large emperor penguin colony nearby. This photograph was taken early in the southern summer, and the penguins appeared to be enjoying their new-found freedom in the sea after a long and difficult winter on the ice."

Nikon F601 with 17mm lens; 1/250 sec at f5.6; Kodachrome 200

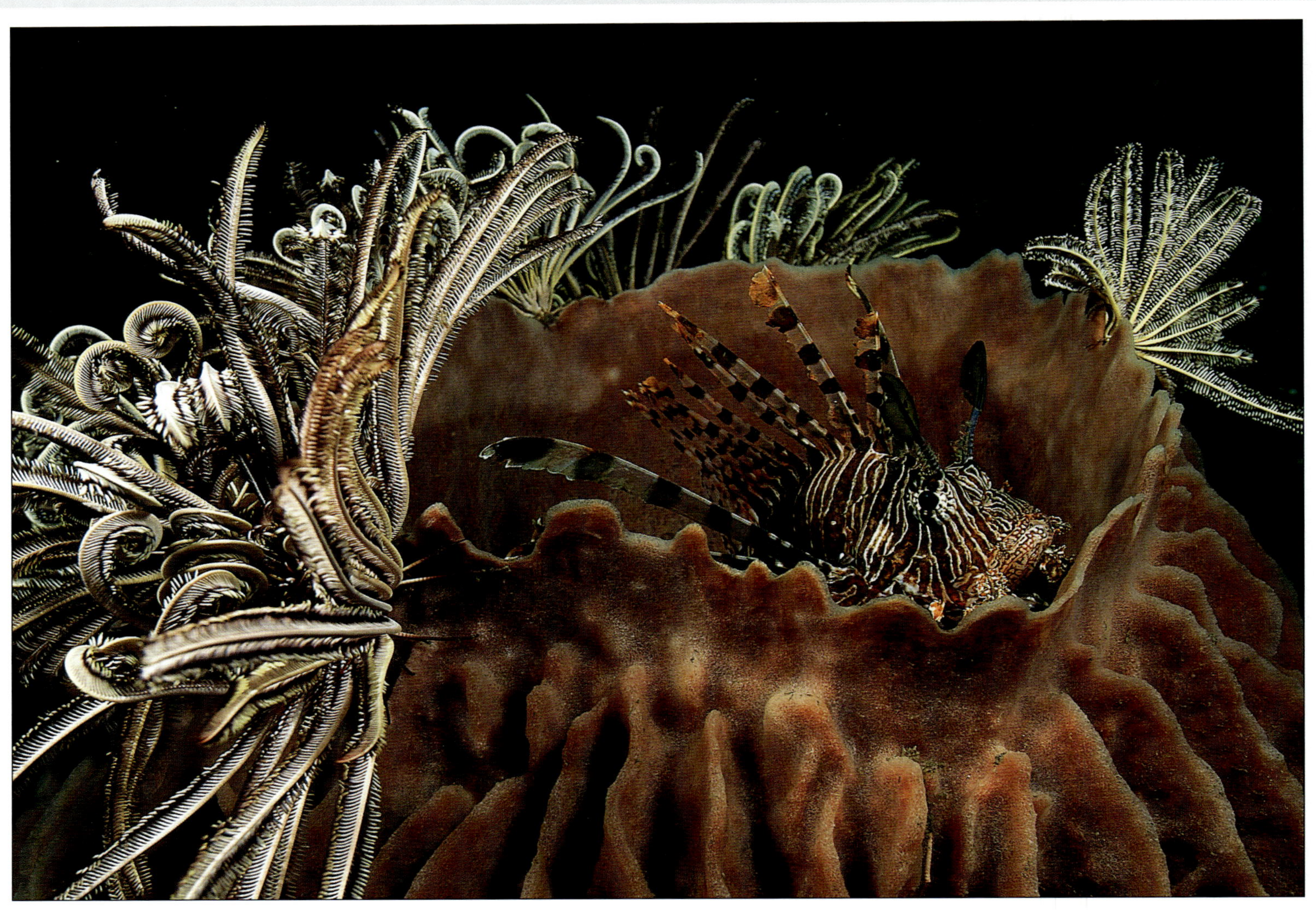

Fred Bavendam
United States of America
HIGHLY COMMENDED

Lionfish in barrel sponge

"The lionfish in the waters off Bali frequently hide among the feather stars at the lips of barrel sponges, as this picture illustrates, where they wait to ambush unsuspecting small fish."

Nikon F4 with 20-35mm lens; underwater housing; two strobes; 1/125 sec at f16

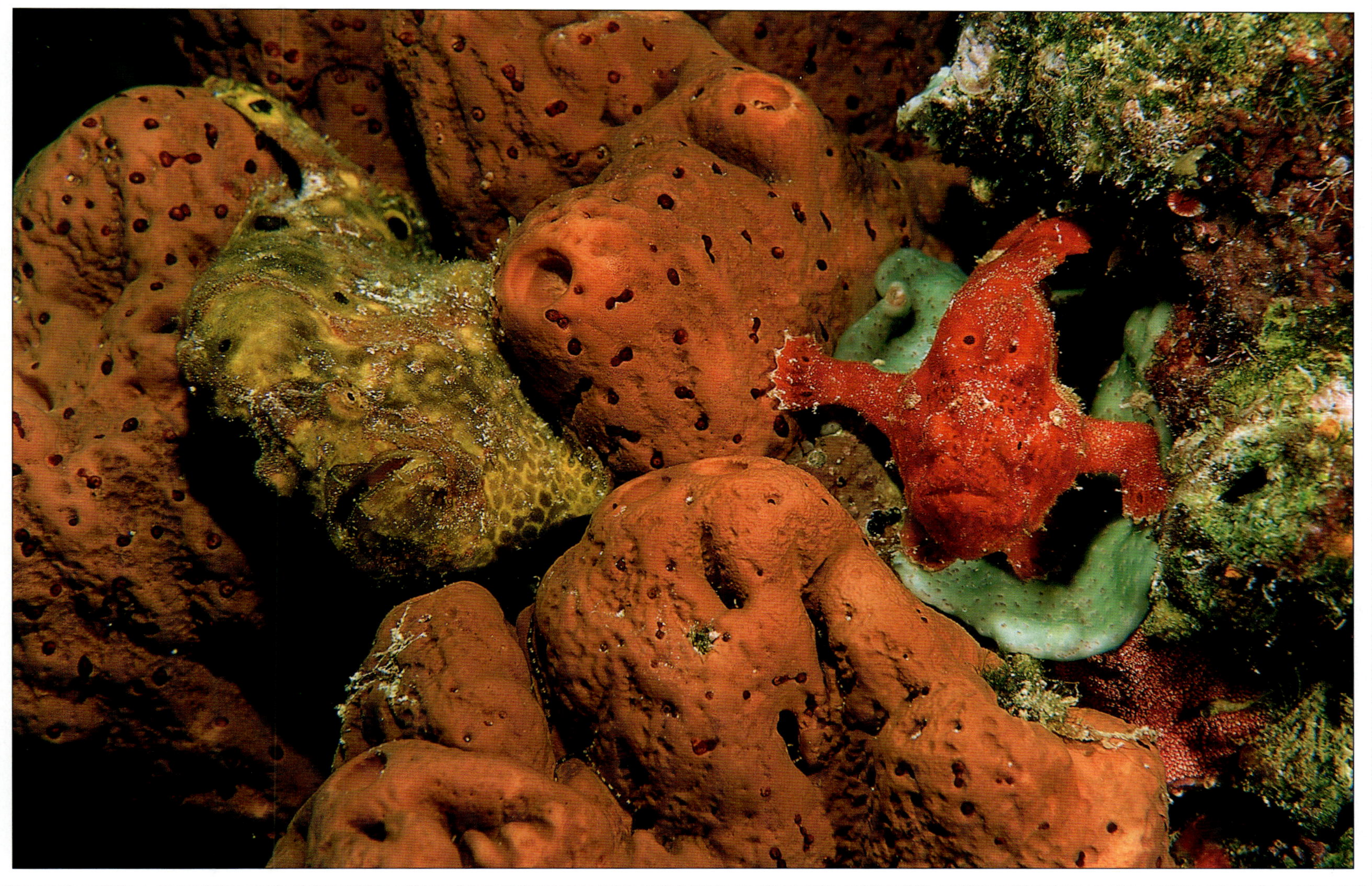

Dennis Liberson
United States of America
HIGHLY COMMENDED

Contrasting frogfish

"Frogfish are able to change colour to blend in with their surroundings, so I was lucky to spot this red one when it was camouflaged against a similar coloured sponge. Disturbed by my camera and flash, it hopped over the top of the sponge and joined its partner."

Nikon F5 with 60mm lens; underwater housing; two strobes; 1/125 sec at f16; Fujichrome Velvia

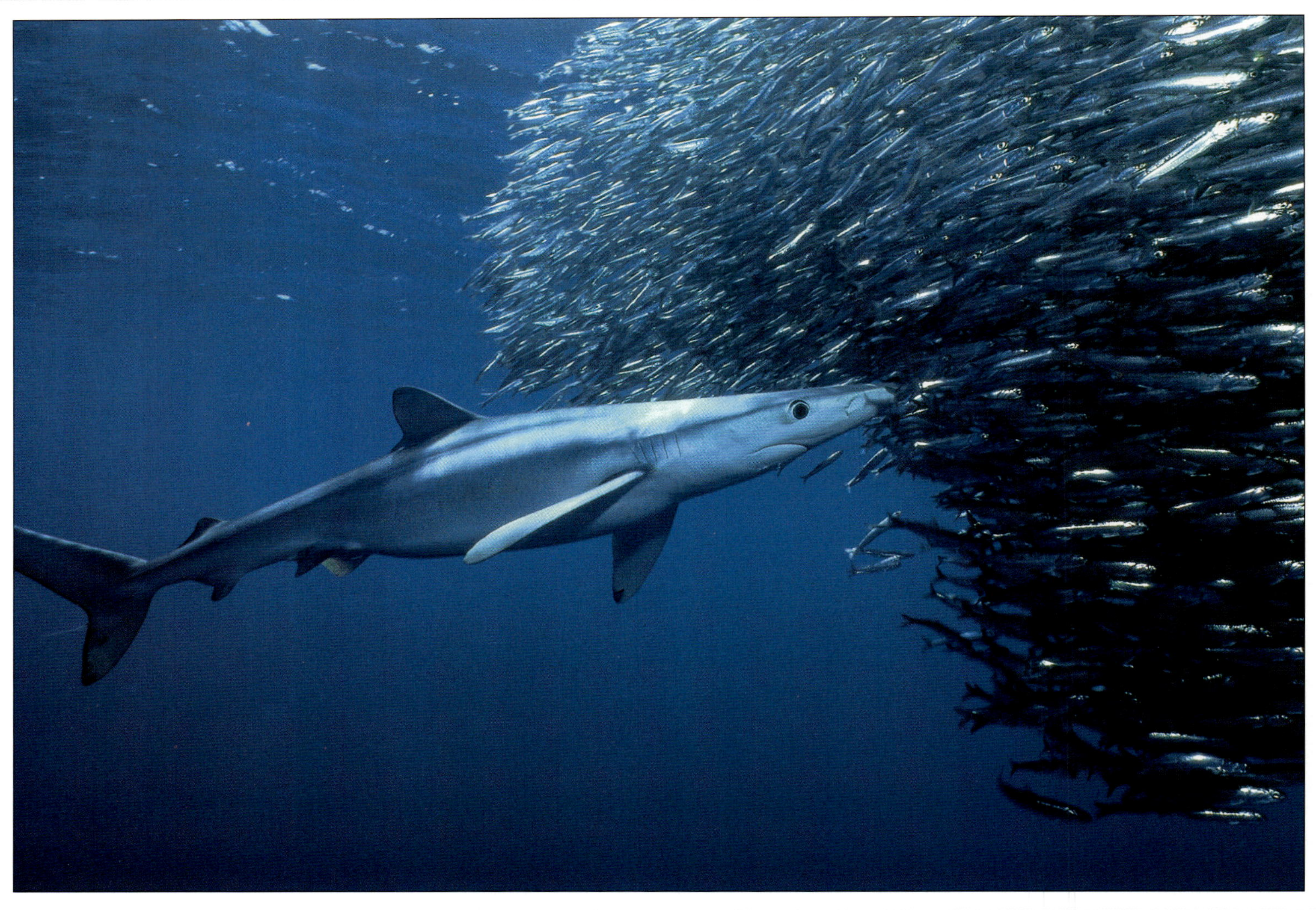

Richard Herrmann
United States of America
HIGHLY COMMENDED

Blue shark feeding on anchovies

"Seven blue sharks, yellowfin and skipjack tuna were feeding on this 'baitball' of anchovies from below, while pelicans and gulls plunged down from above. There was no escape and within four hours the shoal was reduced from the size of a small car to the size of a basketball. The sea, just off the San Diego coast, was littered with scales and body fluids."

Nikonos 5 with 20mm lens; strobe; 1/90 sec at f8; Fujichrome Provia 100

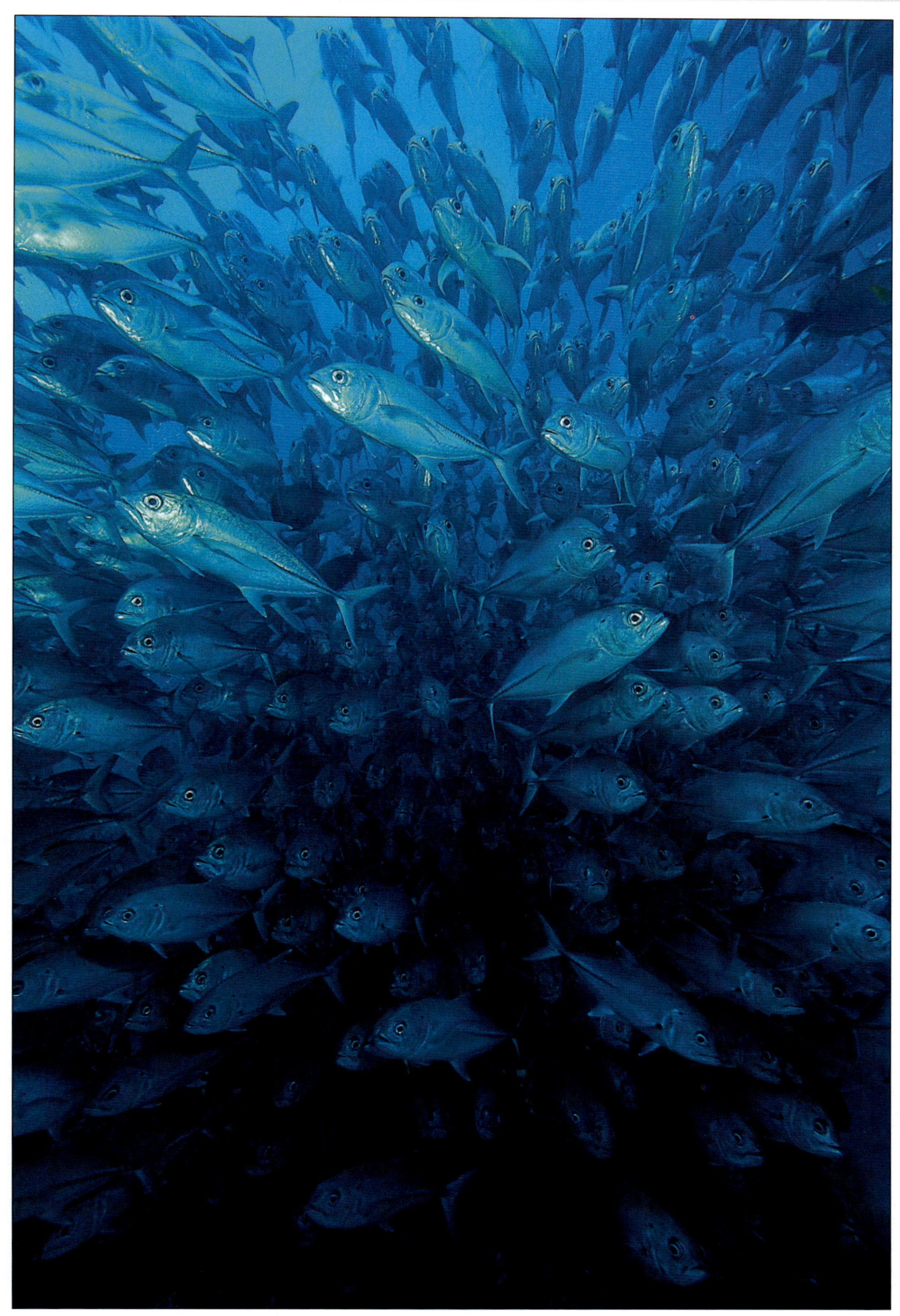

Martin Edge
United Kingdom
HIGHLY COMMENDED

School of jacks

"I must have used up more than 30 rolls of film on jacks in Sipadan, Borneo, but this shot is a 'one off'. The school swam towards me, and I fired the shutter at the moment when all the fish seemed to look into the lens."

Nikon F801s with 16mm fisheye lens in underwater housing; flash; 1/125 at f8; Ektachrome Elite 100

Urban & Garden Wildlife

Pictures must show animals or plants in a garden or an obviously urban or suburban setting.

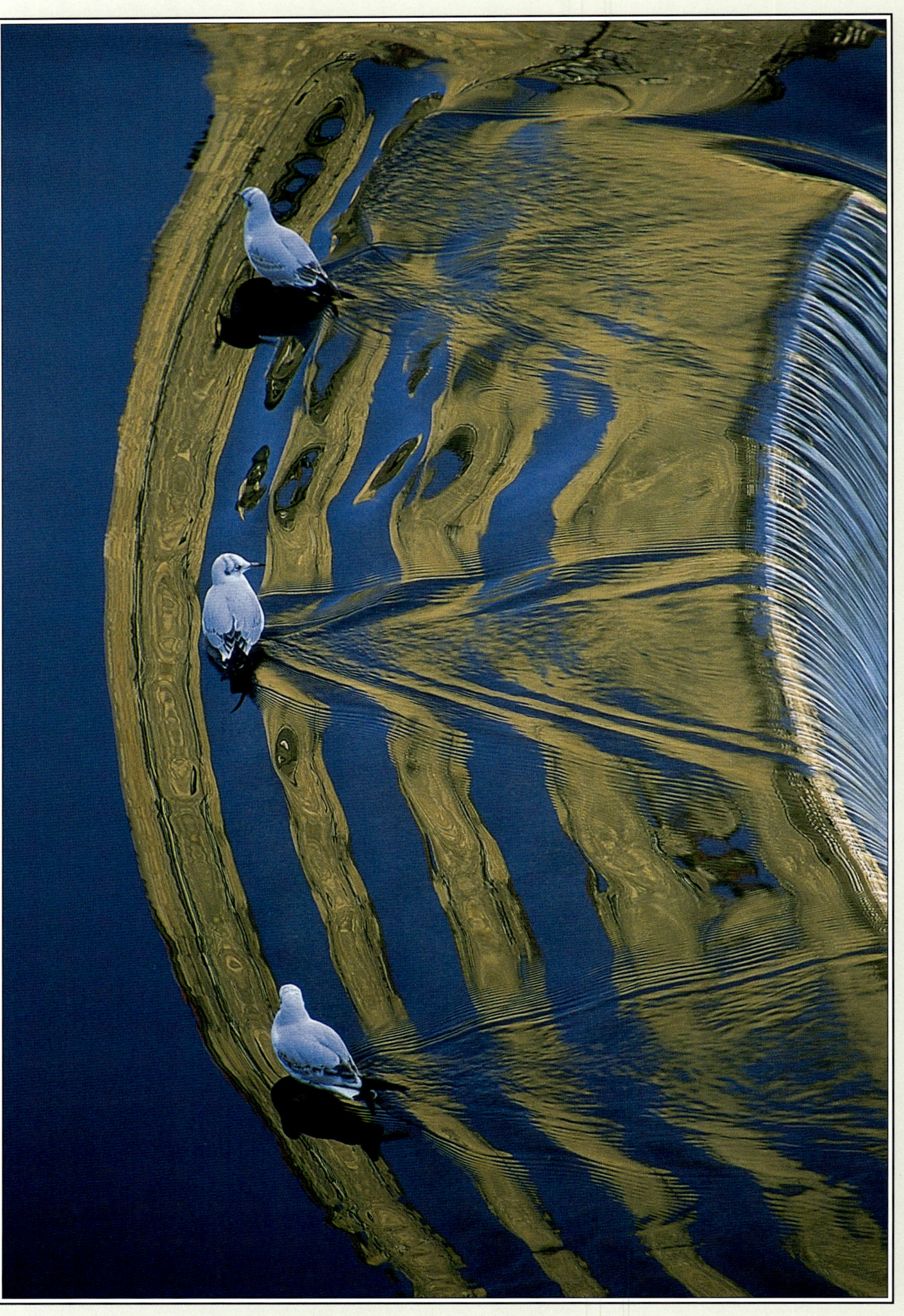

Raoul Slater
Australia
WINNER

Black-headed gulls on weir

"The famous stone Pulteney Bridge in Bath had caught the late autumn sunshine and reflected golden light onto the elegant weir below. These black-headed gulls braved cold feet and stood on top of the weir creating a wonderful pattern."

Canon EOS A2 with 75-300mm lens; 1/30 sec at f 5.6; Fujichrome Velvia

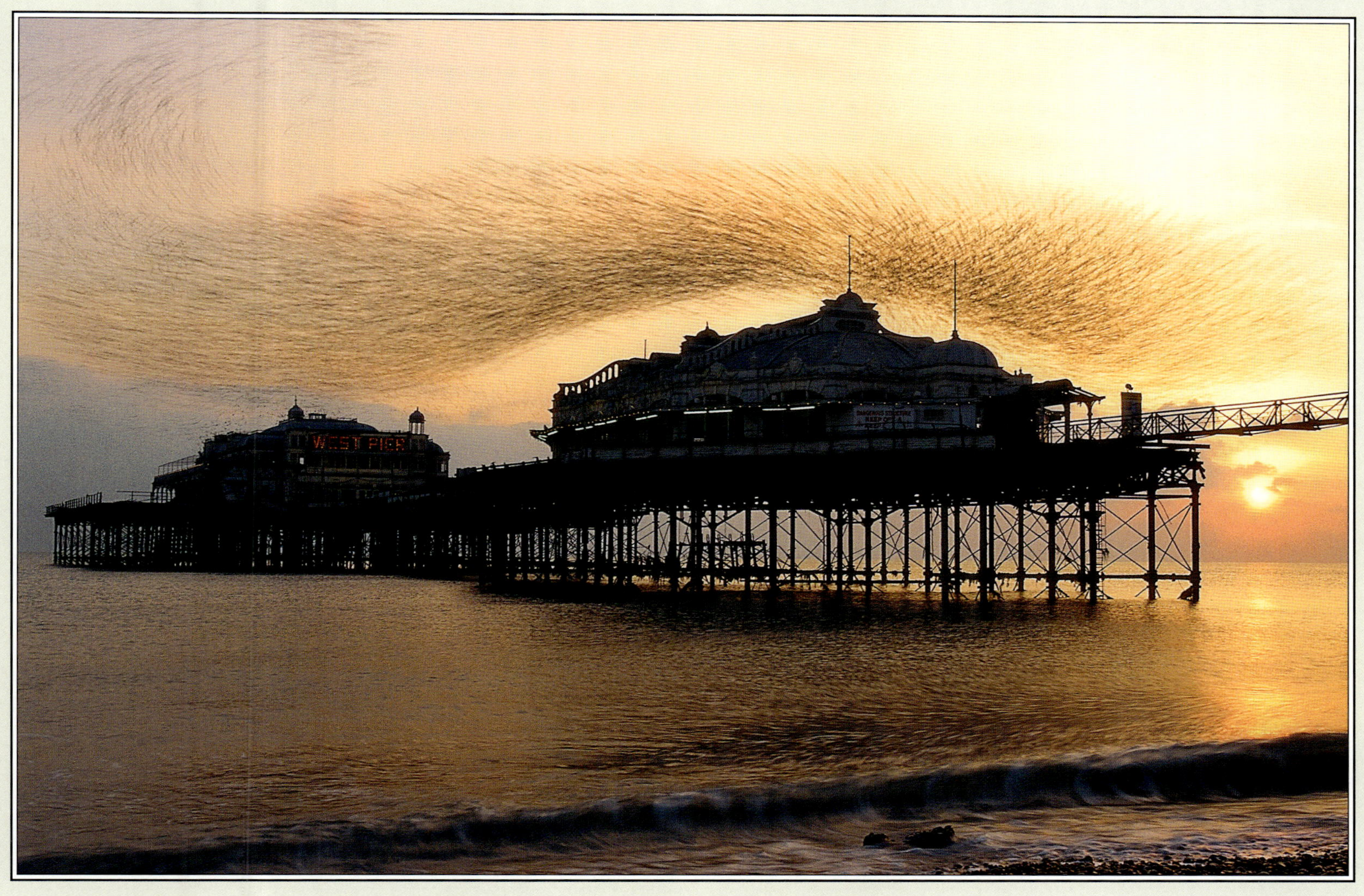

James Warwick
United Kingdom
RUNNER-UP

Starling flock above Brighton Pier

"Every evening the starlings congregate on Brighton's derelict West Pier. Small flocks would arrive first, from all directions, but before settling down for the night, the whole gathering would perform the most wonderful acrobatic displays. They were like iron filings in a magnetised sky. A slow shutter speed and the muted, winter light gave an Impressionistic feel to the composition."

Nikon F90x with 28-80mm lens; tripod; Fujichrome Sensia 100

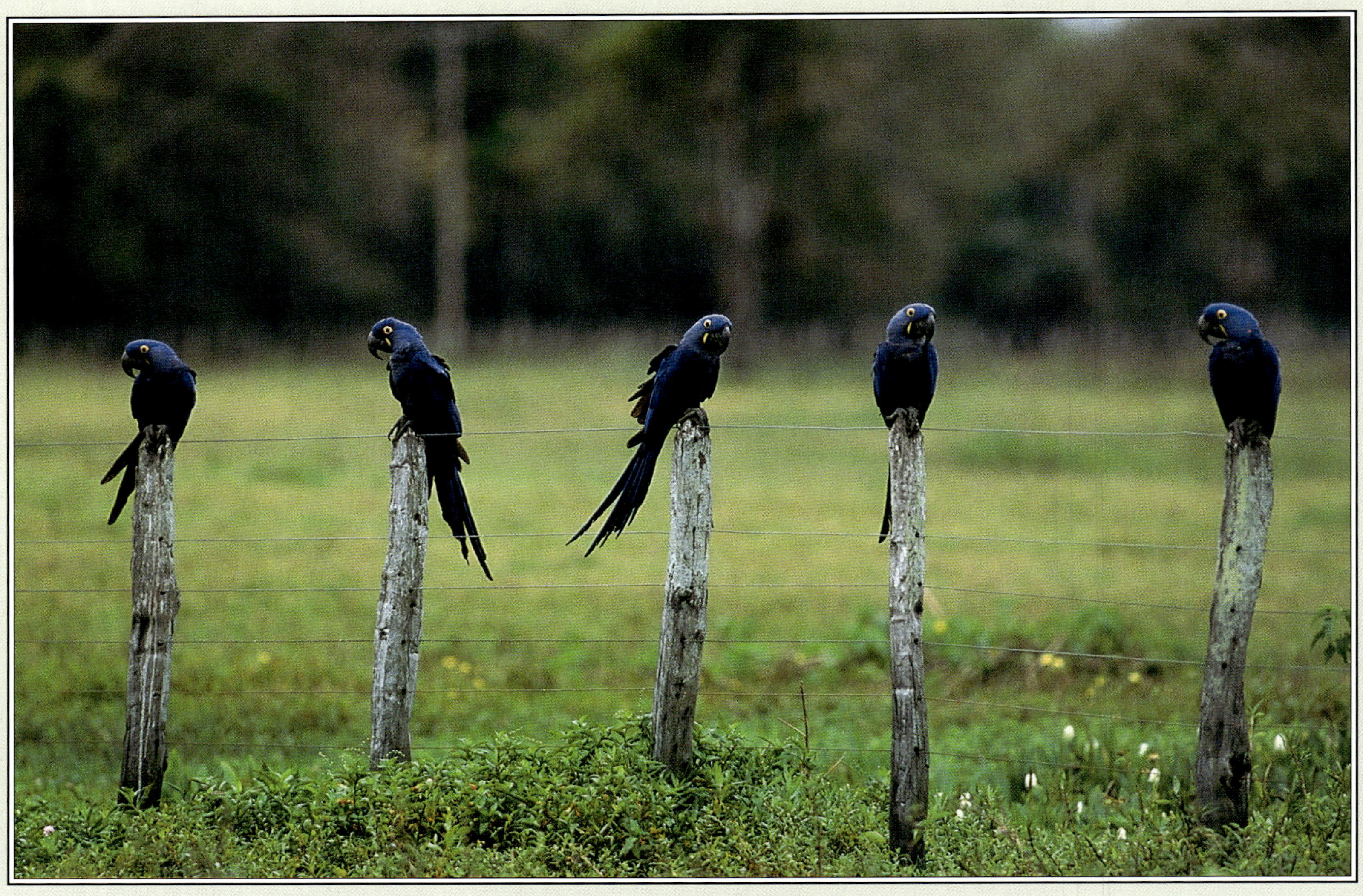

Olivier Grunewald
France
HIGHLY COMMENDED

Hyacinth macaws

"The endangered hyacinth macaws at the Caïman Ecological Refuge, in the South Pantanal, are used to humans and range freely round the lodge. Each morning they follow a regular routine, leaving their man-made nests in the trees to bath in the marsh and then perch on the fence posts to dry their wings."

Nikon F4 with 500mm lens; monopod; 1/250 sec at f5.6; Fujichrome Provia 100

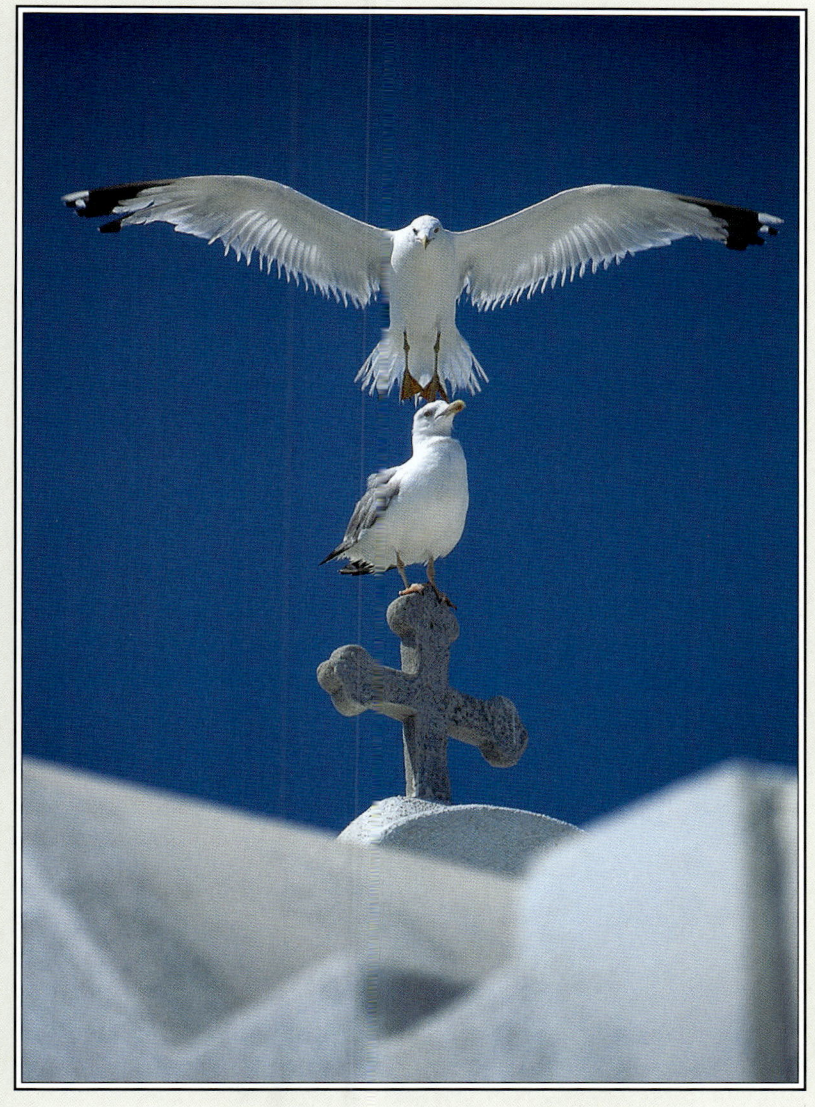

Ewald Neffe
Austria
HIGHLY COMMENDED

Herring gulls on church spire

"I watched these two gulls for a long time, taking turns to perch on the spire of a church on the Greek island of Paros. Eventually I managed to capture this shot of them forming a perfect shape."

Canon EOS 100 with 35-350mm lens; 1/3[illegible]0 sec at f5.6; Fujichrome Velvia

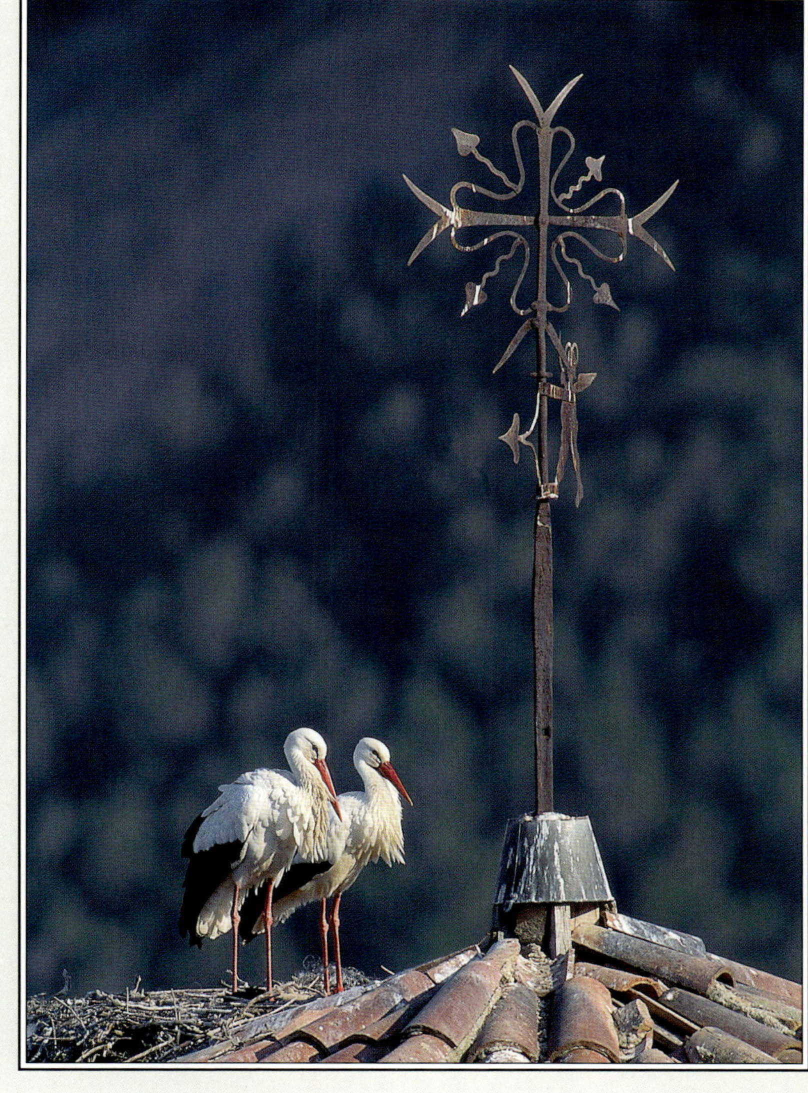

Christof Wermter
Germany
HIGHLY COMMENDED

White storks on roof

"This pair of storks were standing on the roof of the church in the small town of Baloba, Spain. From the rock where I stood, the picture was one of perfect harmony."

Nikon F90 with 500mm lens and x1.4 converter; tripod; 1/250 at f4; Fujichrome Sensia 100

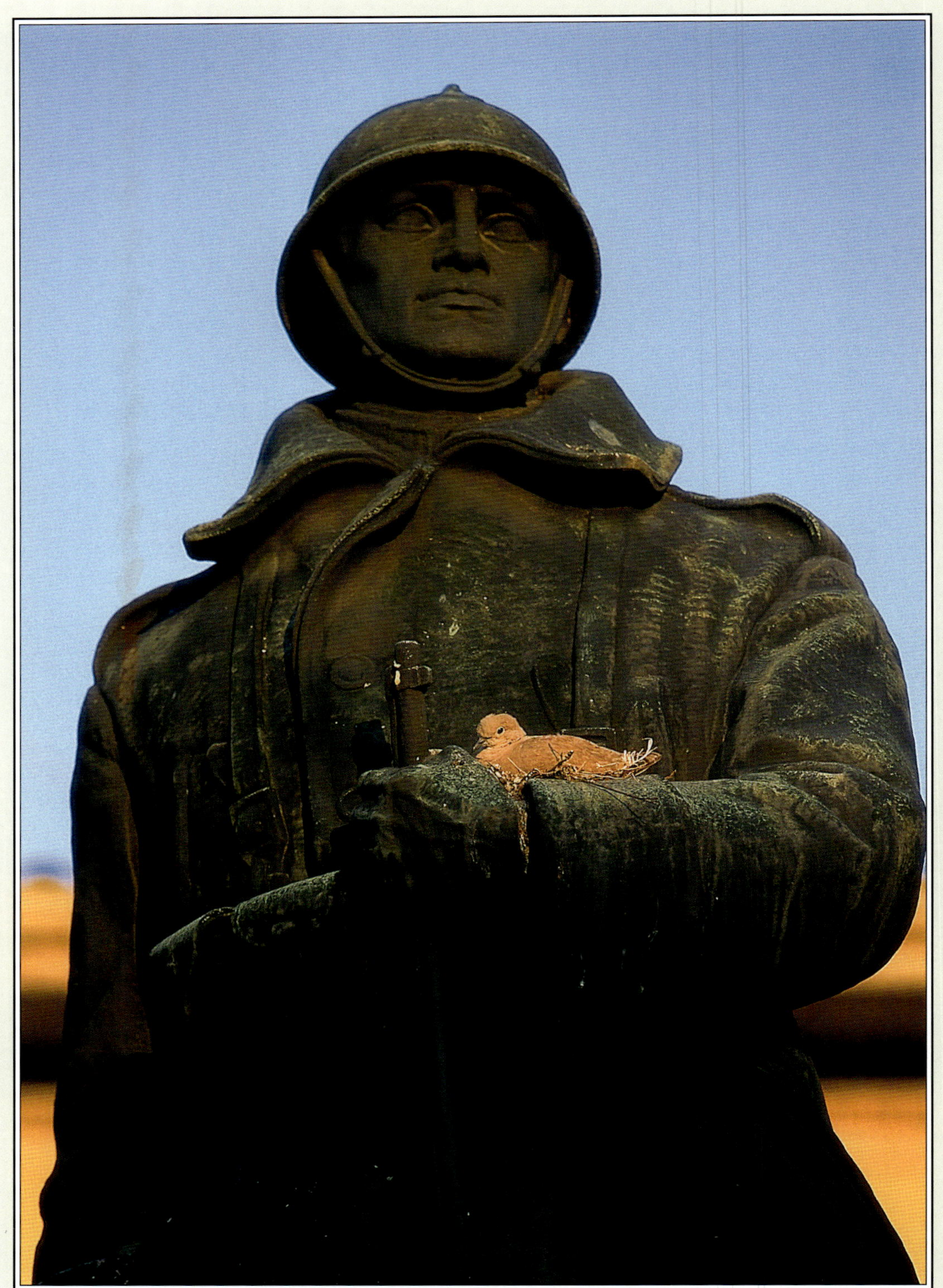

Paolo Cortesi

Italy

HIGHLY COMMENDED

Dove on statue

"This collared dove had deserted her nest on the war memorial in my home town of Bologna because of the annual fair. A few days later she returned to the arms of the soldier, and I took this picture. But, a week later restoration work started on the memorial and she left for good."

Pentax Z1P with 300mm lens; tripod; 1/125 sec at f8; Fujichrome Velvia

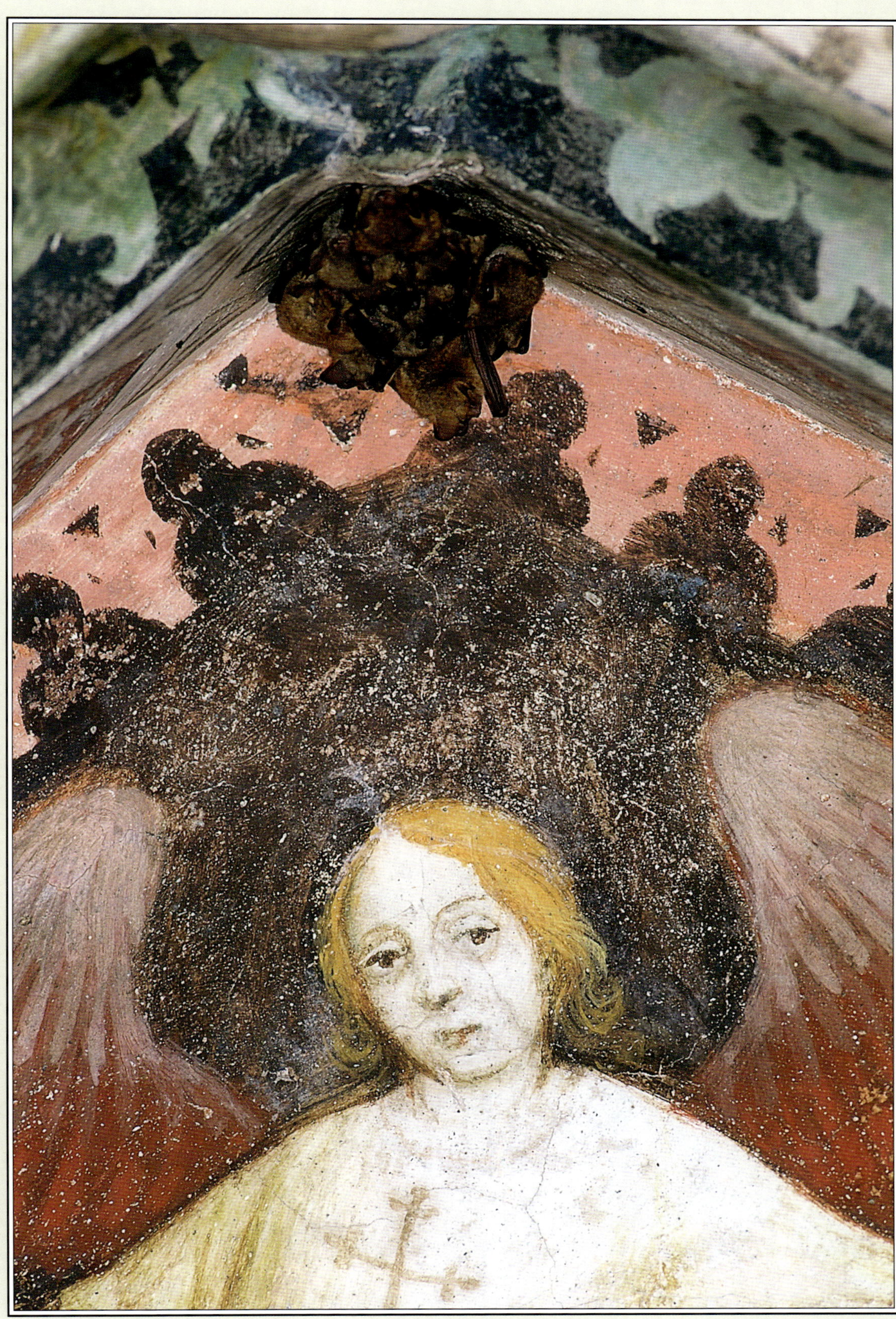

Roberto Siniscalchi
Italy
HIGHLY COMMENDED

Geoffroy's bats

"These bats have found an ideal place to bring up their young in the cloisters of the cathedral in my home town of Bressanone. Hundreds of tourists visit the building every year but never notice these small residents. However, I was fascinated by the contrasting images of the bats and the angel."

Canon EOS 1N with 300mm lens; flash; 1/30 sec at f5/6; Fujichrome Sensia 100

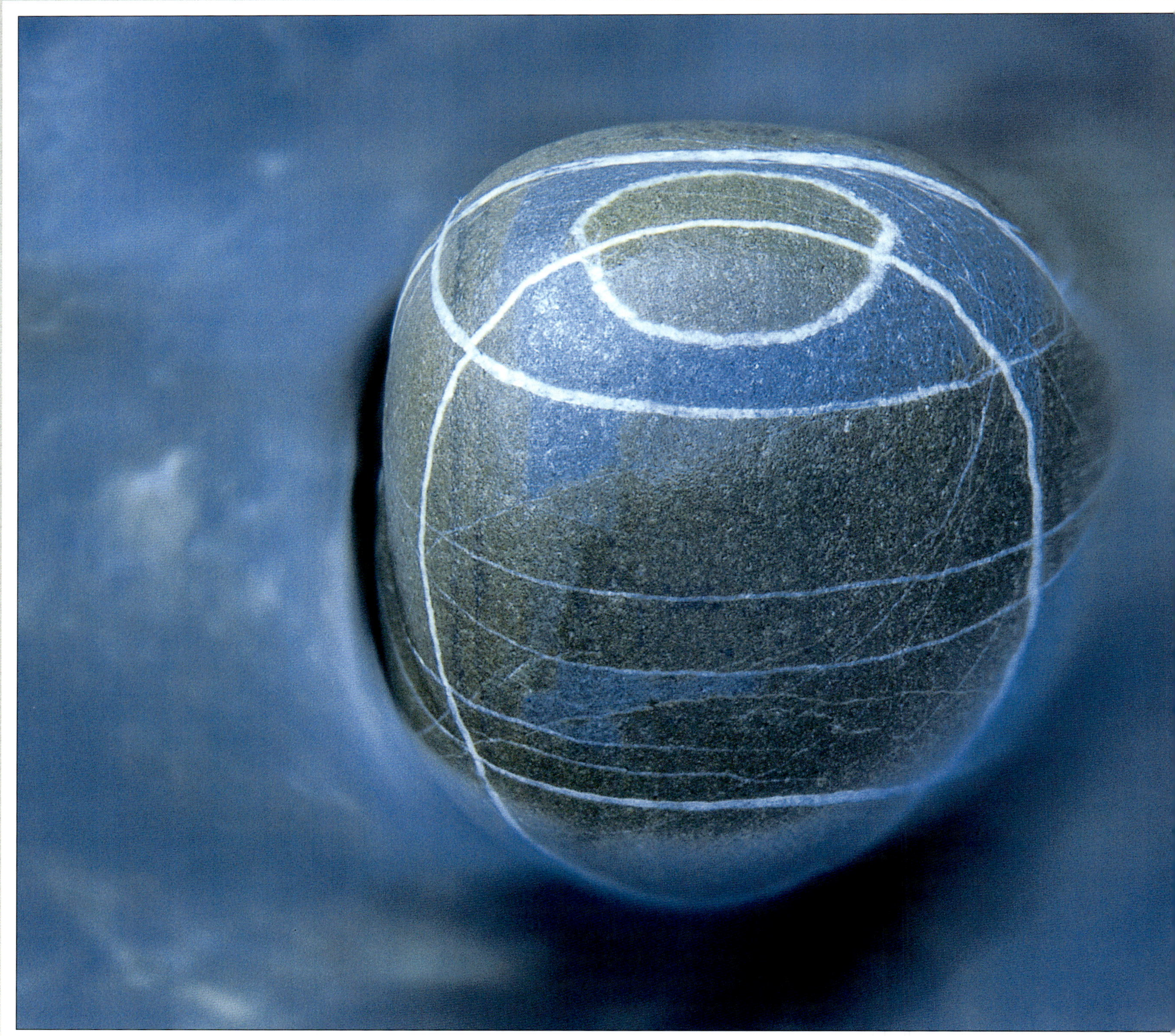

Composition and Form

Pictures in this category must illustrate natural subjects in abstract ways and are judged for their aesthetic values.

Adriano Turcatti
Italy
WINNER

Blue stone

"I found this little stone, only 5cm across, on a beach on the Greek Island of Chios, and was amazed by the perfect circles entwined around it. This beautiful geometrical form must, I thought, have been born from chaos."

Canon EOS 5 with 35-70mm lens; extension tubes; tripod; 3 sec at f22; Fujichrome Sensia 100

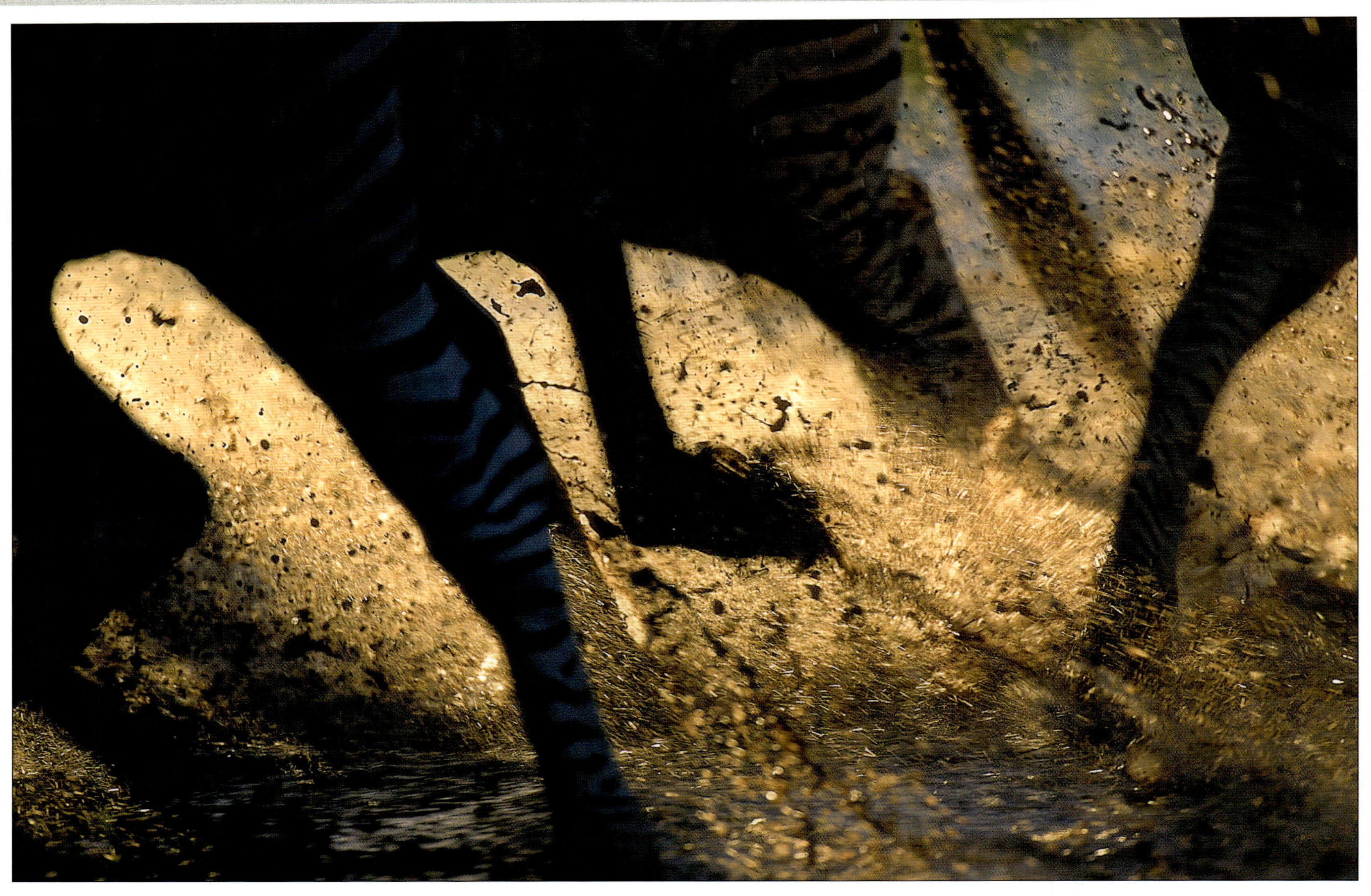

Adrian Bailey
South Africa
RUNNER-UP

Zebras running

"During the rainy season in Northern Botswana, rainwater pools form throughout the mopane woodlands. Each morning, herds of Burchell's zebra would gather at this particular waterhole. The dramatic shafts of early sunlight catching the water was particularly enthralling, and the constant movement of the herds allowed me ample opportunity to capture the spectacle."

Nikon F5 with 500mm lens; Fujichrome Velvia

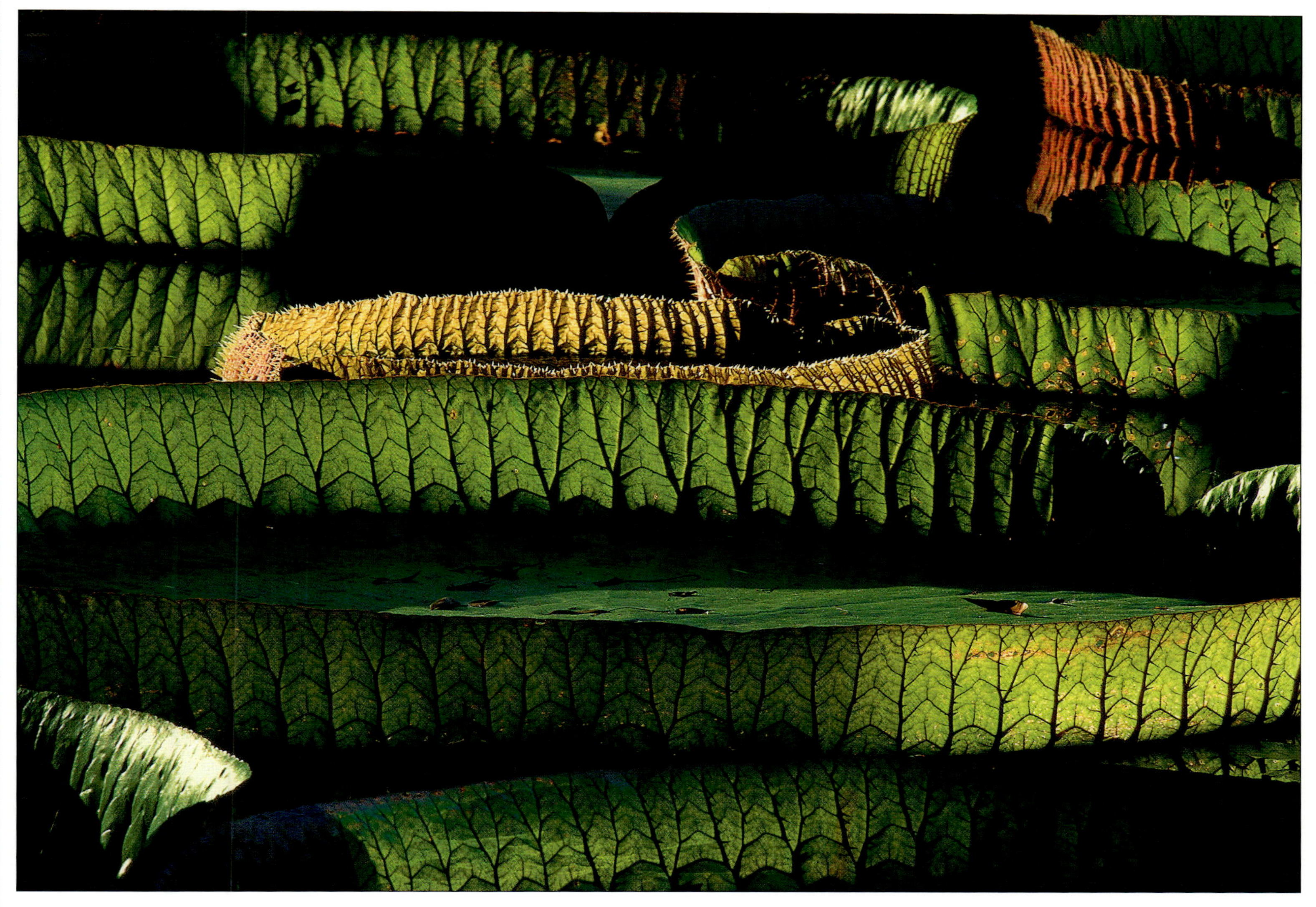

David Lyons
United Kingdom
SPECIALLY COMMENDED

Amazonian lily pads

"I photographed these Amazonian lily pads in the Sir Seewoosagur Ramgoolam Gardens at Pamplemousses, Mauritius."

Mamiya Pro 645 with 210mm lens; tripod;
Fujichrome Velvia rated at 32

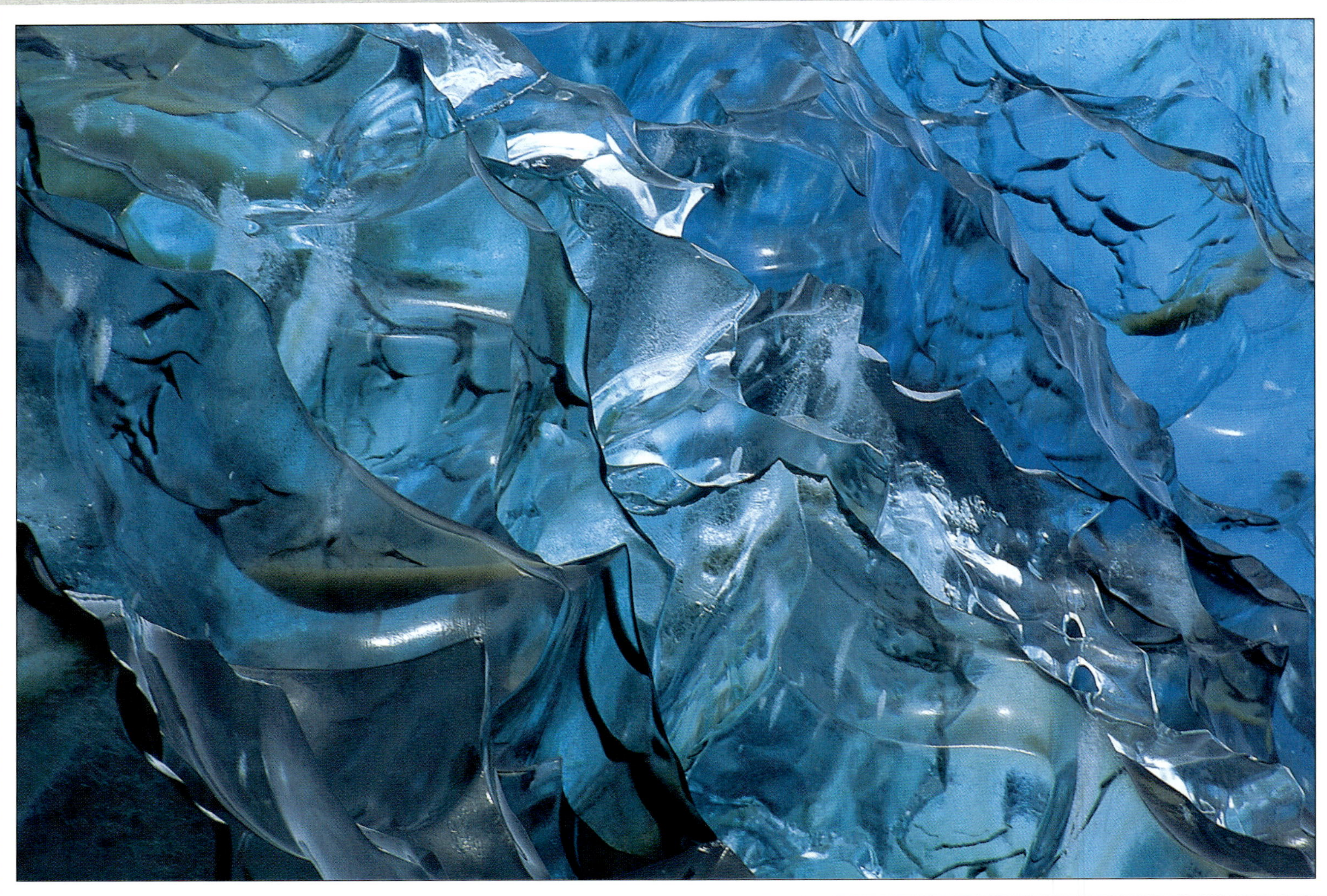

Klaus Kretzer
Germany
HIGHLY COMMENDED

Iceberg sculpture

"An iceberg in the Jökulsárlón glacial lagoon, south-east Iceland, had recently collapsed. The very pure ice, which had been submerged, absorbs all light except the blue, and the different intensities of colour are derived from variations in the thickness. The greyish-blue ice in the foreground is 'polluted' with debris. Once the ice is exposed to the sun, air-filled cracks are formed, which reflect light, and the iceberg turns white."

Nikon F90 with 80-200mm lens; 16 secs at f2.8; Fujichrome Velvia

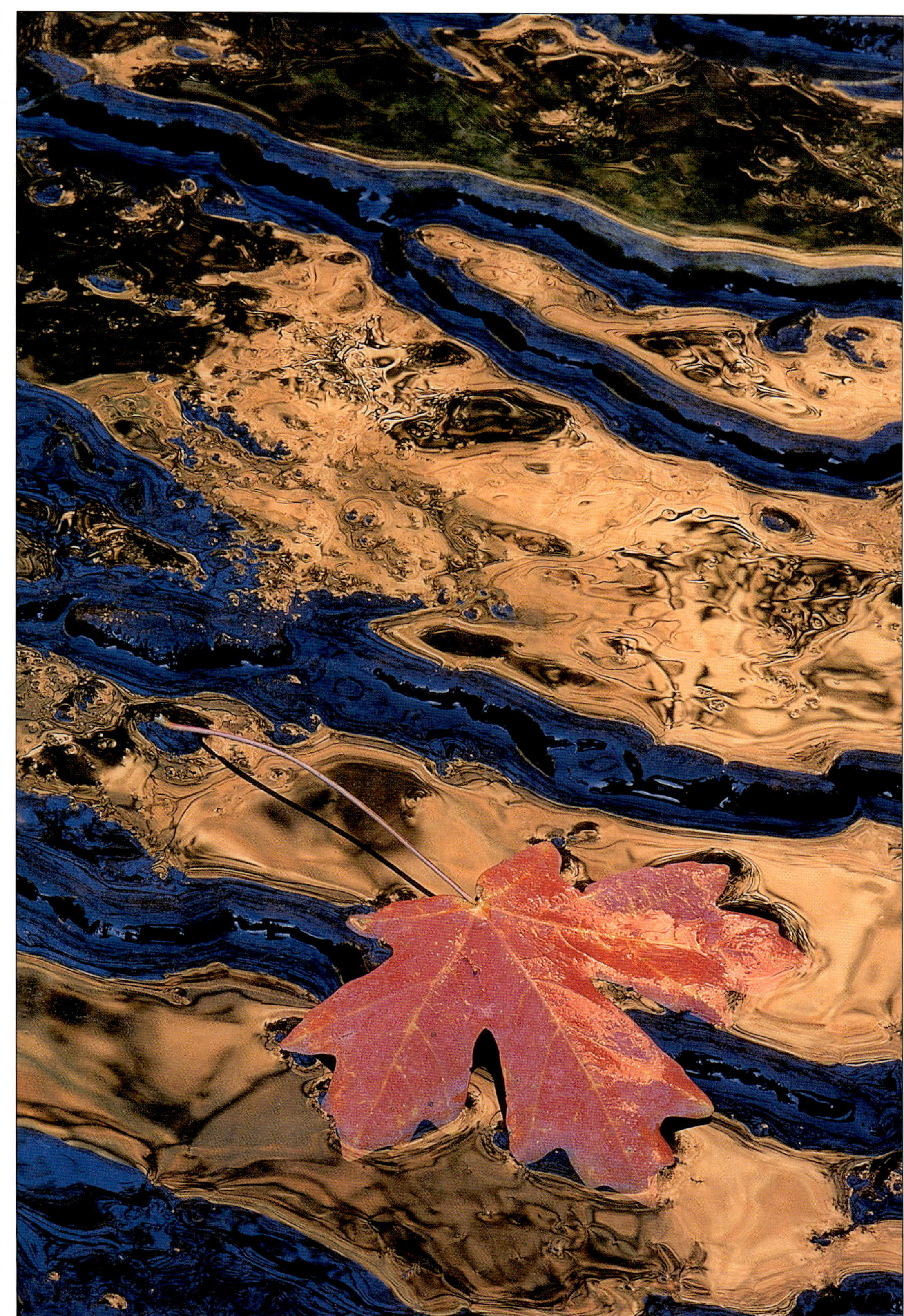

Adam Gibbs
Canada
HIGHLY COMMENDED

Maple leaf

"The combination of warm and cool colours has always interested me. In this image, taken in the autumn in Zion National Park, Utah, a thin veil of water ran down a slab of rock. The golden light is a reflection of sunlit cliffs, and the blue ripples are small ledges catching the reflection of the sky. The leaf anchors the whole composition."

Nikon F4s with 105mm lens; Fujichrome Velvia

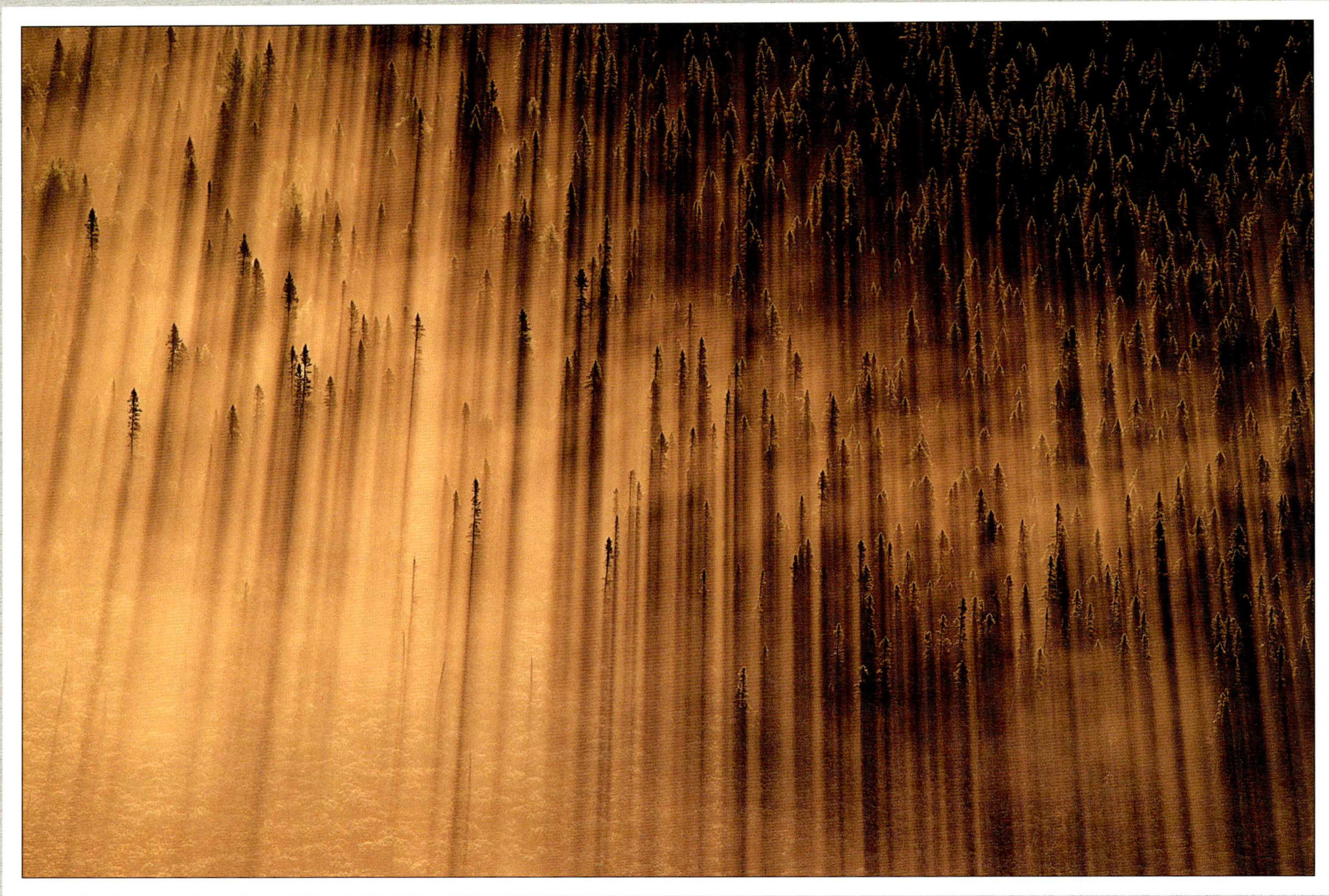

Richard Hamilton Smith

United States of America

HIGHLY COMMENDED

Spruce in morning fog

"This picture was taken at dawn as I flew over Swamp River Preserve in north-eastern Minnesota, near the Canadian border. The pilot and I only passed over the black spruce swamp once before the fog disappeared."

Canon EOS 1N with 70-200mm lens; 1/250 sec at f8; Ektachrome 100 rated at 200

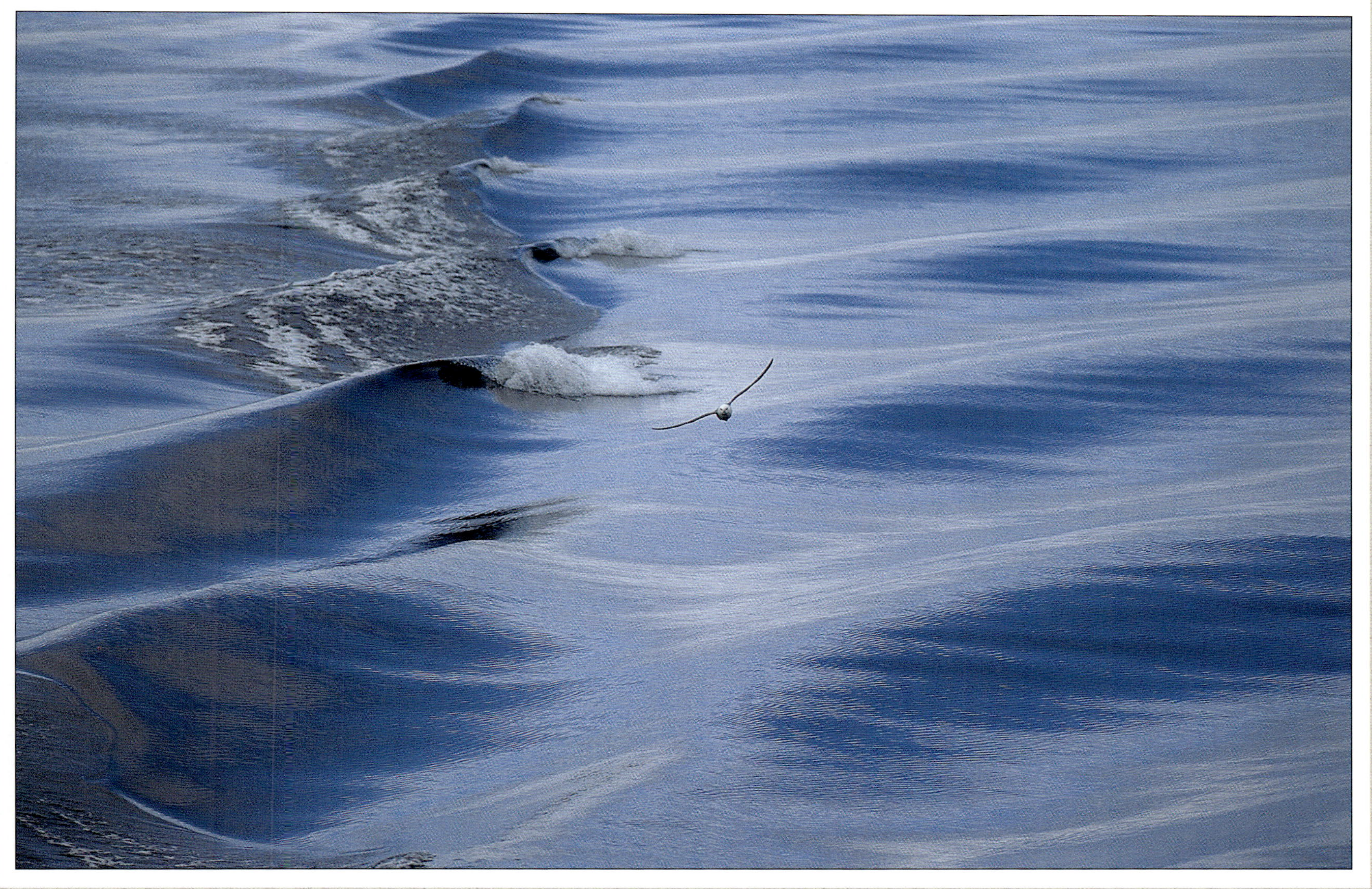

Marc Slootmaekers
Belgium
HIGHLY COMMENDED

Fulmar over waves

"The waves made by the bow of the ship on a dead calm sea caught my attention on a boat trip in Iceland. Seeing the fulmar coming, I used a 300mm lens to make a good composition and closed the diaphragm to obtain the depth of field."

Canon EOS 5 with 300mm lens; hand-held with gun-stock; 1/125 sec at f8; Fujichrome Provia 100

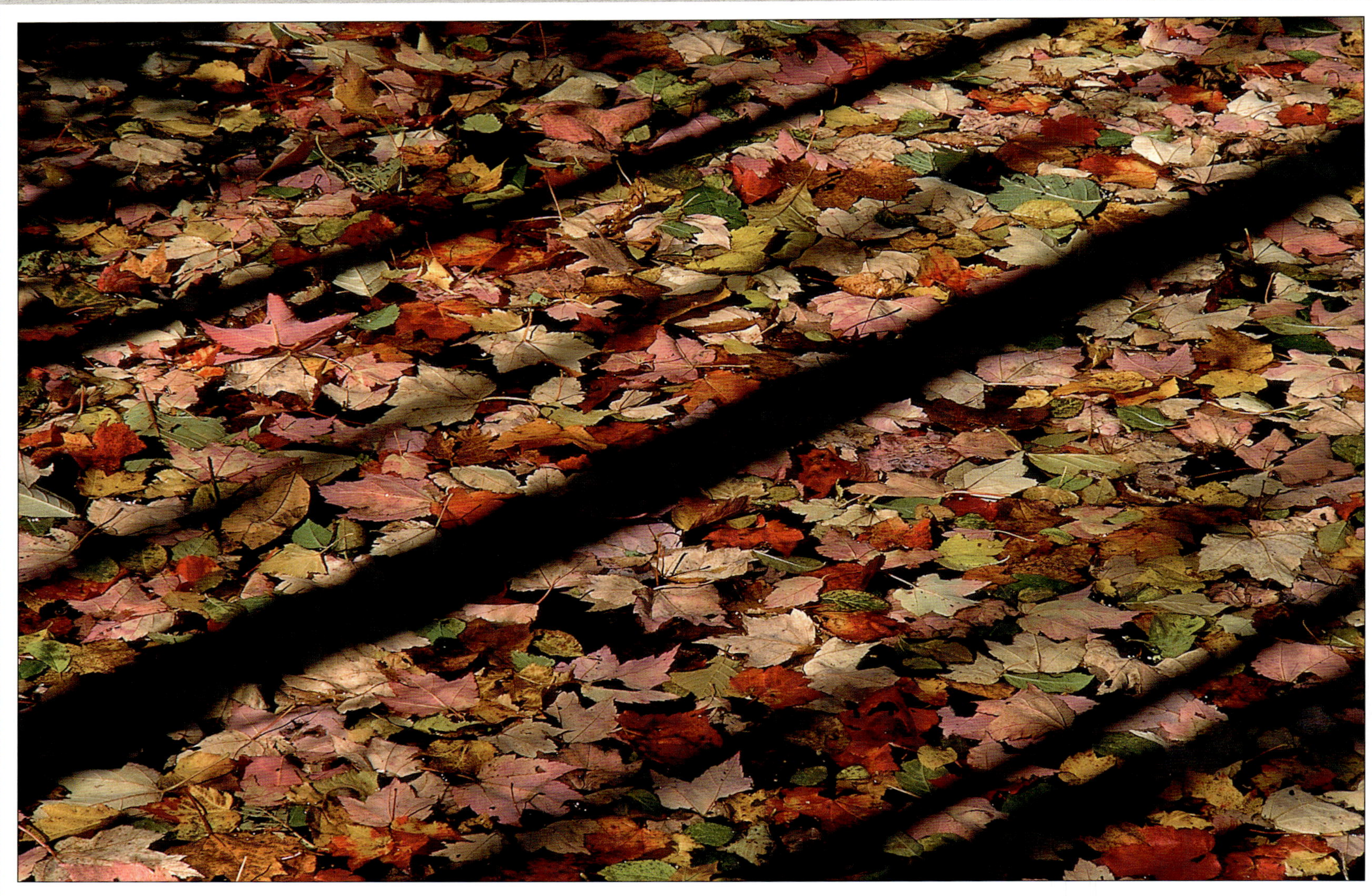

Thomas Wiewandt
United States of America
HIGHLY COMMENDED

Shadows on floating leaves

"This image is one of my favourites taken in autumn in Acadia National Park, New England. The shadows of the naked trees added interest to the pool of water covered with freshly-fallen leaves and also emphasised the immediacy of winter. Heavy winds that had cursed the previous day proved a blessing in disguise."

Nikon F4 with 80-200mm lens; tripod; f32; Fujichrome Velvia

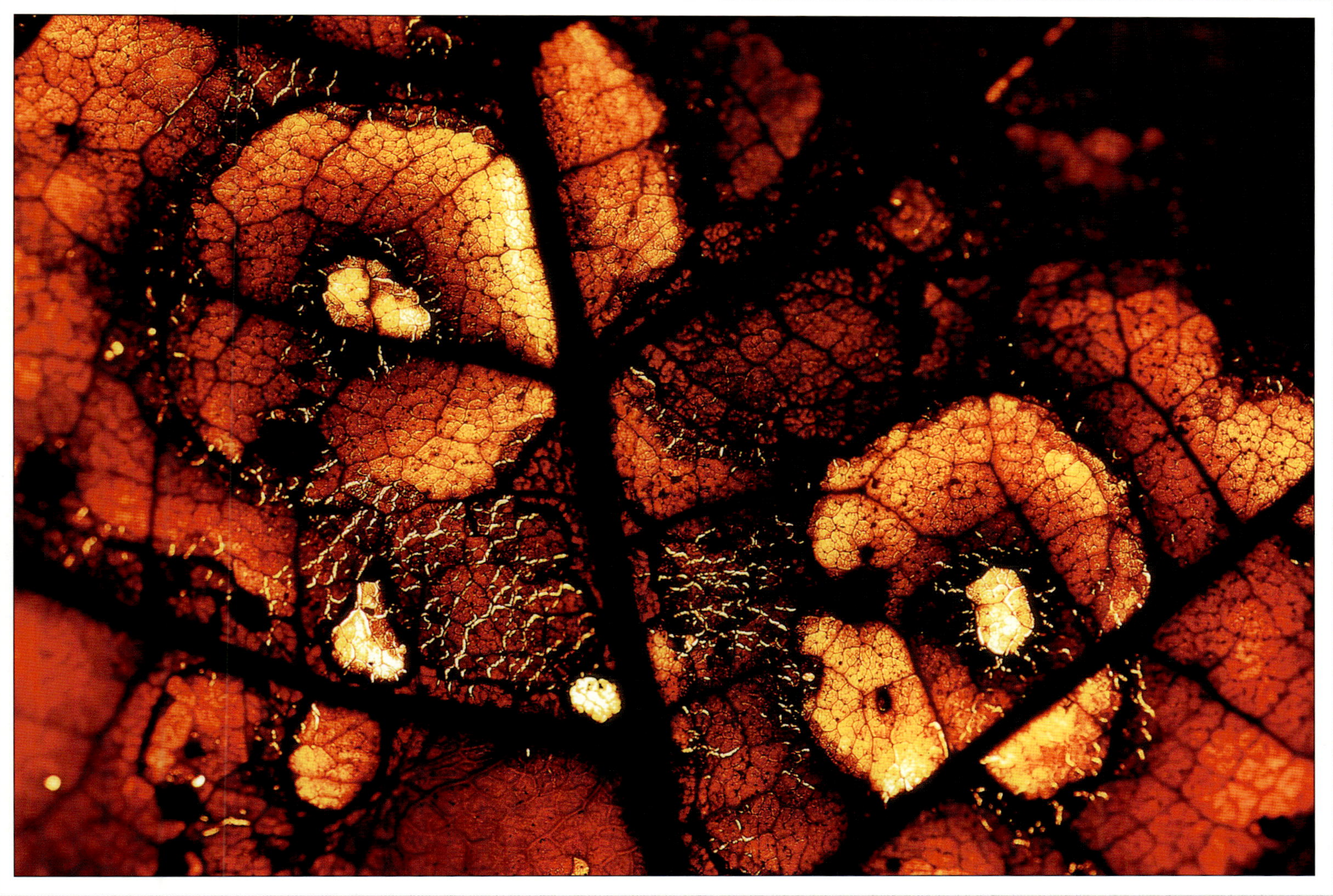

Jan Vermeer
The Netherlands
HIGHLY COMMENDED

Leaf detail

"I was on a botanical expedition to Guyana with the University of Utrecht. Having travelled as far as we could by vehicle, we walked for a day to reach the rainforest base camp. On the ground was an old Secropia leaf with this wonderful structure and amazing colours."

Canon EOS 5 with 100mm lens; 1/15 at f8; Fujichrome Velvia

Wild Places

Landscapes must convey a feeling of wildness and create a sense of wonder or awe.

Andreas Leemann
Switzerland
WINNER

Mesa Arch, Utah

"I arrived at Mesa Arch, in Canyonlands National Park, just before sunrise on a clear autumn morning. As the dark blue night sky slowly became brighter, I noticed that the arch was being lit by light reflected from the cliff below. The sunlight gradually became stronger until the whole arch was literally glowing. The spectacle was over in a few minutes."

Mamiya 645 Pro with 35mm lens; tripod; 1/15 sec at f22; Fujichrome Velvia

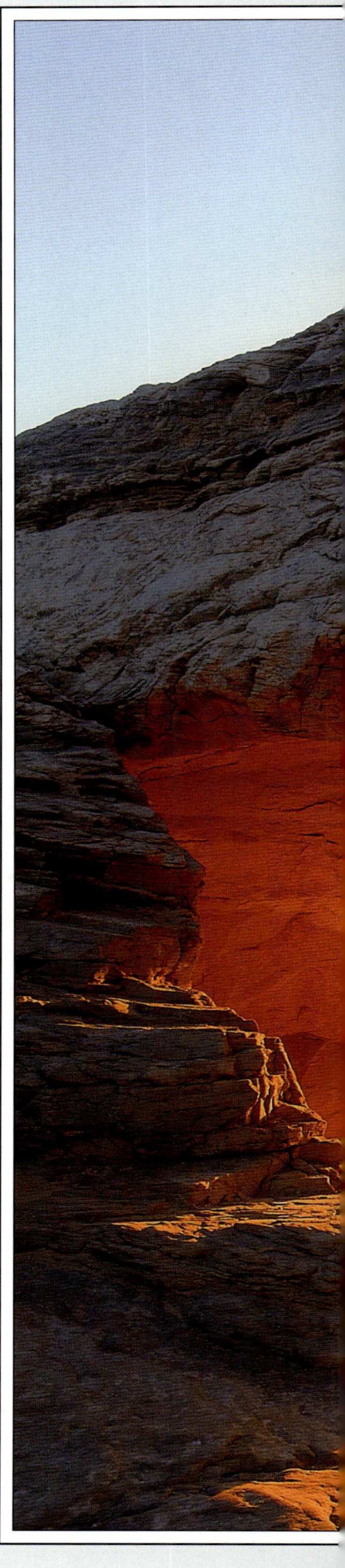

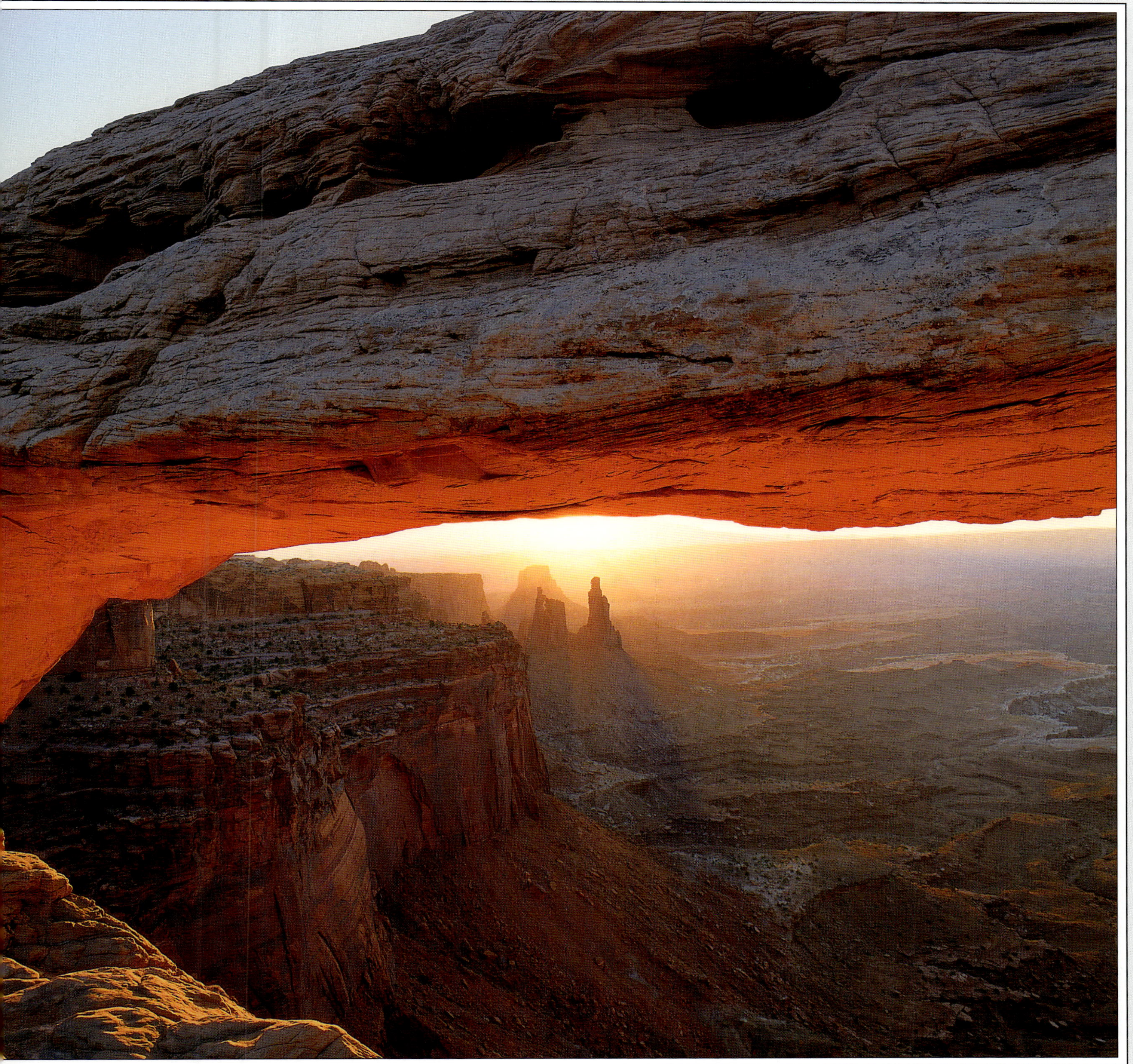

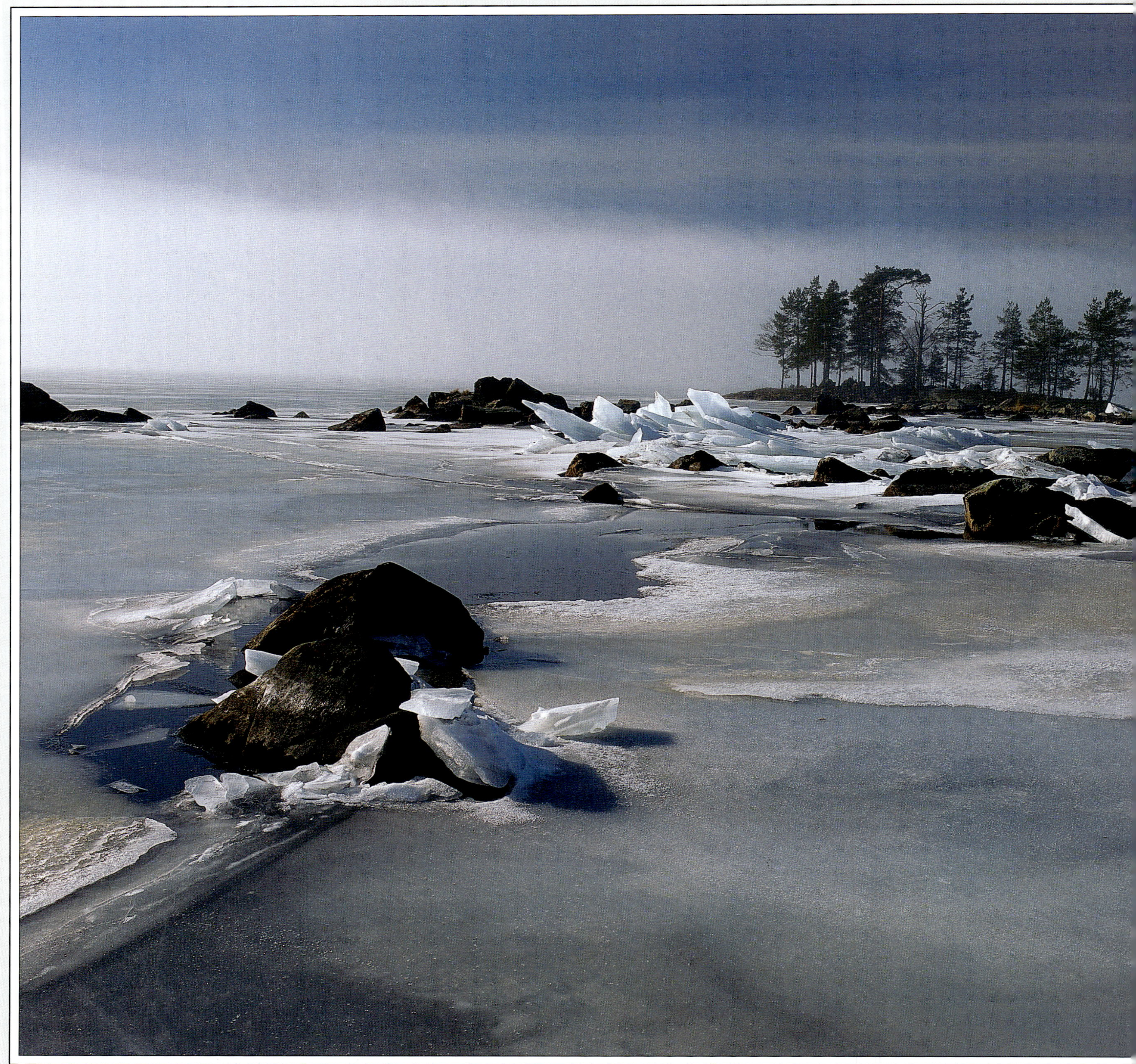

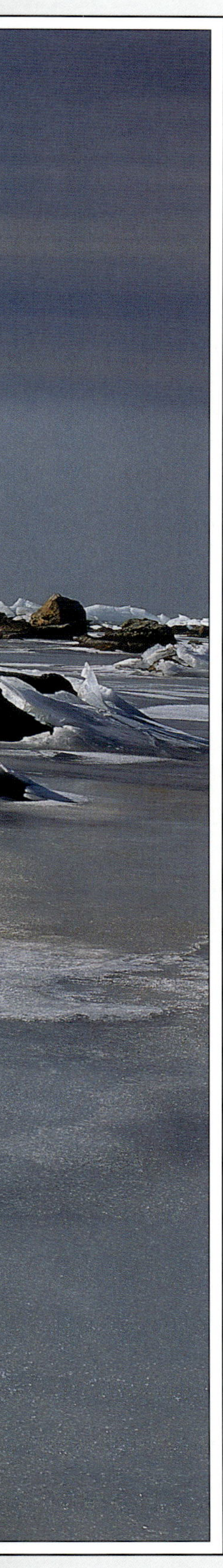

Janos Jurka
Sweden
RUNNER-UP

Lake Väsman, Sweden

"After a few days of mild weather with strong winds, the ice on the lake started to move. During the night, the skies cleared, the wind died down and a bank of fog floated over the lake. The morning was wonderful."

Hasselblad with 60mm lens; tripod; 1/15 sec at f8; Fujichrome Velvia

Geoff Doré
United Kingdom
HIGHLY COMMENDED

Shags, spray and cliffs

"The wild, windy weather off Caithness, Scotland, had whipped up a tumultuous sea. The spray from the huge breakers was sparkling in the sun as it rose high into the cavernous cleft of the cliffs. The shags, oblivious to the waves crashing around them, continued their preening. I, however, was more perturbed, perched on an exposed cliff-top ledge."

Nikon F4s with 80-200mm lens; tripod; 1/250 sec at f5.6; Kodachrome 64

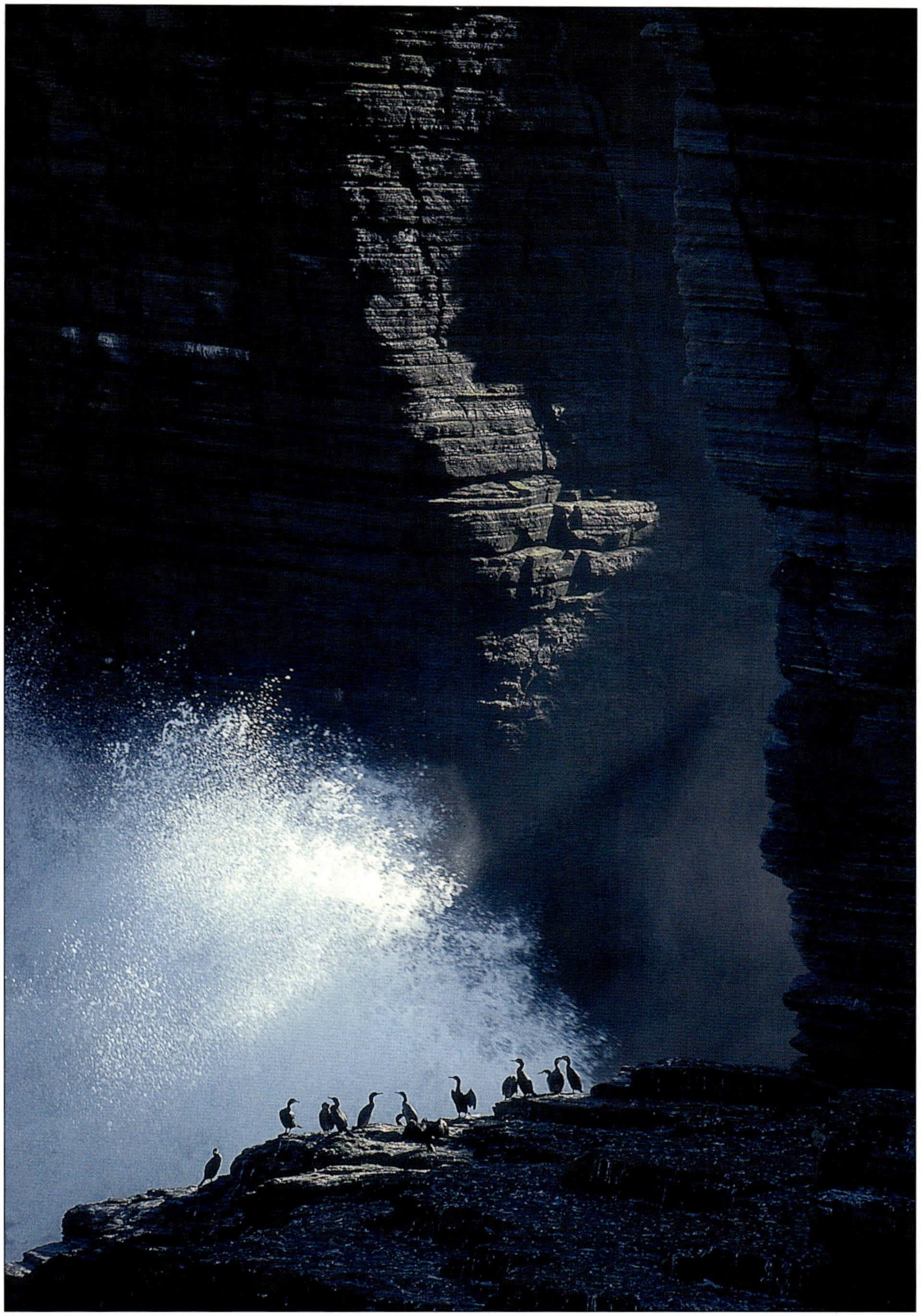

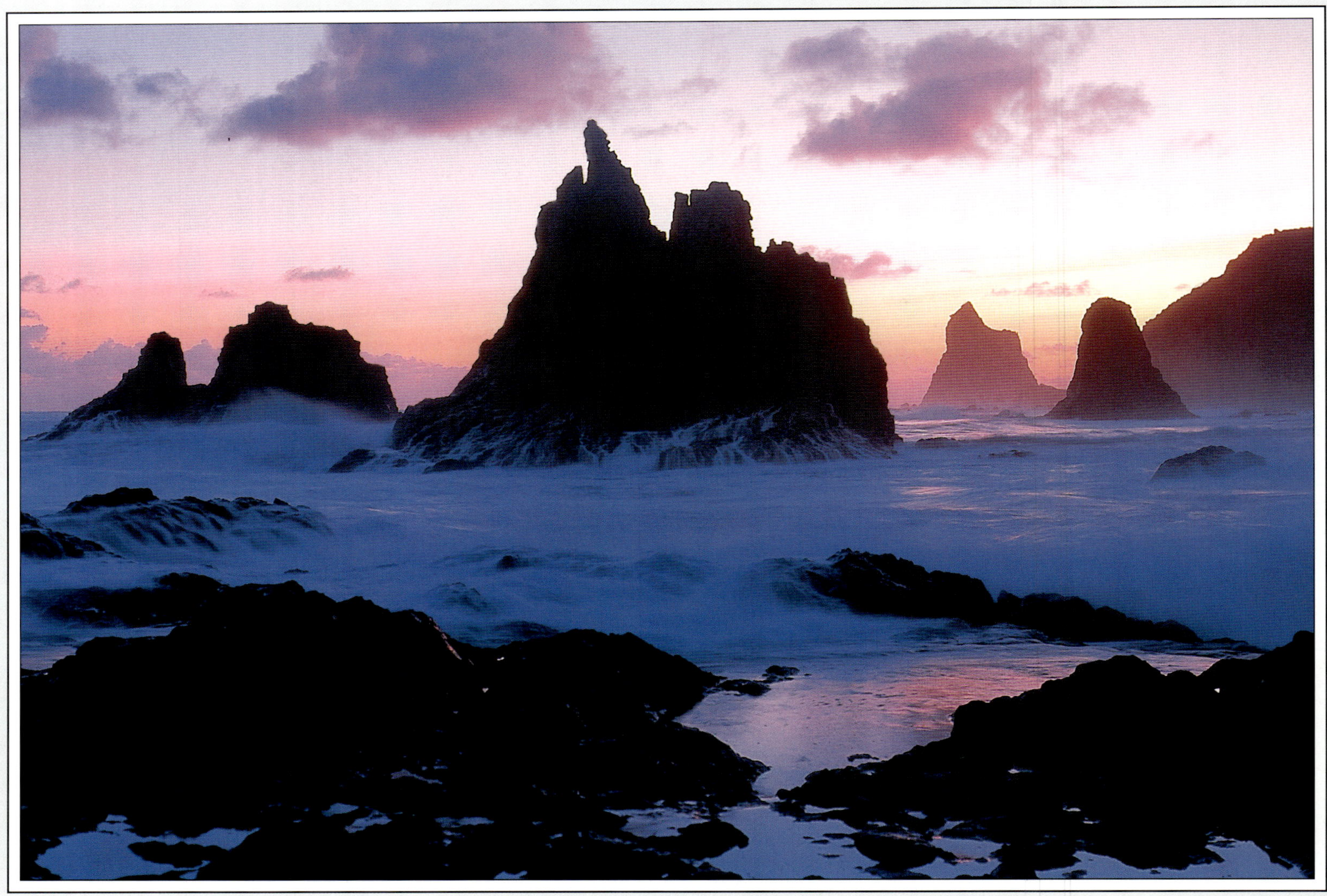

José B Ruiz
Spain
HIGHLY COMMENDED

Benijo coast, Tenerife

"Much of the coastline on Tenerife has been damaged by tourist developments, but a few inaccessible places remain wild and unspoilt. The large rock formations are called 'Los Roques de Anaga'."

Nikon FM2 with 50mm lens; tripod; 1/2 sec at f16; Fujichrome Velvia 50

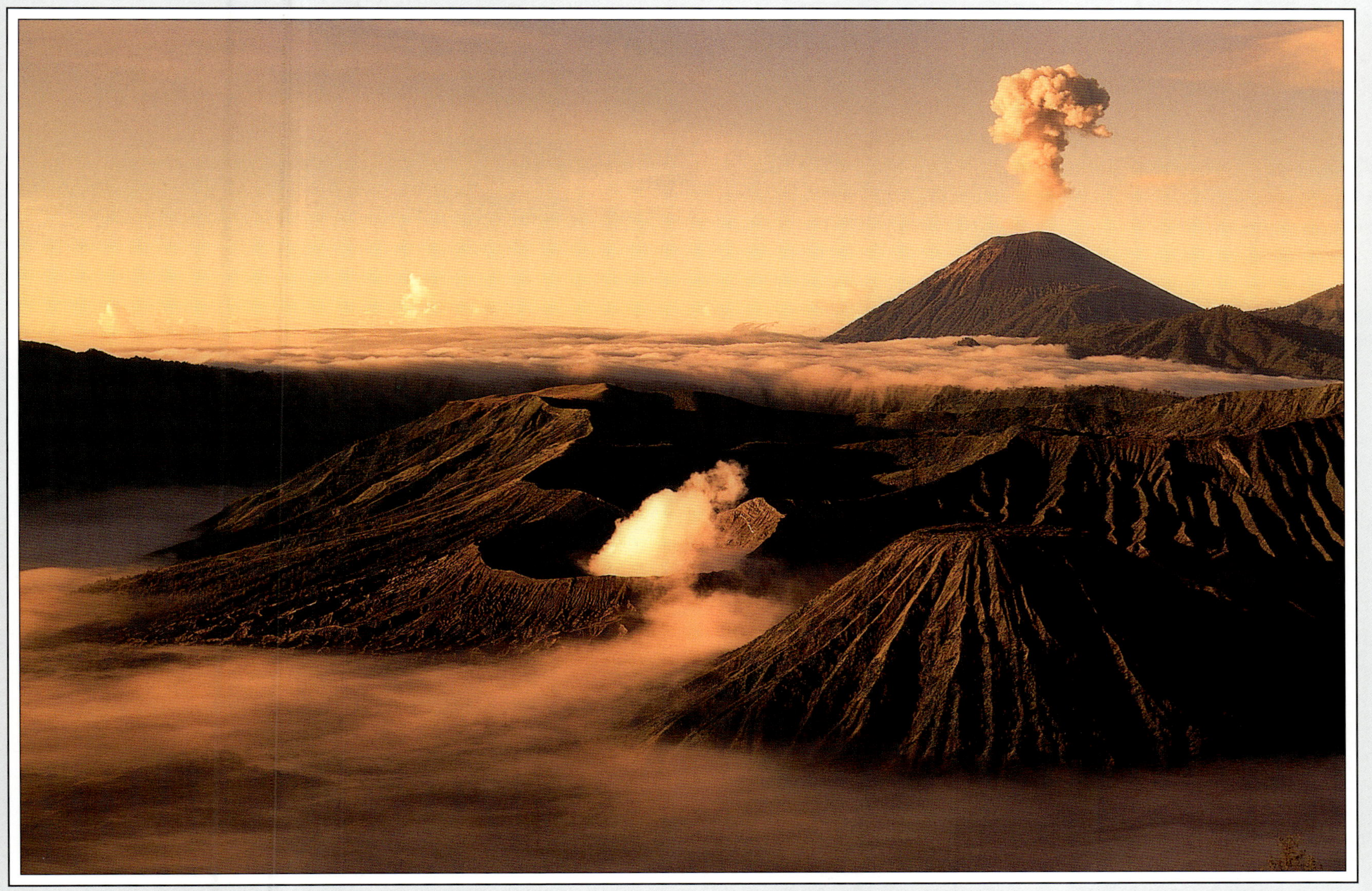

Dan Bool
United Kingdom
HIGHLY COMMENDED

Mount Bromo, Java

"The central peak is Mount Bromo, flanked by the perfect cone of Mount Kursi and the remains of Mount Batok. In the past, Tenggerese Hindus climbed Mount Bromo at sunrise to throw offerings into the crater to pacify the god of the volcano. The smoke plume in the background is from Mount Gunung, Java's highest mountain, which erupts every 30 minutes."

Canon EOS 1N with 28-70mm lens; tripod; 1/15 sec at f8; Fujichrome Provia 100

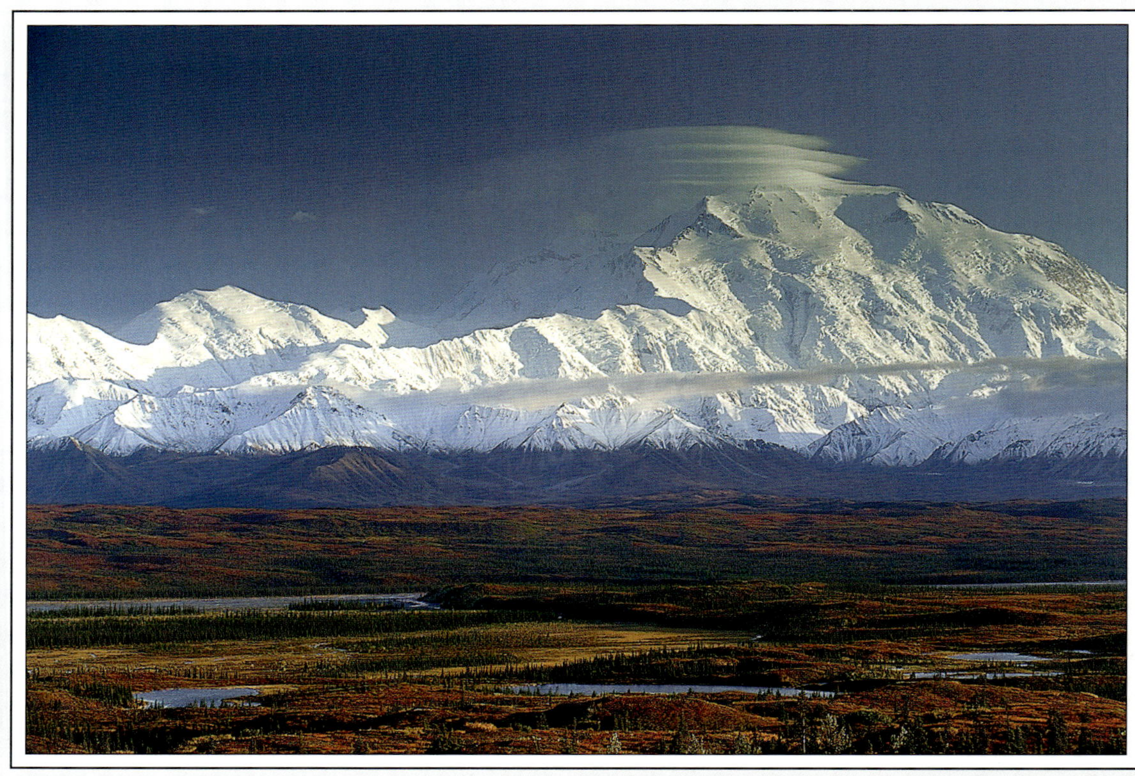

Howie Garber
United States of America
HIGHLY COMMENDED

Mount McKinley, Alaska

"This photograph was taken shortly after sunrise in early September, near Wonder Lake, Denali National Park, Alaska. The tundra was in its autumn colours and cirrus clouds capped Mount McKinley."

Nikon 8008S with 28-70mm lens; tripod; Fujichrome Velvia

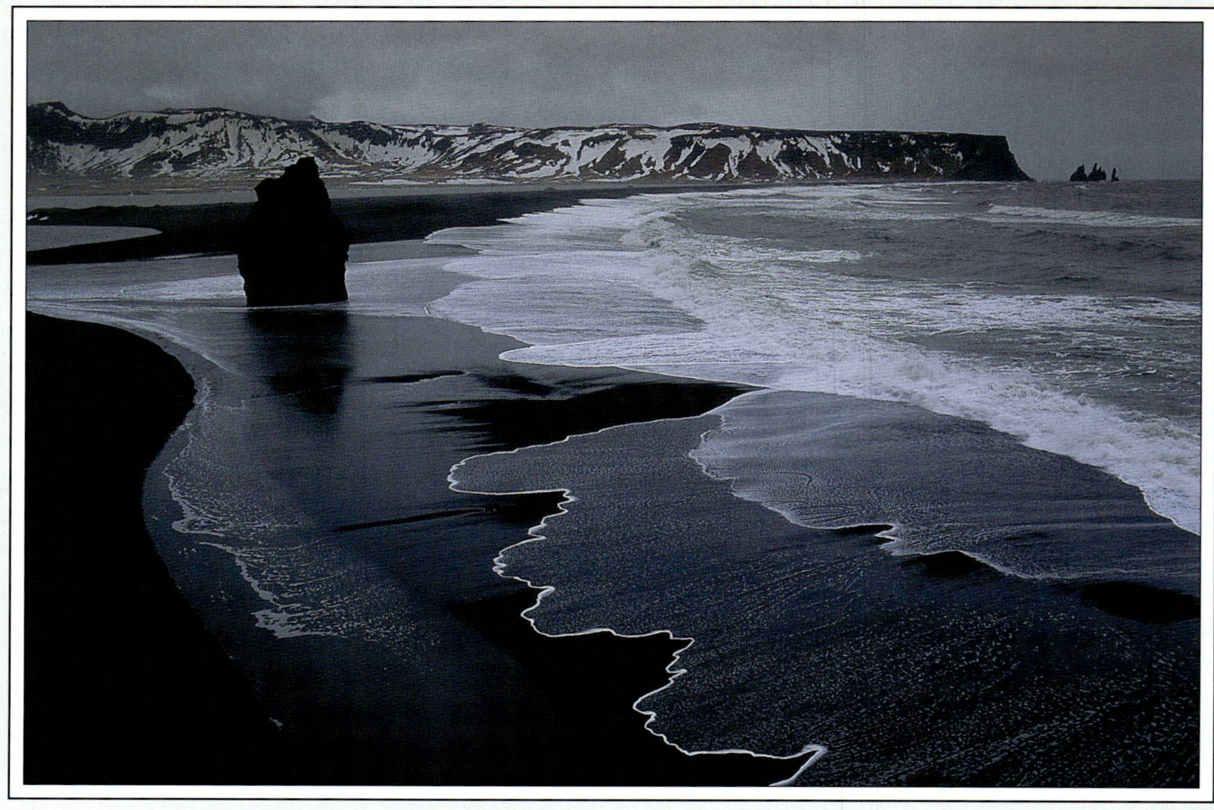

Andy Horner
Finland
HIGHLY COMMENDED

Reynisfjara beach, Iceland

"Nestling below the giant Myrdalsjökull Glacier at the southernmost tip of Iceland, the beach of Reynisfjara is frequently lashed by Atlantic storms. As the light faded on this stormy, April evening, I was struck by the contrast of the ever-changing lacy foam patterns against the black volcanic sands."

Pentax MX with 28mm lens; 1/30 at f4; Fujichrome Velvia

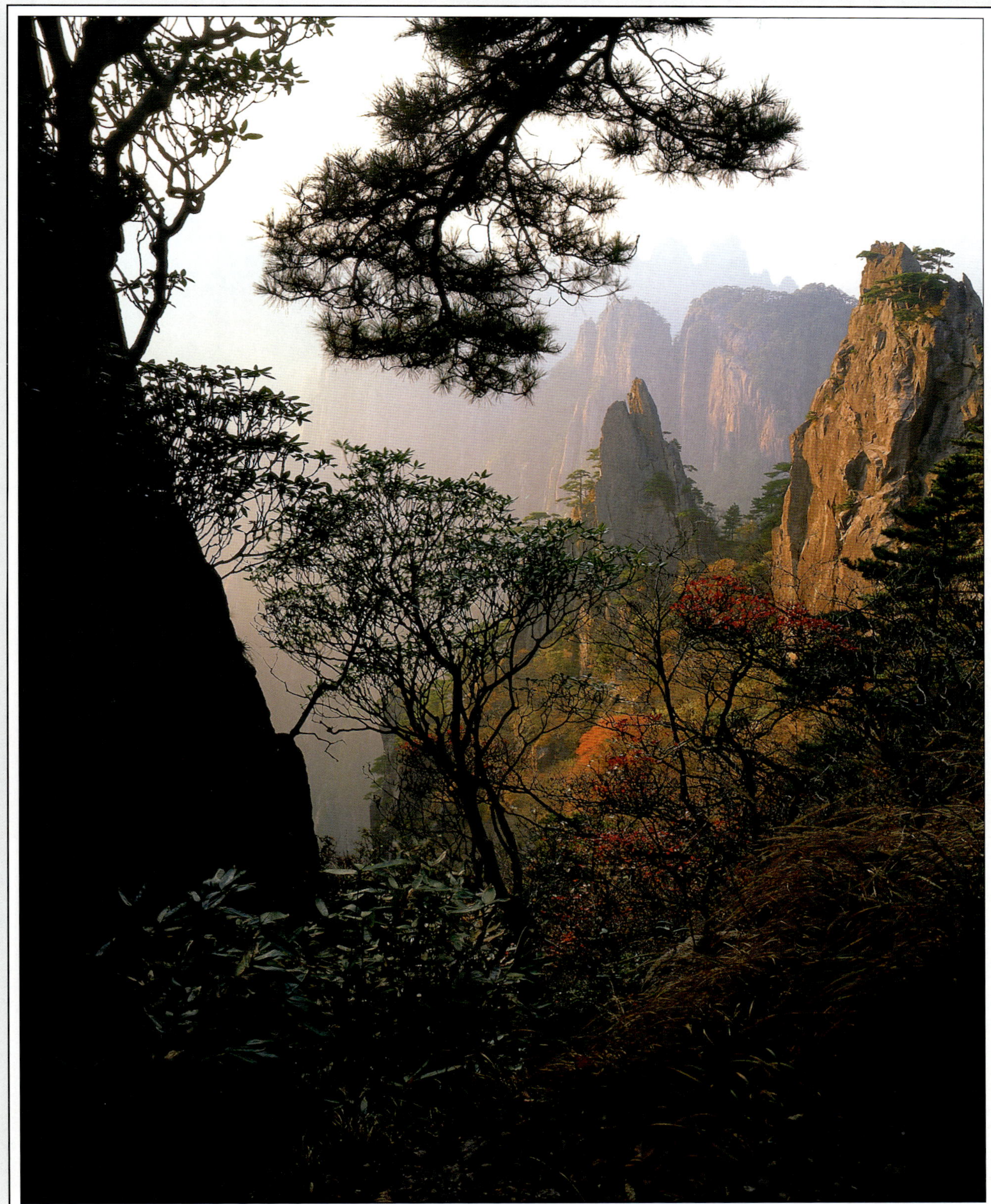

Jan Töve Johansson
Sweden
HIGHLY COMMENDED

Huang Shan mountains, China

"I was running around wildly looking for the right position to capture the sunset in these mountains. Then I realised I must relax and forget preconceived images. So, slowing down, I opened my mind and eyes to the landscape that was there - the real China. Suddenly I saw the picture I was seeking both in reality and image."

Mamiya 7 with 65mm lens; Fujichrome Velvia

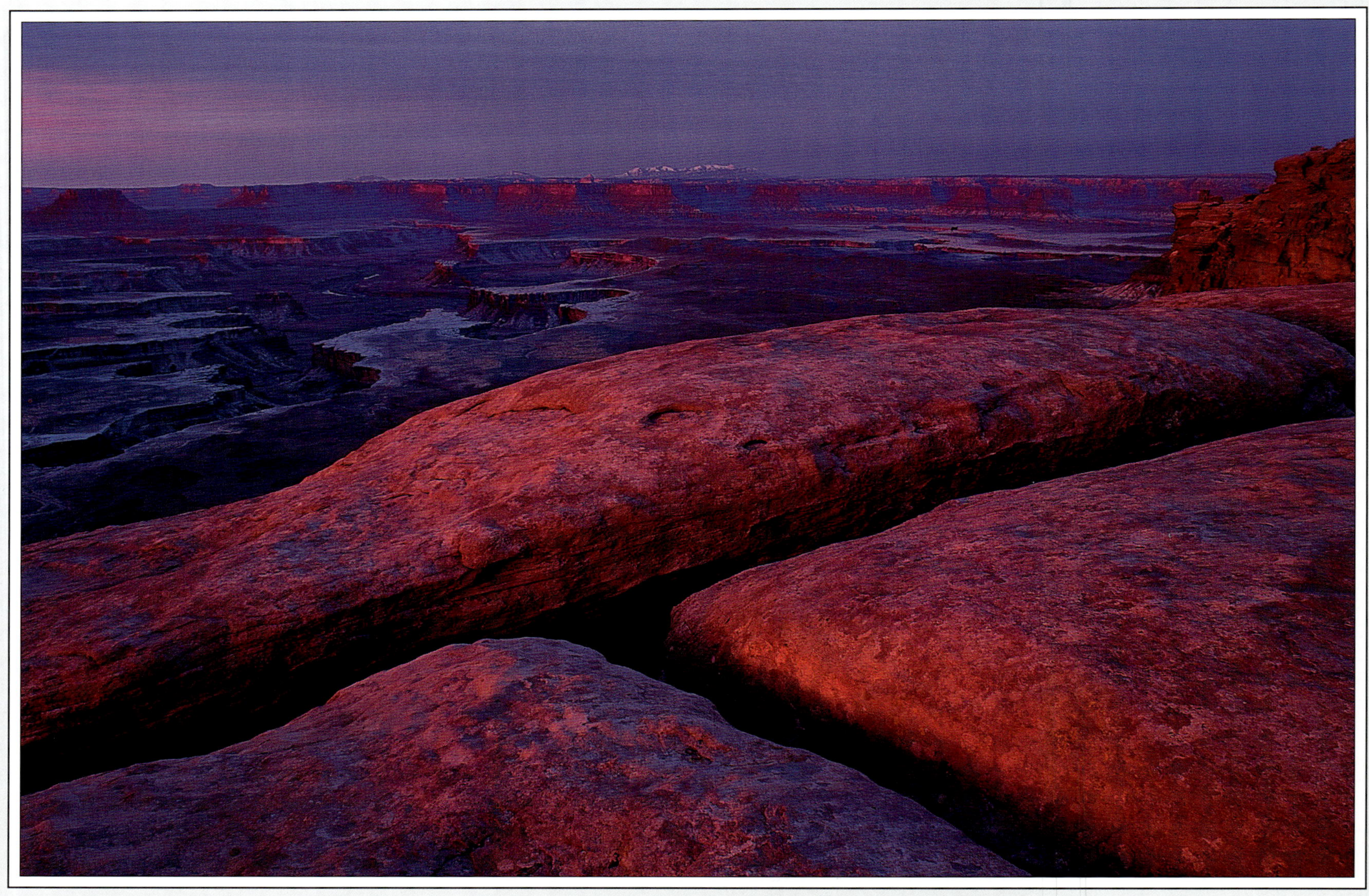

Shaun Cunningham
Canada
HIGHLY COMMENDED

Canyonlands dawn

"As the autumn sun rose over the Green River canyon in the 'Islands of the Sky' district of Canyonlands National Park, Utah, the light was reflected from the partially cloudy sky. I used a wide-angle lens to accentuate the rock formations in the foreground. In the distance, across the vast canyon, are the Henry Mountains."

Canon A2 with 20-35mm lens; tripod; 10 sec at f16; Fujichrome Velvia

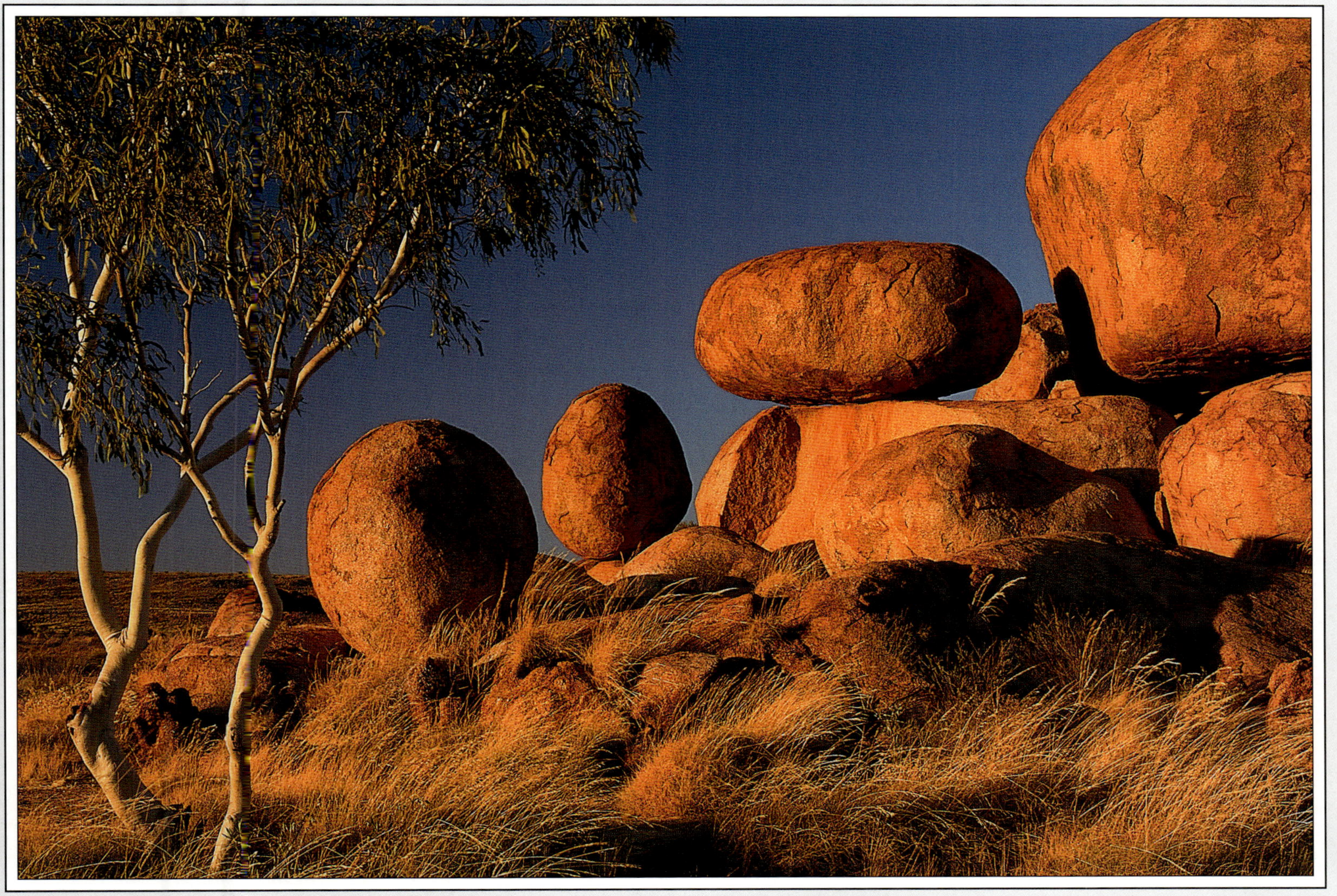

Daniel Zupanc
Austria
HIGHLY COMMENDED

Devil's Marbles, Australia

"I woke just before sunrise to photograph the Devil's Marbles in Australia's Northern Territory in the first morning light to emphasise the rich, warm colour of the boulders. It was a great experience to walk between the elegantly-shaped rocks, which have been formed by wind and rain erosion. Aboriginal mythology says they are the eggs of the rainbow snake."

Nikon F4 with 35-70mm lens; tripod; f16;
Fujichrome Velvia 50 rated at 40

The World In Our Hands

Pictures must illustrate in a symbolic or graphic way our dependence on the natural world or our capability of inflicting harm on it.

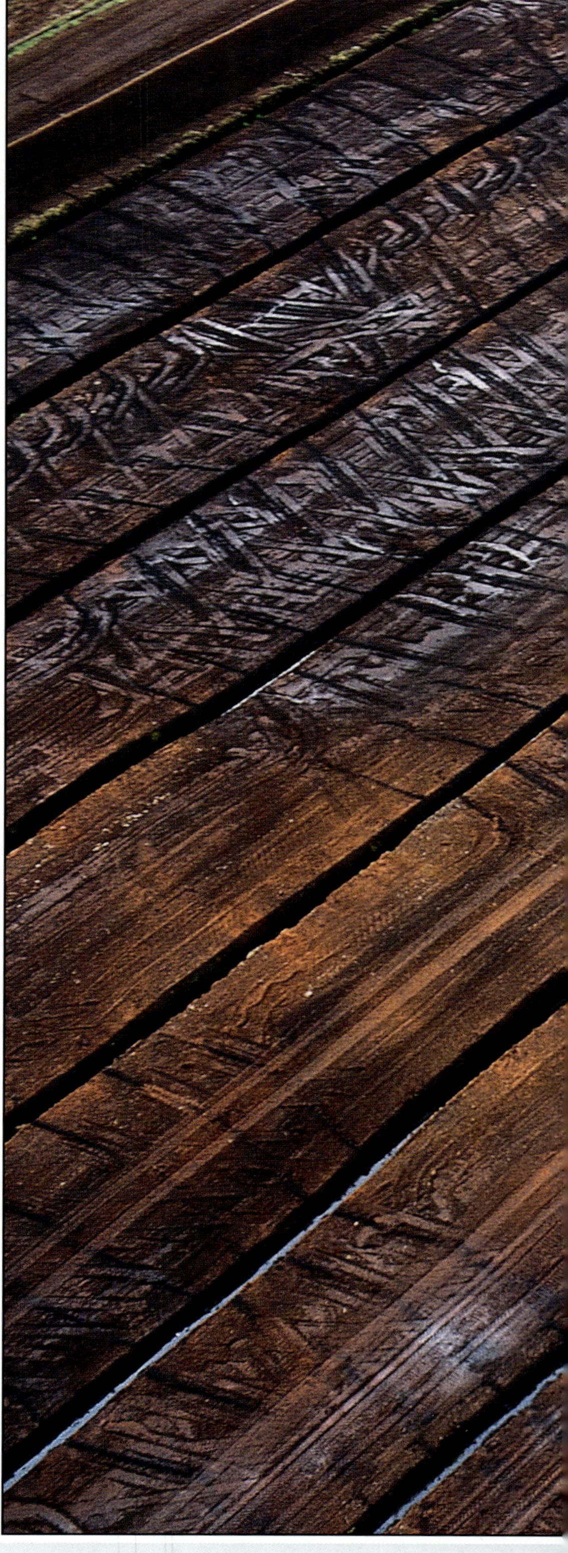

Lorne Gill
United Kingdom
WINNER

Commercial peat extraction

"The entire surface of Letham Moss, Scotland, has been stripped of vegetation and drains cut to dry out the peat for commercial extraction. This process totally destroys the rare bog habitat, as it can never regenerate. Britain has lost 95 per cent of its raised bogs, but Scotland's central lowlands now have one of the most significant surviving concentrations in Western Europe."

Nikon F4 with 24mm lens; 1/500 sec at f4; Fujichrome Velvia

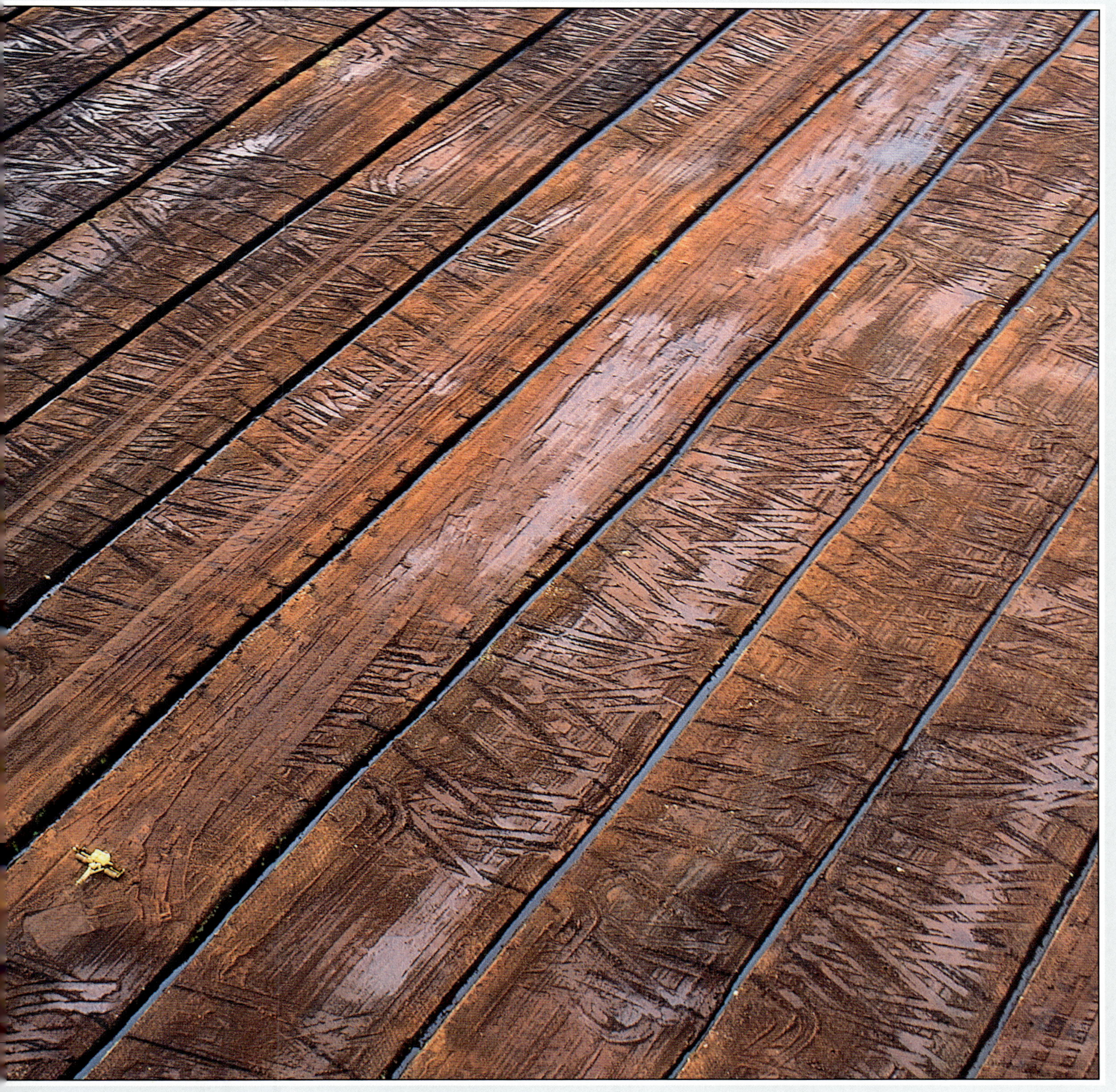

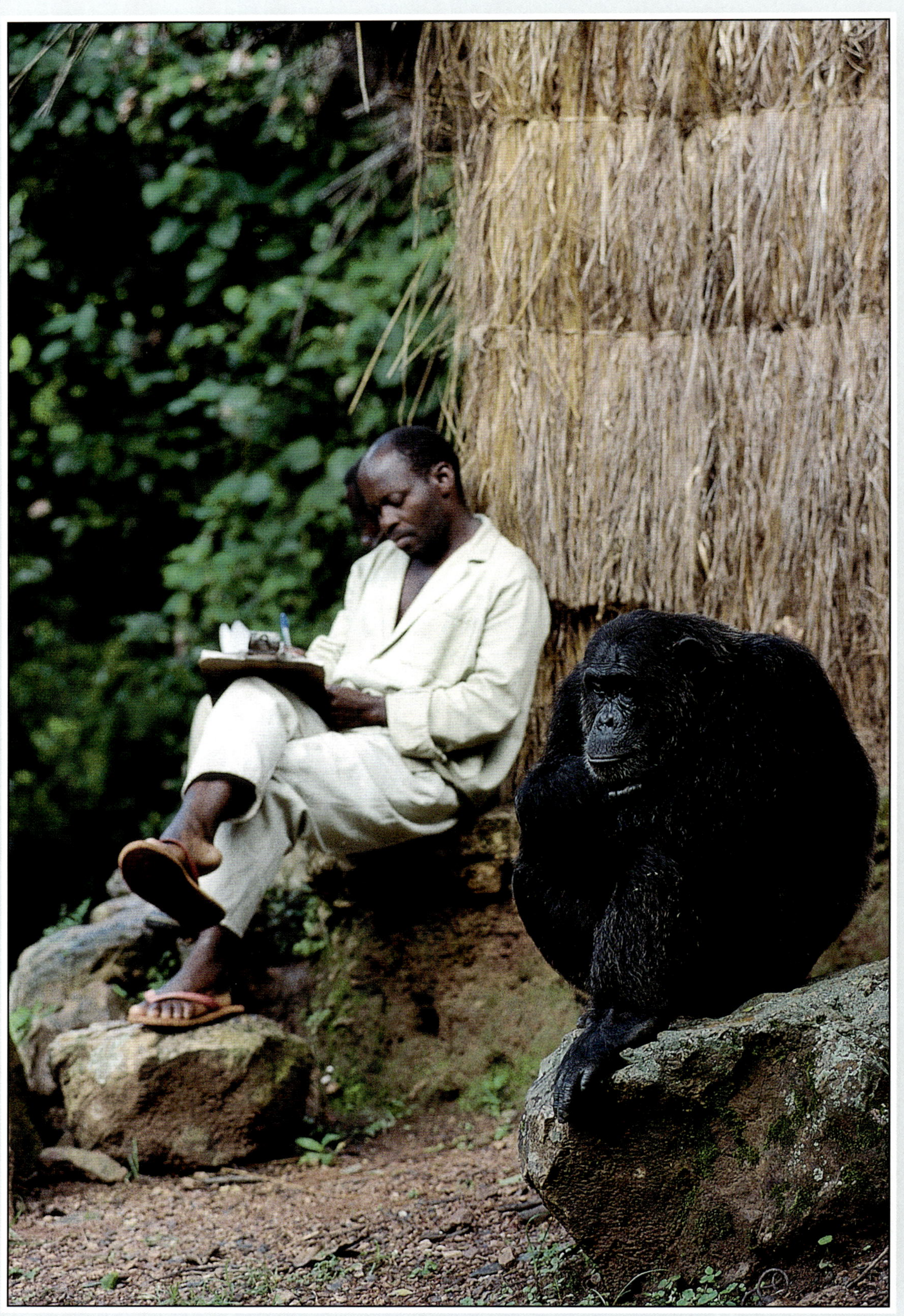

Fritz Pölking
Germany
RUNNER-UP

Gombe chimpanzee study

"This chimpanzee is one of the individuals that the Jane Goodall research group has been studying in the Gombe Stream National Park, Tanzania. I thought this wonderful image showed how similar we are to the great apes. There is a special, silent humour in this picture."

Nikon F5 with 80-200mm lens; tripod; Fujichrome Sensia 100

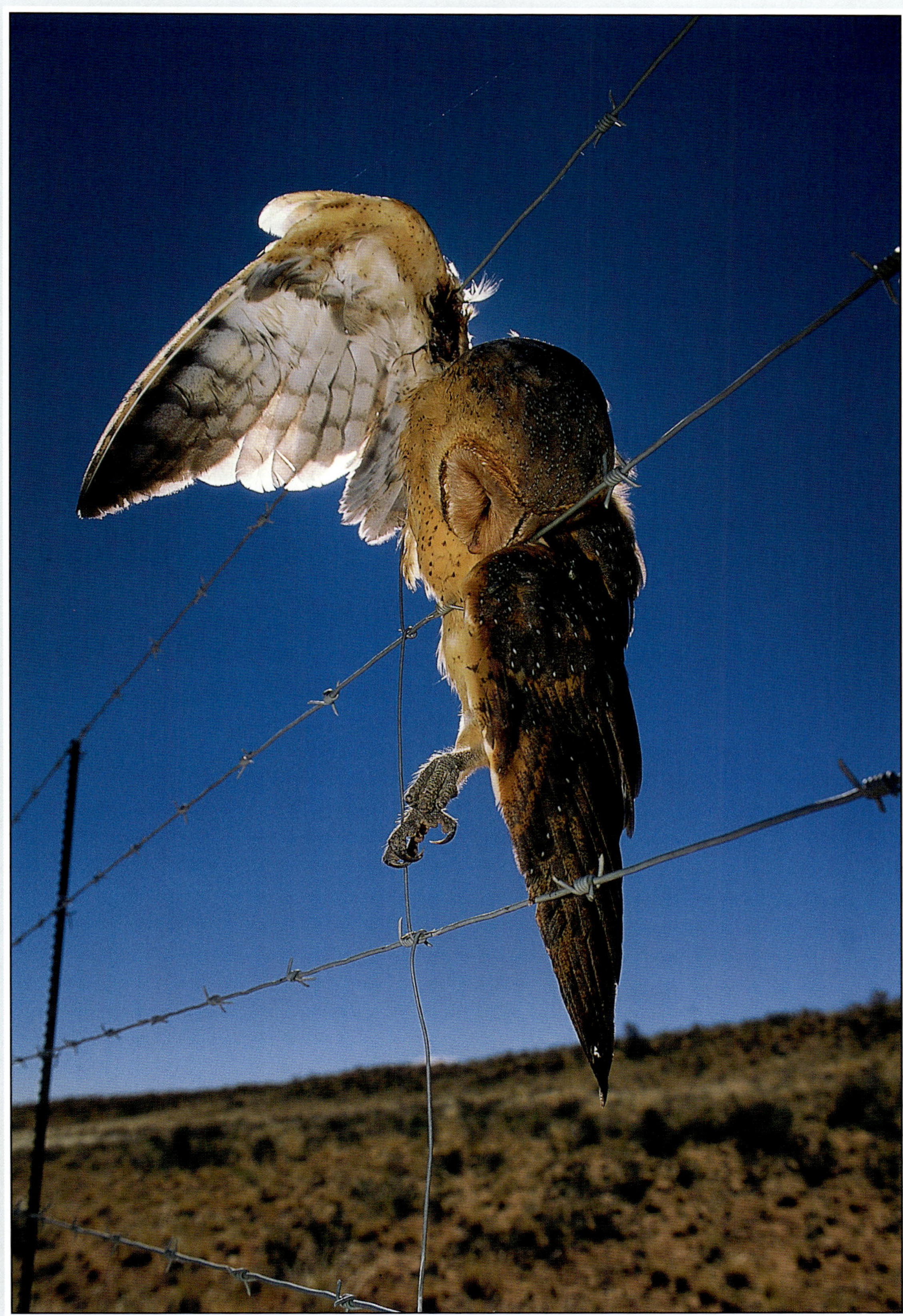

Richard du Toit
South Africa
SPECIALLY COMMENDED

Owl caught on barbed wire

"I found this barn owl hanging by the roadside when driving in the Kalahari. It struck me as particularly ironic that such a beautiful and beneficial bird should die like this on a farmer's fence."

Canon EOS 1N with 17-35mm lens; flash; Fujichrome Velvia

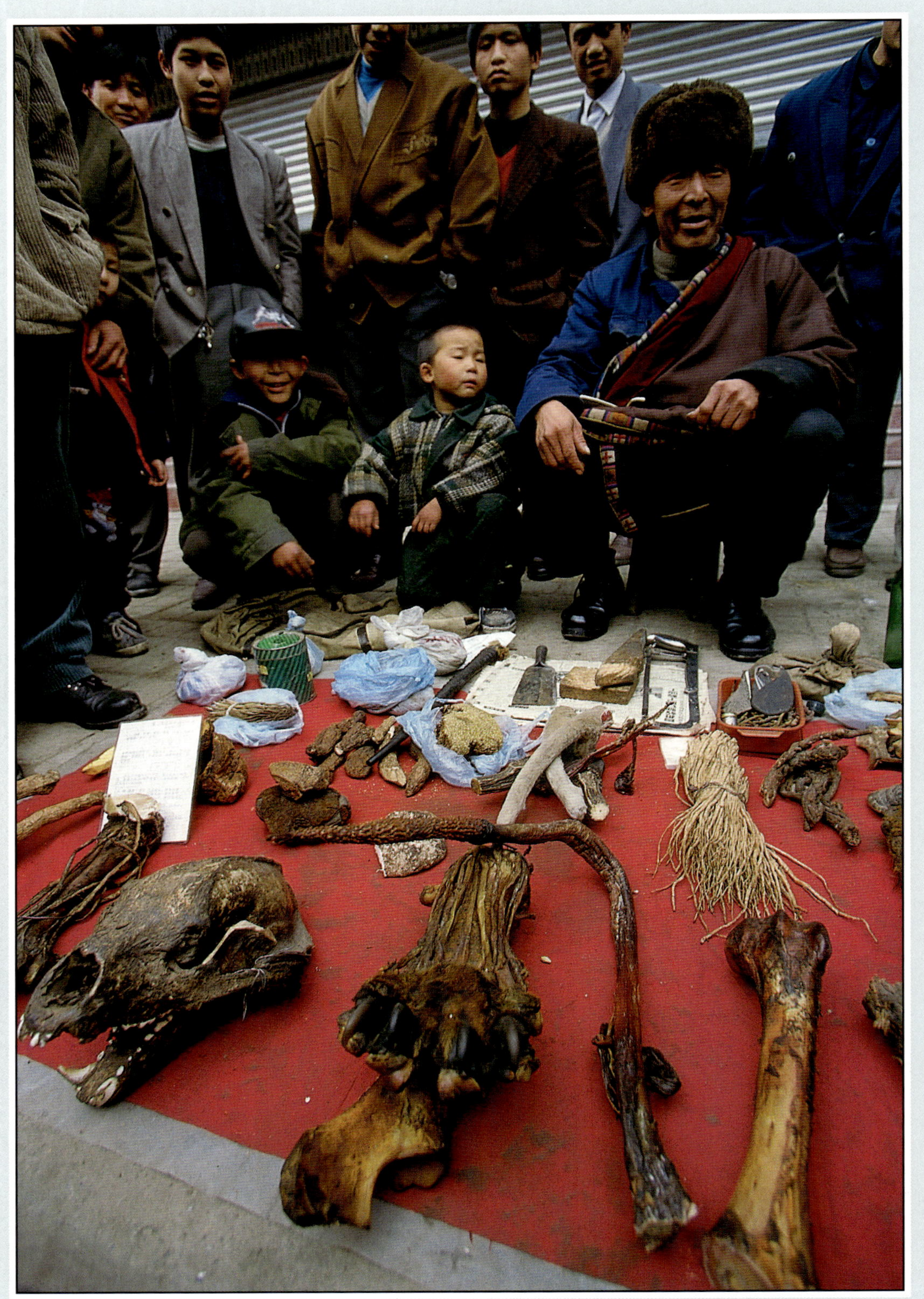

Konrad Wothe
Germany
HIGHLY COMMENDED

Chinese traditional medicine

"Tiger paws and penises, a leopard skull, and other horns and bones were being sold as potency remedies in a street market in Chengdu, China. The trader objected to being photographed and became quite aggressive, asking for a large amount of money. He knew of course that trading in tiger parts was illegal."

Canon EOS 1N with 17-35mm lens; 1/30 sec at f8; Fujichrome Sensia

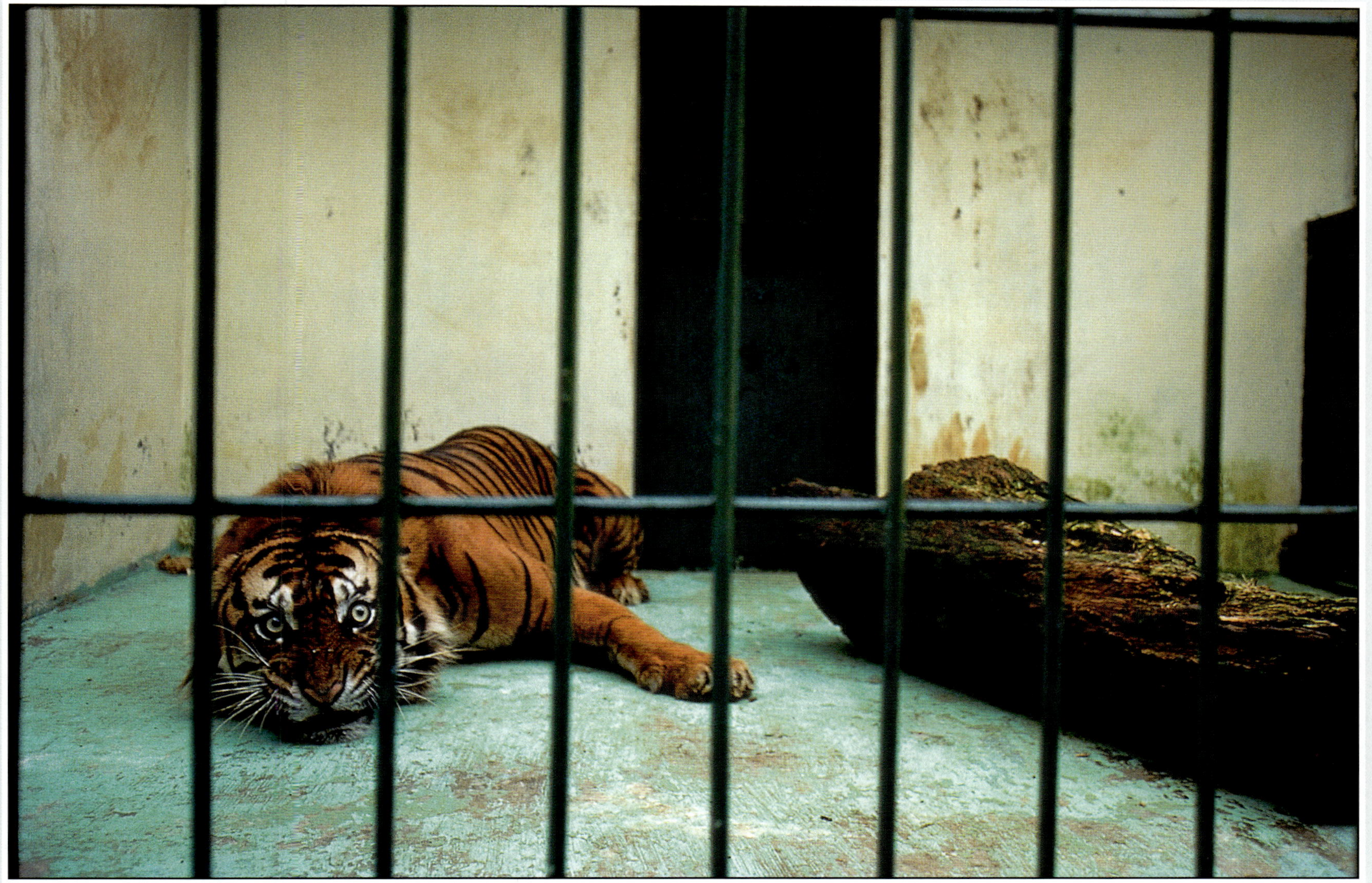

Michael Nichols
United States of America
HIGHLY COMMENDED

Caged Sumatran tiger

"The look of fear still remains in this tiger's eyes after nine years of captivity in Taman Safari Park, near Jakarta, Indonesia. This magnificent animal was brought in from the wild to be placed in their captive breeding program, which is part of a concerted worldwide effort to boost the precariously low populations of all five remaining tiger species."

Canon EOS 1N; Kodak E100SW

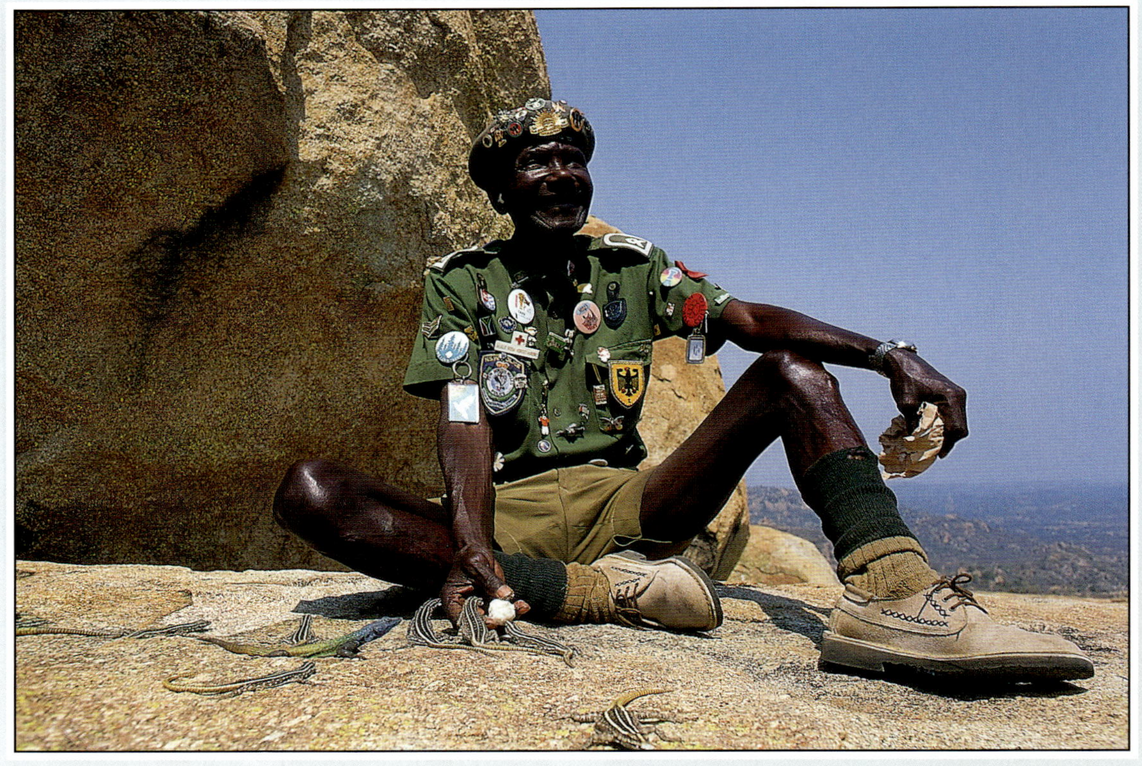

José B Ruiz

Spain

HIGHLY COMMENDED

Lizard feeding time

"Every afternoon this man climbed up to the tomb of Cecil Rhodes in Matopos National Park, Zimbabwe, to feed the lizards. It is a popular event with the tourists."

Nikon FM2 with 24mm lens; 1/30 sec at f16; Fujichrome Velvia 50

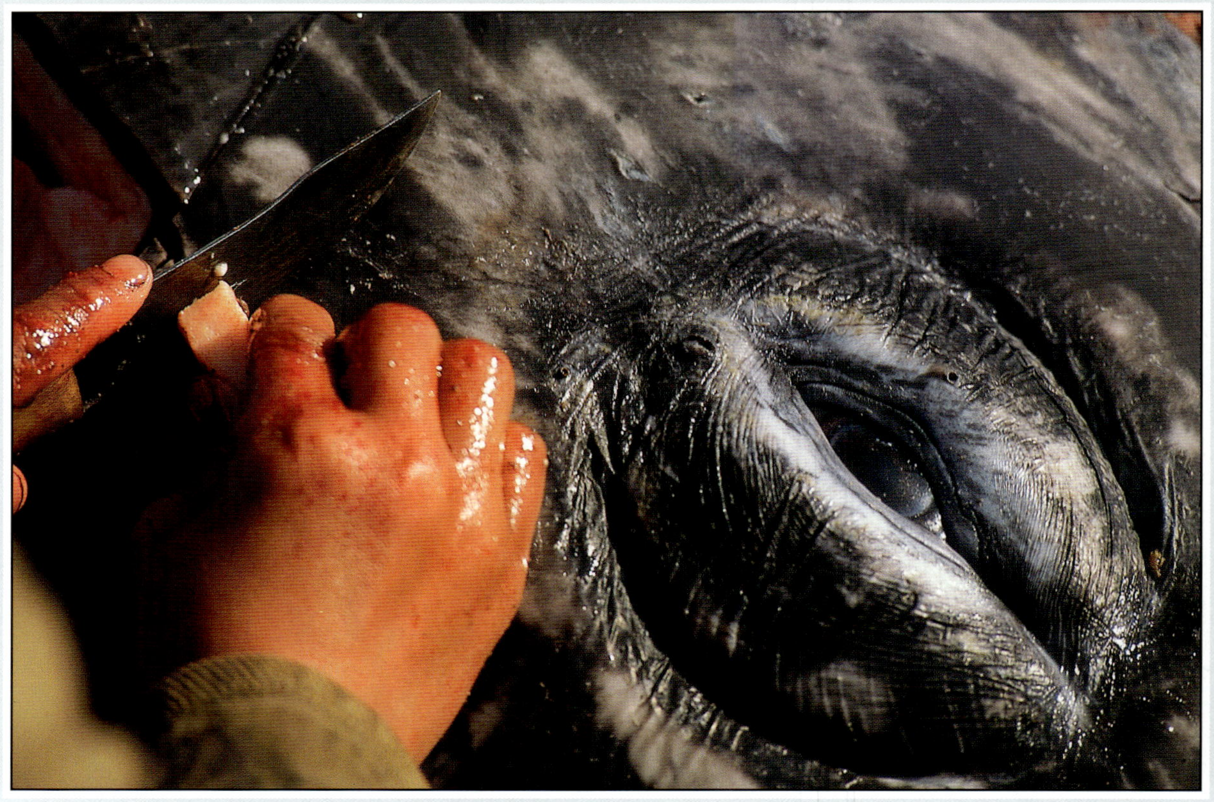

Staffan Widstrand

Sweden

HIGHLY COMMENDED

Whale skin

"A Chukchi hunter cuts a piece of skin from a freshly-caught grey whale – an important source of vitamin C for Arctic hunting people. The whale is one of the year's legal quota of 75 greys for the Lorino community in Russia. Half the meat is consumed by the village, but the authorities insist the rest goes to the Arctic fox farm despite there being no market for the pelts."

Nikon F4 with 105mm lens; 1/125 at f5.6; Fujichrome Velvia 50

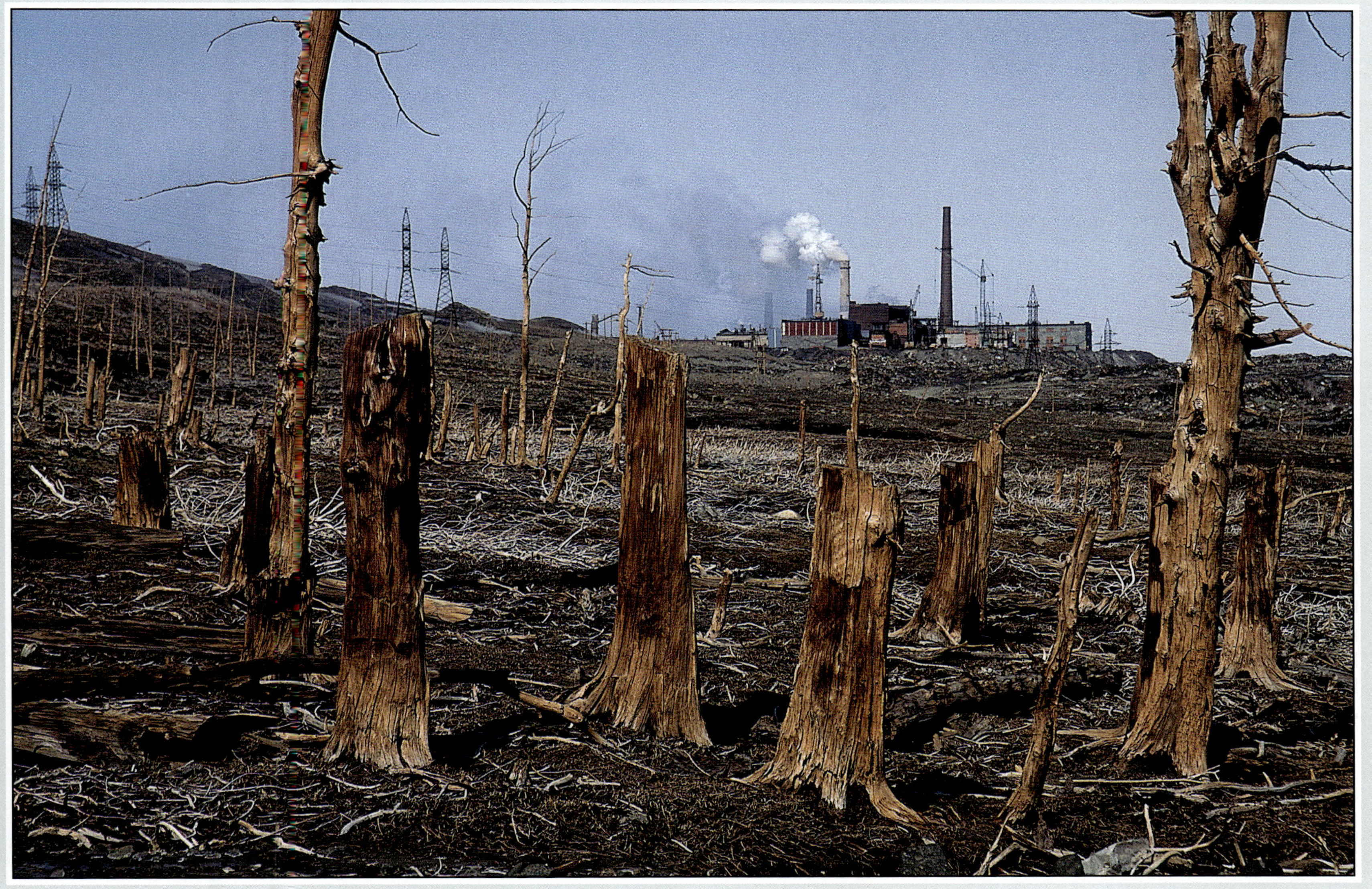

Pål Hermansen
Norway
HIGHLY COMMENDED

Polluted forest

"In the nineteen thirties this area just outside Norilsk in Russia was a dense larch forest. The soil is now so badly polluted that not a single speck of green vegetation can be found, and the forest has been destroyed."

Nikon F4 with 80-200mm lens; 1/8 sec f22; Fujichrome Velvia

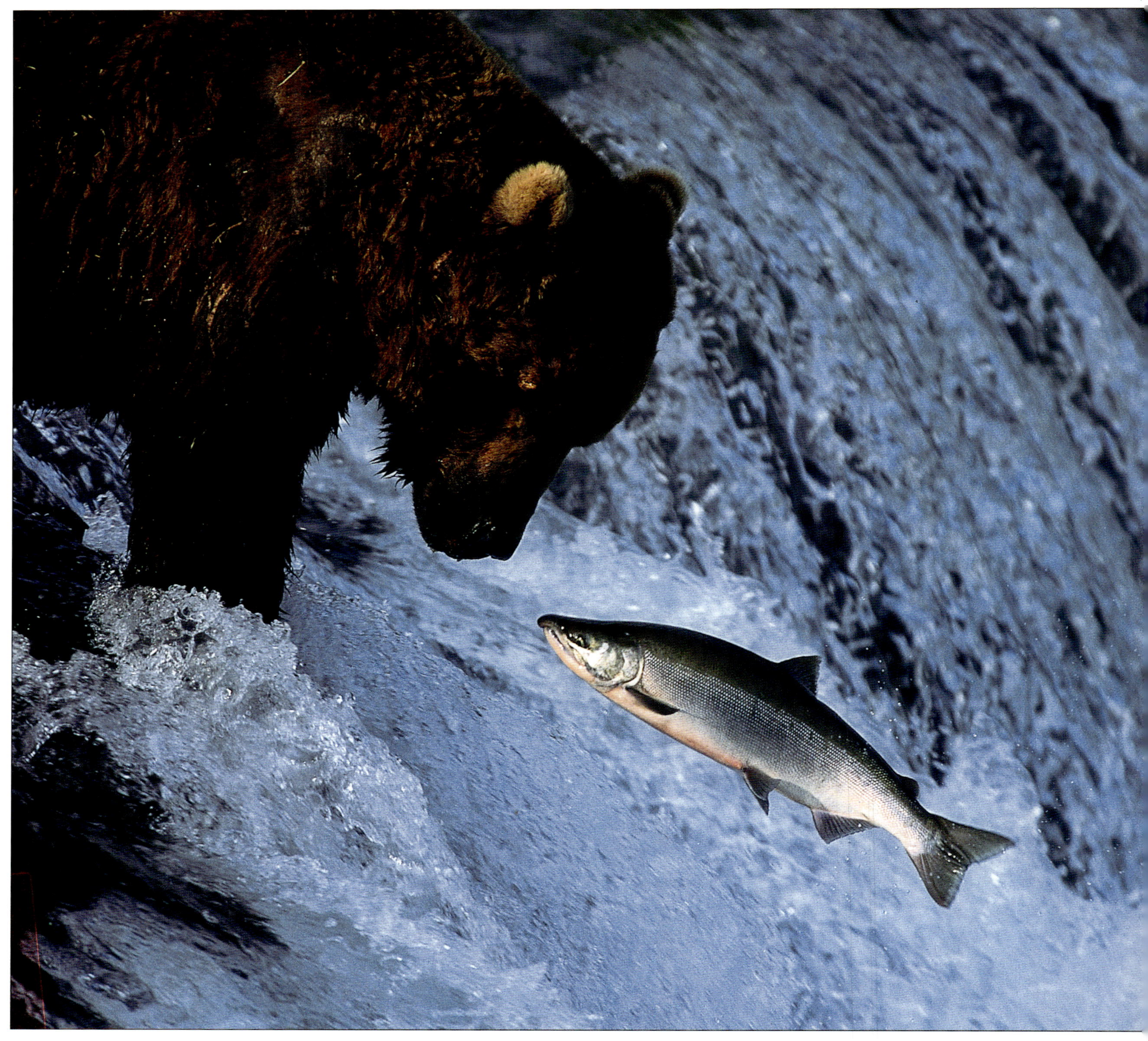

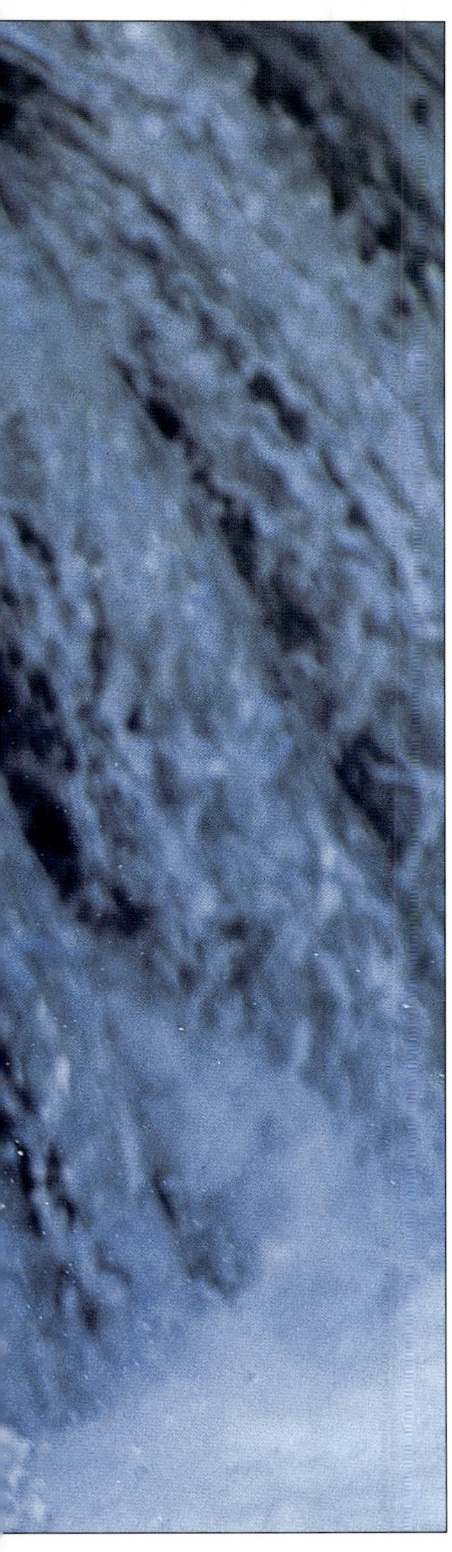

Young Wildlife Photographer of the Year

This section of the Competition is open to photographers aged 17 and under. It is divided into three age categories: 10 years and under, 11 to 14 years and 15 to 17 years. Photographers are able to enter up to six images of any wildlife subject. The winner and runner-up in each age-group receives a cash prize.

This year, there was a special category in association with YOC, the winner receives a cash prize and a trophy.

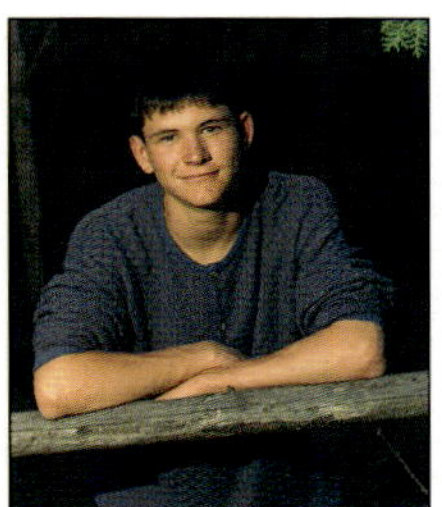

Brandon T Garland
United States of America
YOUNG WILDLIFE PHOTOGRAPHER OF THE YEAR 1998

Brown bear fishing for salmon

"The brown bears at Brooks Falls on the Katmai Peninsula, Alaska, use various fishing techniques. This individual is employing the 'sit and wait for the fish to come to you' method. She sat, as I did, for three hours waiting for the fish to jump. Finally it did, and the catch made a great shot and a fine meal for her three waiting cubs."

Canon EOS1 with 300mm lens and x2 teleconverter; clamp; Fujichrome Provia 100

The overall winner of the Competition, 17-year-old Brandon Tyler 'Ty' Garland from the United States of America, received the BG Award - a bronze trophy of an ibis - a cheque for £500 and the opportunity to spend a day on location with wildlife photographer Heather Angel.

Ty began photographing on family outings with the guidance of his mother, Alice Garland, a nature photographer. These early photographic and outdoor influences set the stage for his continued interest in wildlife photography. As an ambitious, young mountaineer, Ty also photographs his climbs in the Northwest, Canadian Rockies and Alaska.

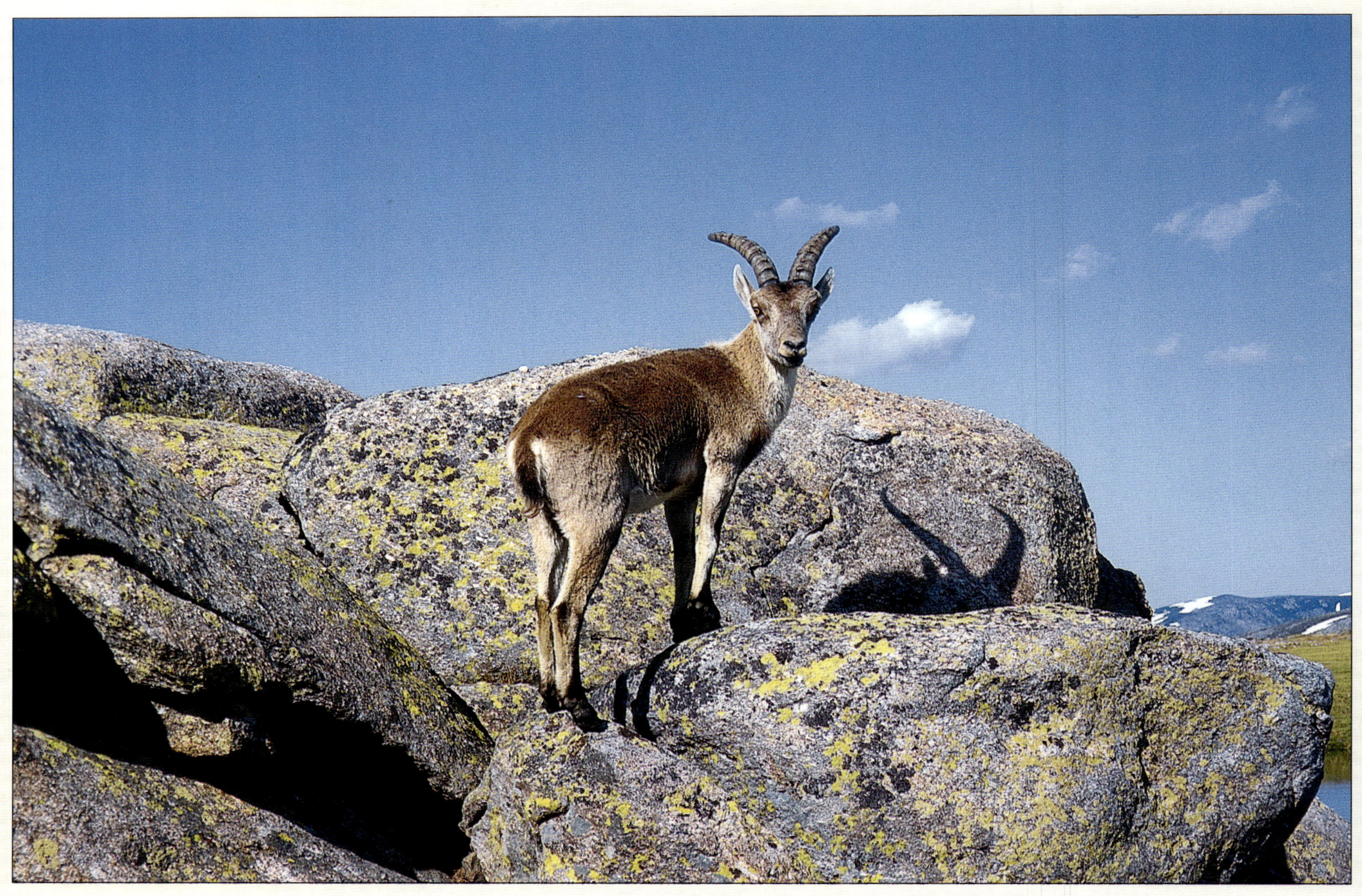

María Cano

Spain

WINNER
10 YEARS AND UNDER

Ibex

"After walking for several kilometres through the snow in the Sierra de Gredos in central Spain, I spotted some grazing ibex. I spent about half an hour creeping close to them. At first they were frightened and fled up onto the rocks, but eventually they got used to me and came down to graze."

Panasonic C-2200 ZM with 35-70mm lens; Fujichrome Sensia

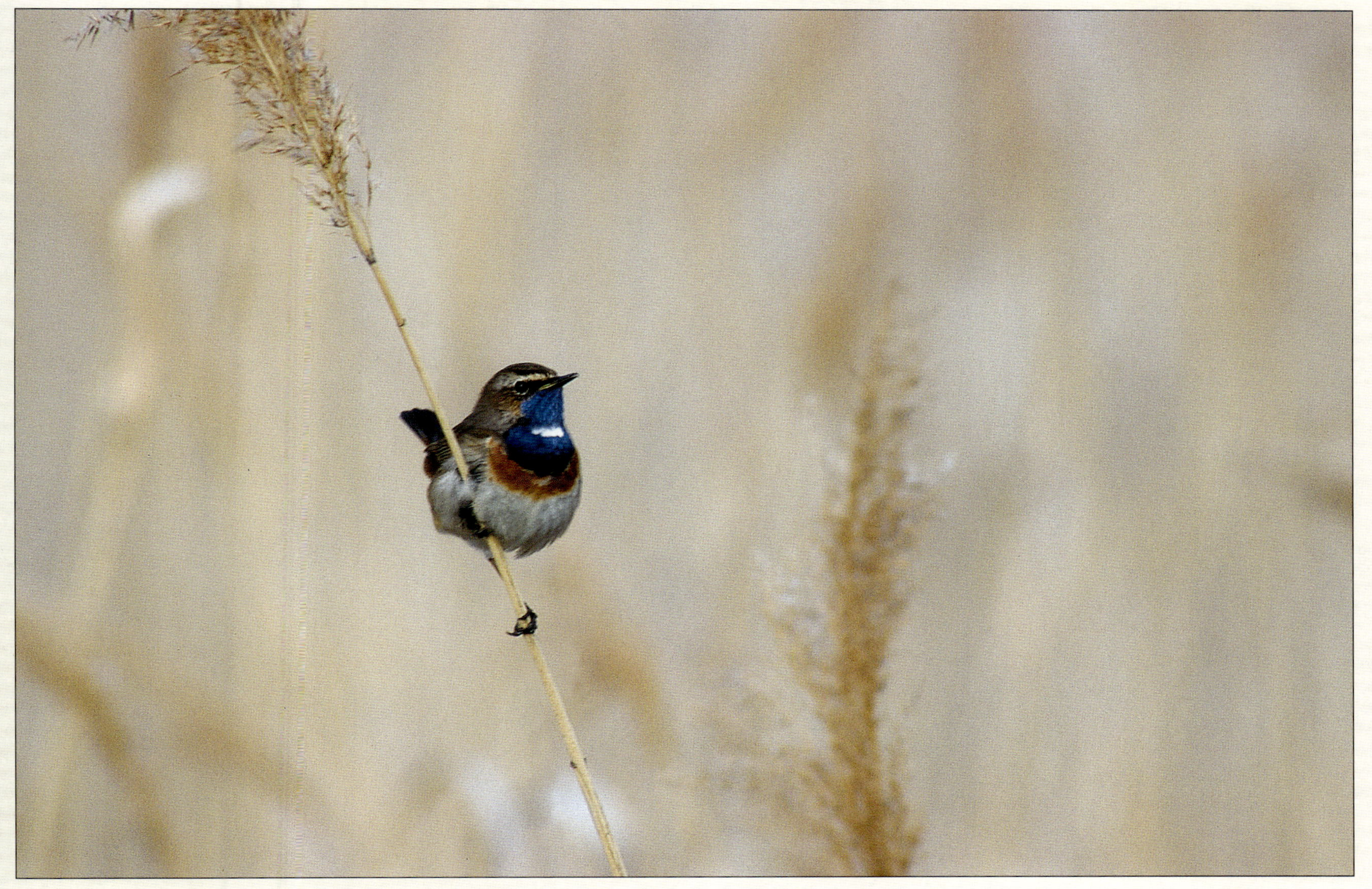

Verena Hahl
Germany
WINNER
11-14 YEARS OLD

Bluethroat

"In April, bluethroats defend their territories by singing loudly from prominent song-posts and showing off their throat-patches. The weather was bad this spring, and I had only two opportunities to photograph the displaying males. This spectacular bird, with his insistent song and intense colour, is a great advocate for the importance of reedbeds."

Nikon F801 with 135-400mm lens; tripod; 1/125 sec at f9; Fujichrome Sensia

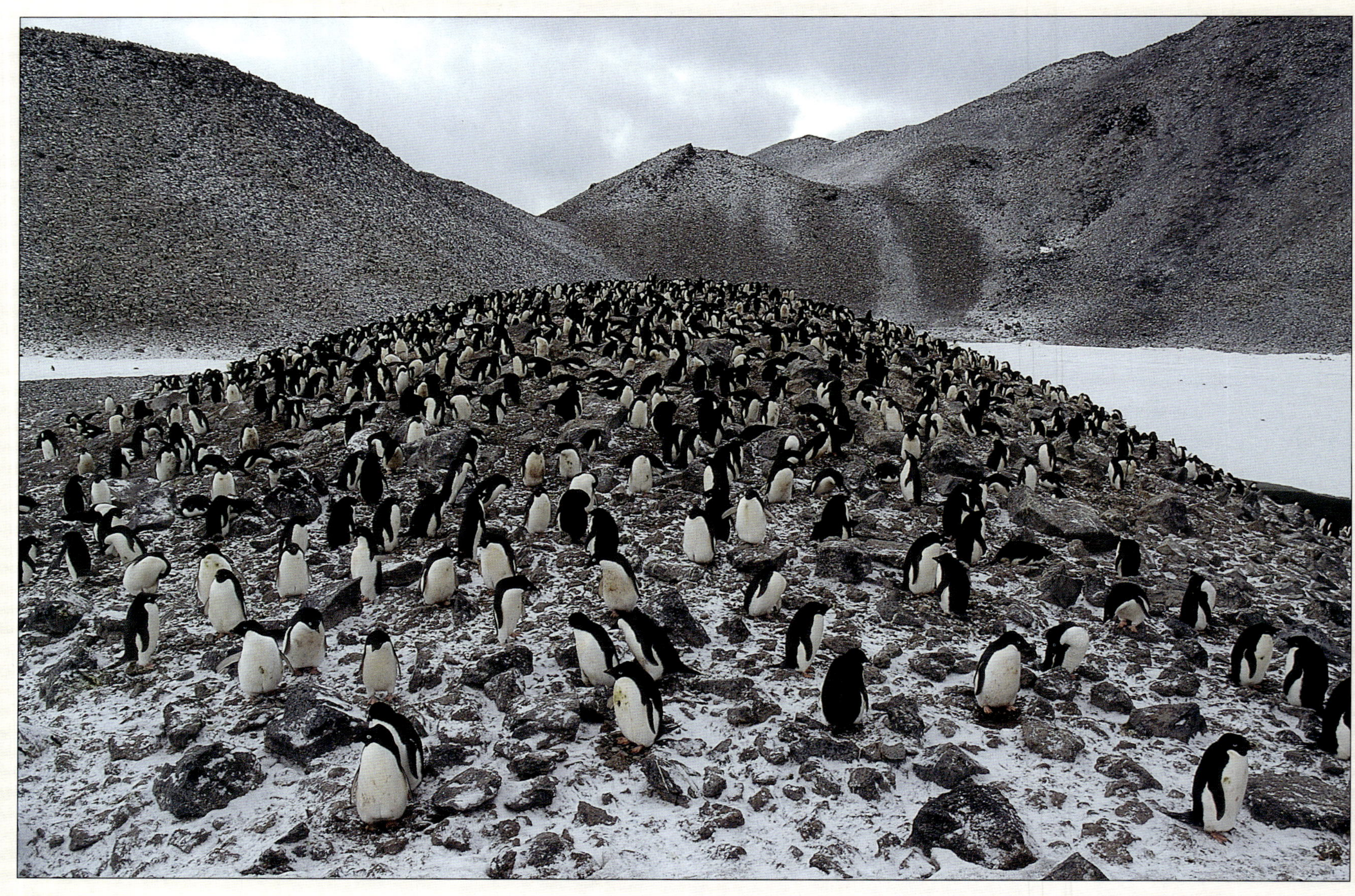

David Scott
United Kingdom
RUNNER-UP
11-14 YEARS OLD

Adélie penguin colony

"It was a grey morning when we climbed into the Zodiacs to be ferried ashore to Paulet Island, off the Antarctic Peninsula. Snow had just fallen and added a pleasing brightness to this penguin rookery. I loved the shapes of the rocks, which were crammed full of displaying and calling birds."

Canon EOS 10 with 28-70mm lens; 1/60 sec; Fujichrome Sensia 100

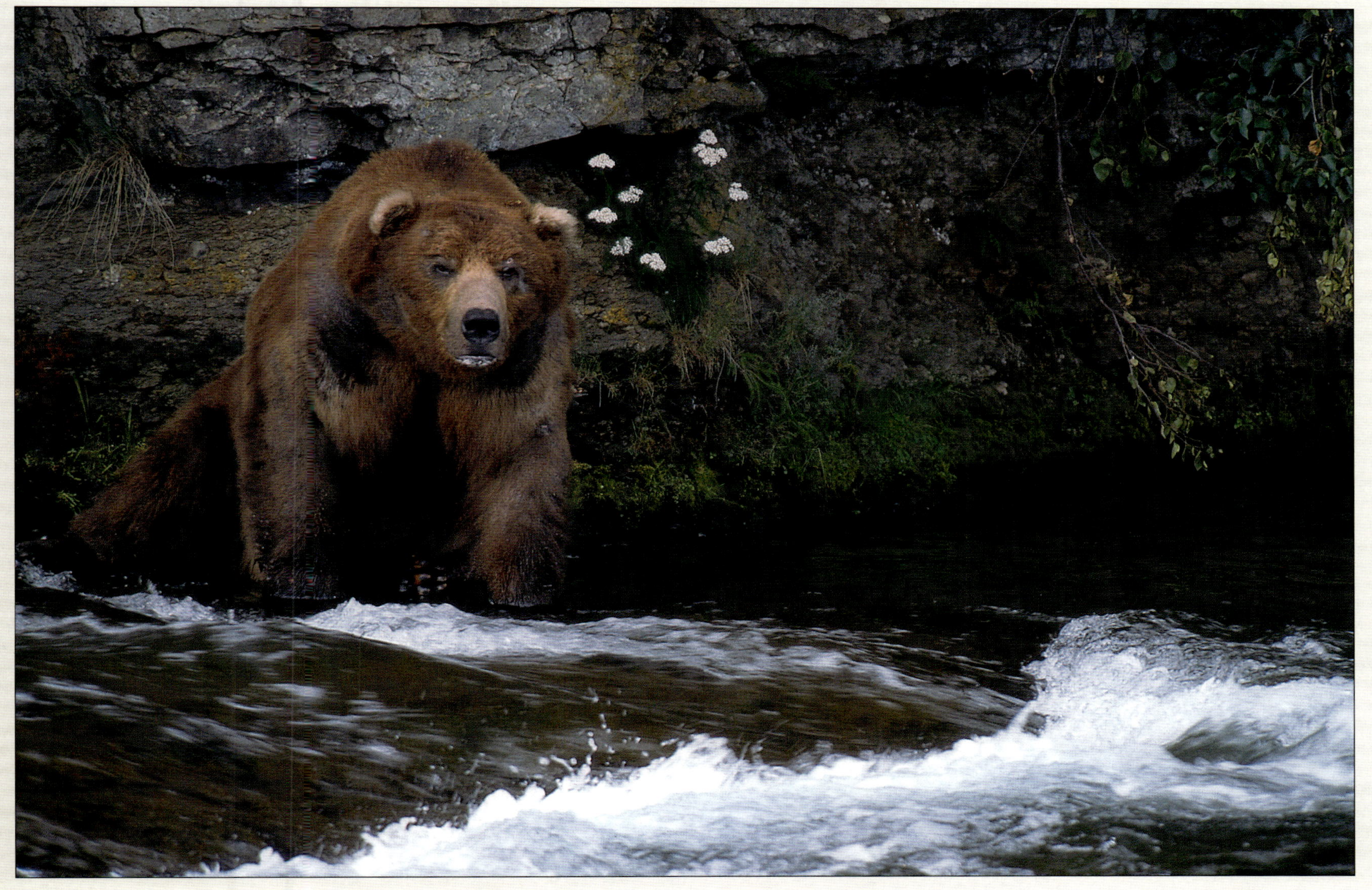

Brandon T Garland
United States of America
WINNER
15-17 YEARS OLD

Brown bear

"This gigantic bear was once the top male, but age has taken its toll. He was forced by the younger males to fish on the far bank of the river. This misfortune for him was perfect for me, as he sat in a nice light next to some daisies."

Canon EOS1 with 300mm lens and x2 converter; tripod; Fujichrome Provia 100

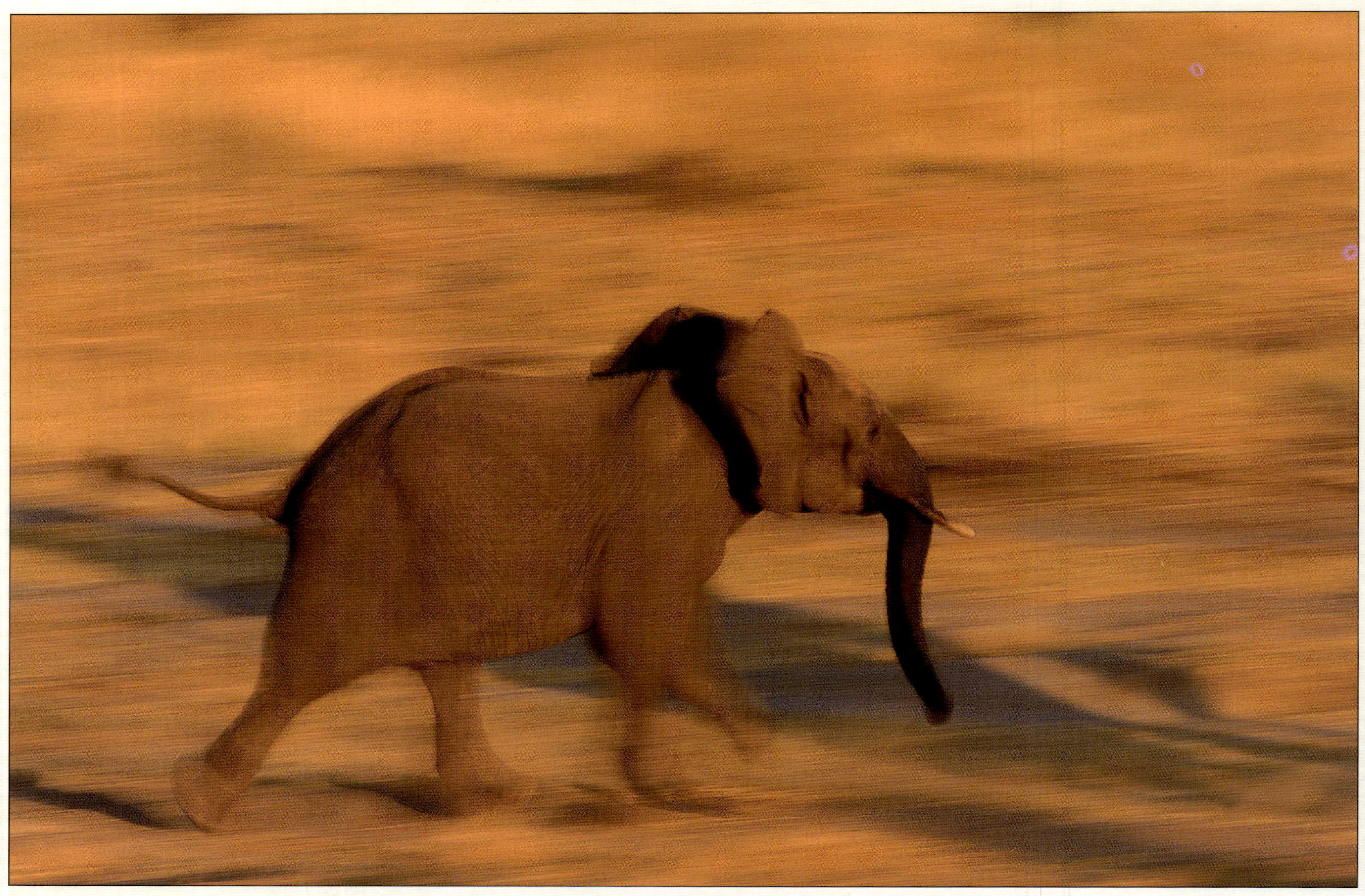

Fabian Fischer
Germany
RUNNER-UP
15-17 YEARS OLD

Elephant running

"Robin's Camp, in Zimbabwe's Hwange National Park, has a viewing platform for watching wildlife. I noticed that whenever a motor started, the elephants fled. So I waited for a car to drive off to take this shot."

Nikon F90x with 300mm lens and x2 converter; tripod; 1/10 sec at f16; Fujichrome Sensia II 100

Rachel Hingley
United Kingdom
SPECIALLY COMMENDED
15-17 YEARS OLD

Grey squirrel gathering bedding

"It was late April and I'd gone to Stewart Park, Middlesborough, to photograph squirrels. I noticed this one collecting bedding material and taking it up to its drey."

Contax 167MT with 300mm and x1.4 converter; tripod; Fujichrome Provia 100

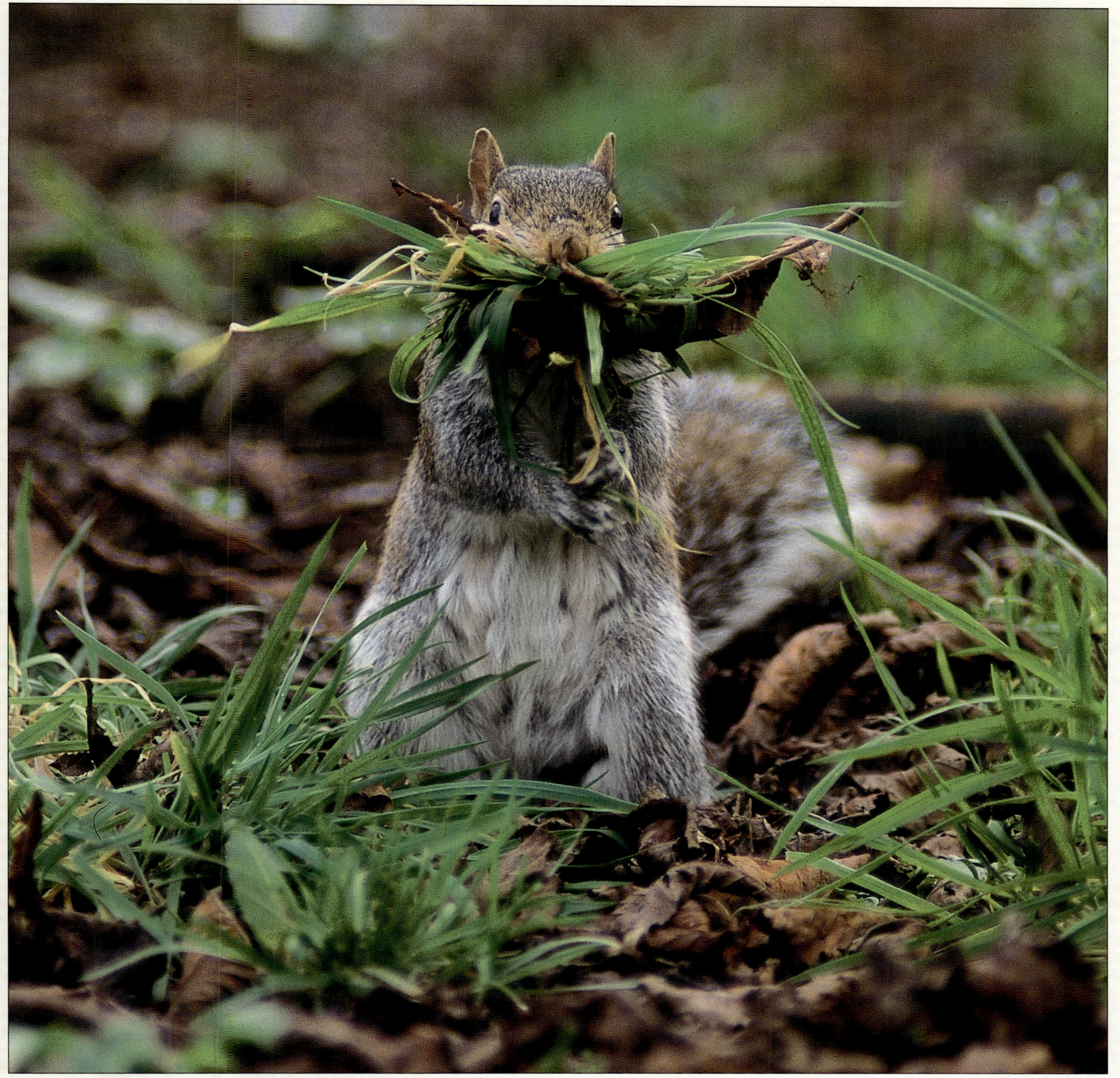

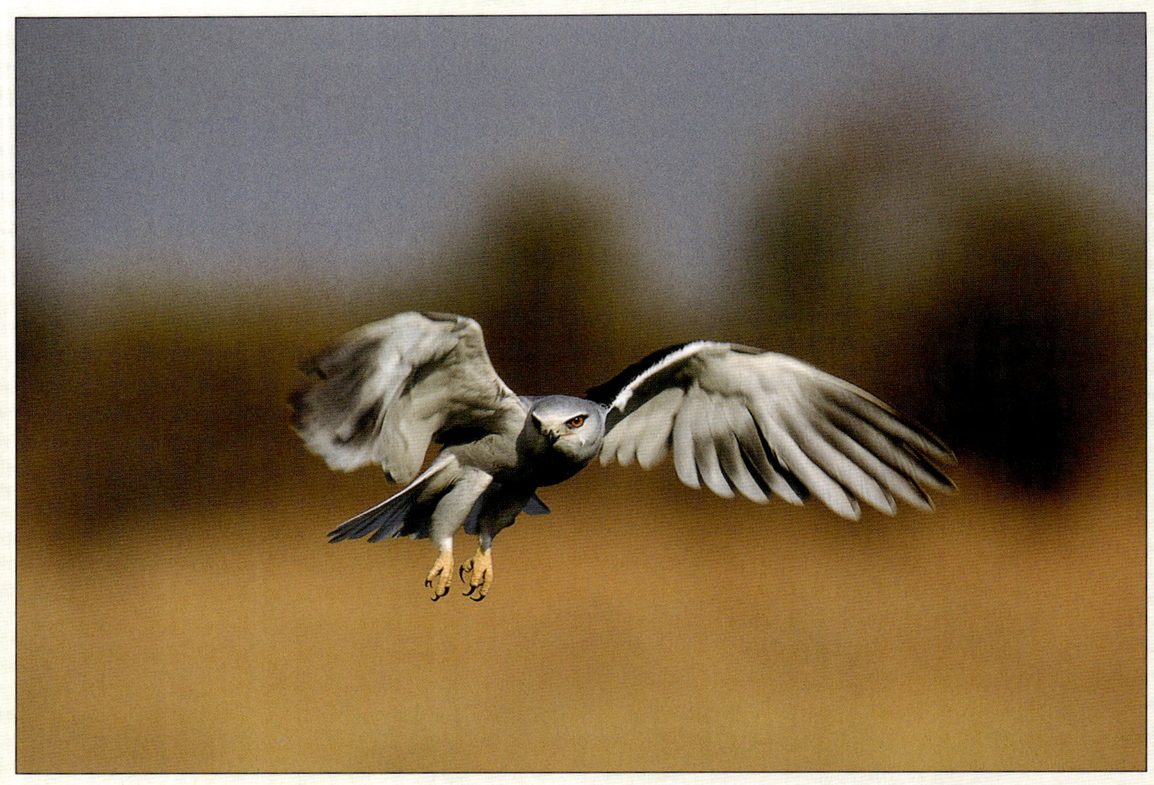

Fabian Fischer
Germany
HIGHLY COMMENDED
15-17 YEARS OLD

Black-shouldered kite

"This kite was hunting insects over a salt pan in Hwanga National Park, Zimbabwe. It was concentrating so intensely on its prey that it paid no attention to our car."

Nikon F90x with 300mm lens and x2 converter; 1/400 sec at f5.6; Fujichrome Velvia 50

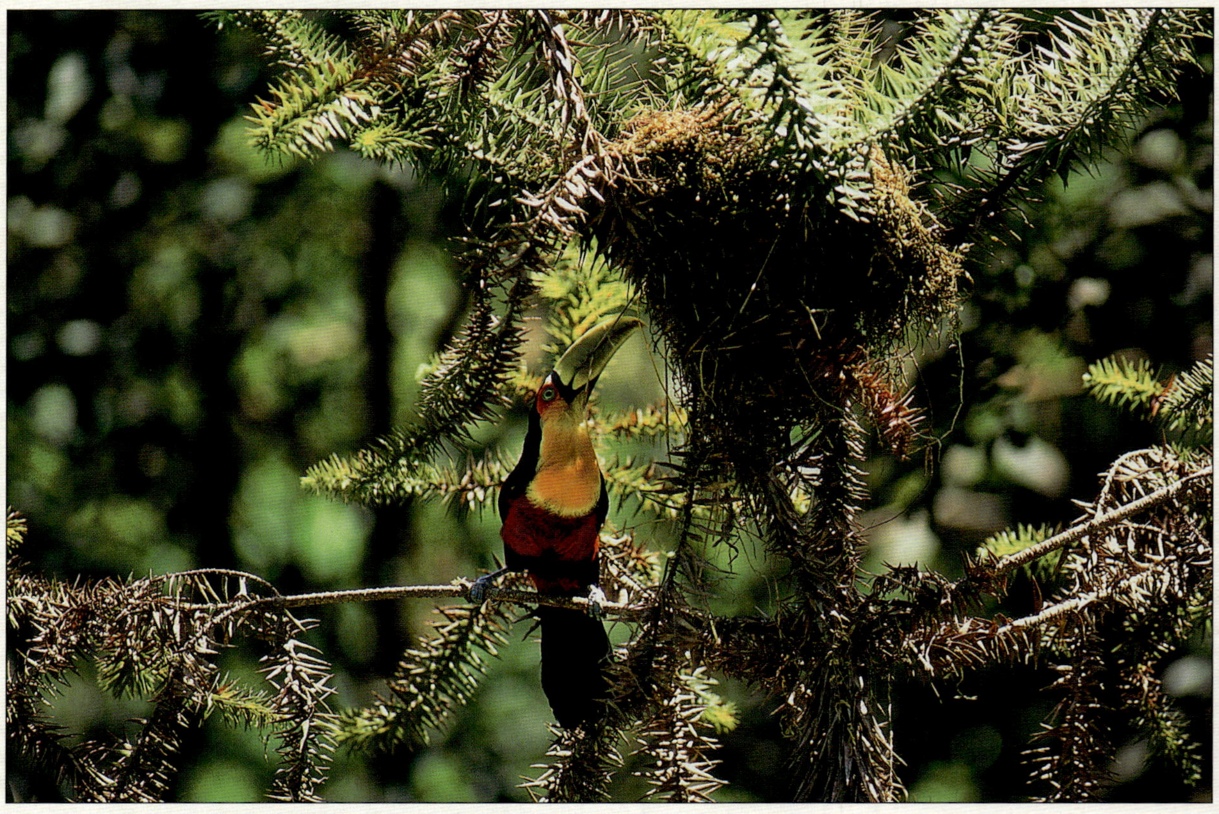

Gustavo Banhara Marigo
Brazil
HIGHLY COMMENDED
15-17 YEARS OLD

Red-breasted toucan

"In the Atlantic rainforest near Resende, Brazil, I heard great kiskadees calling in alarm. Rushing out with my camera, I saw the parent birds attacking a toucan which was trying to raid their nest. More birds came to help, stooping like small falcons around the toucan's head. Despite their efforts, the toucan demolished the nest."

Nikon N90 with 300mm lens; 1/125 sec at f5.6; Fujichrome Velvia 50 rated at 100

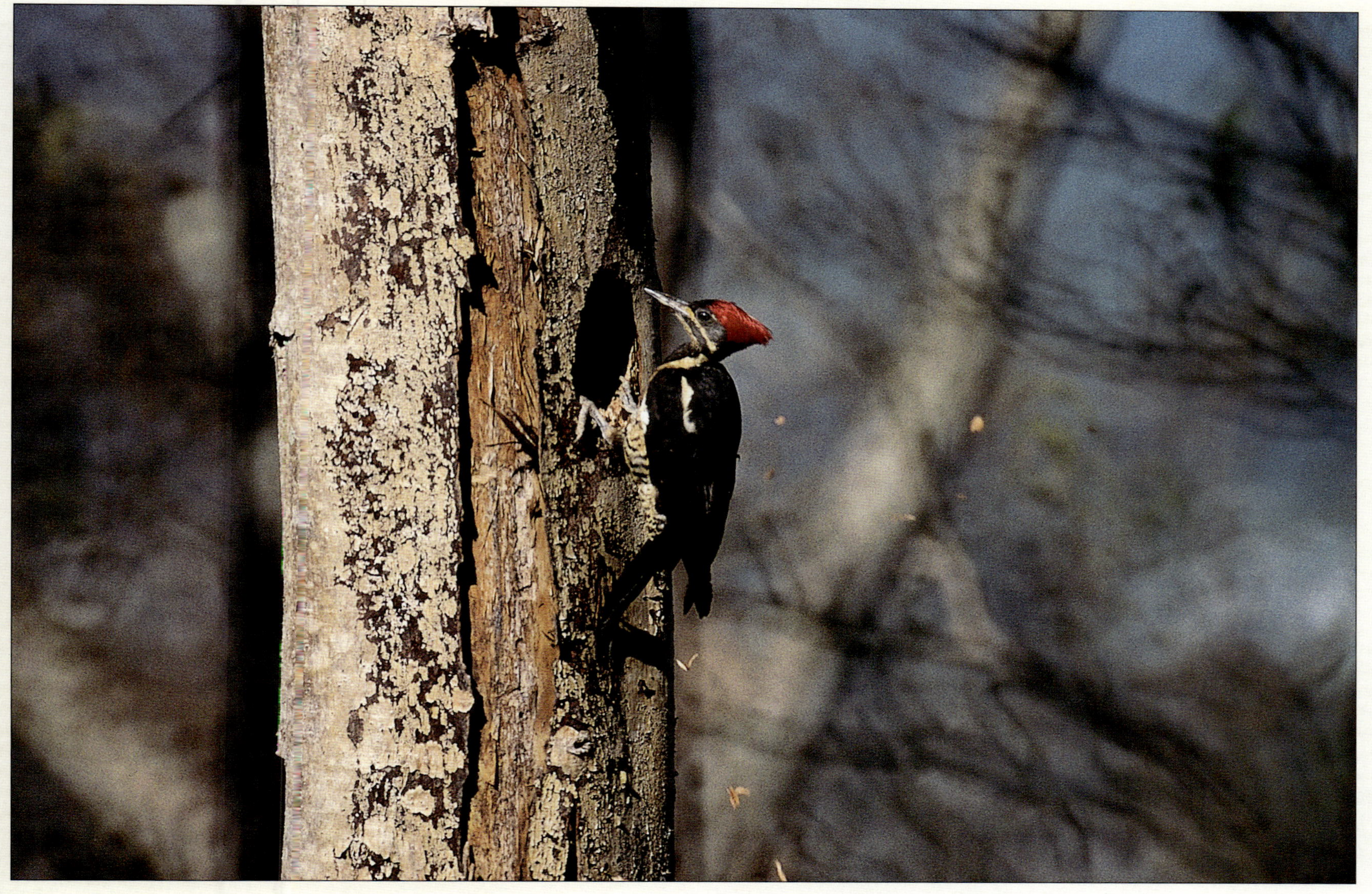

Rebecca Dean
United Kingdom
WINNER
YOC AWARD

Woodpecker excavating nest hole

"I spent several mornings taking photographs of a pair of lineated woodpeckers on Mount St Benedict in Trinidad, but ironically this was the first shot I took. I particularly liked the flying chippings. The bird in the picture is the female, but the male also spent time excavating the hole."

Olympus OM2N with 500mm lens; tripod; 1/250 sec at f8; Kodachrome 200

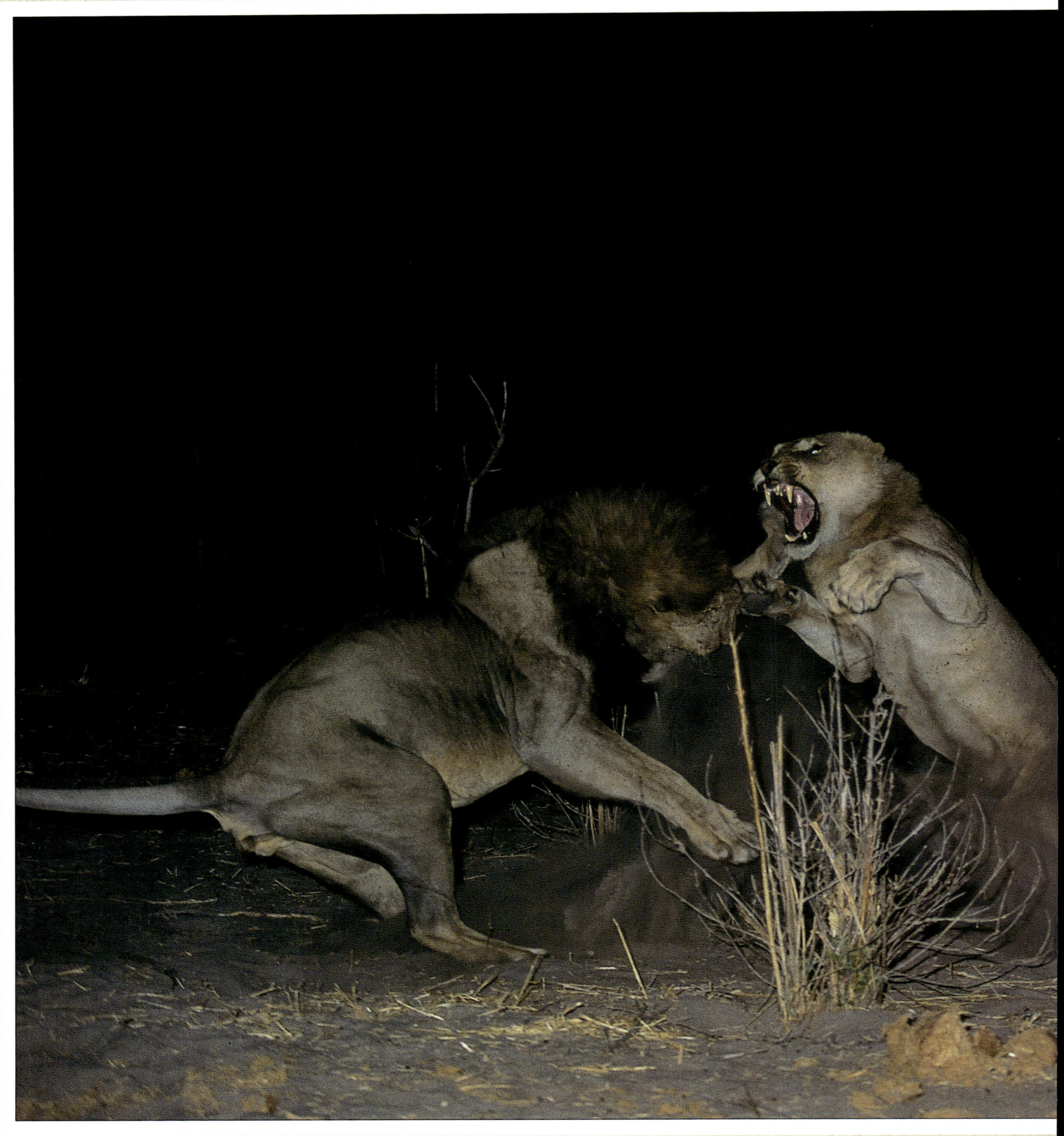

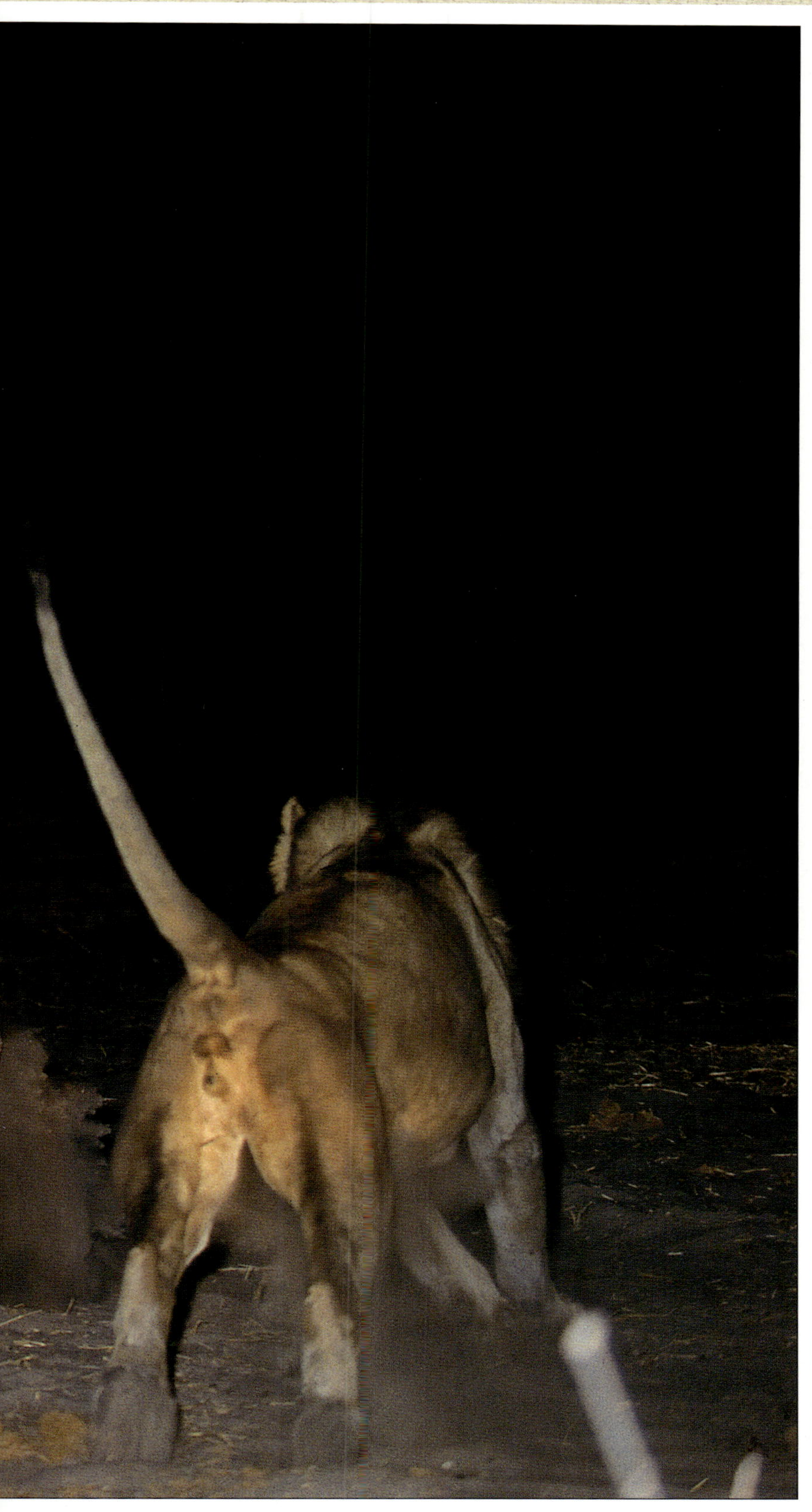

From Dusk to Dawn

Pictures must have been taken between sunset and sunrise (the sun may be on but not above the horizon) and must feature animals.

Beverly Joubert
South Africa
WINNER

Lions fighting at night

"A young nomadic male lion was being attacked by two territorial pride lions and he courageously fought back. But the two males successfully chased him from their area. He limped off in search of a vacant territory elsewhere in the Chobe National Park, Northern Botswana."

Canon EOS with 70-200mm lens; flash; 1/250 at f2.8; Fujichrome 100

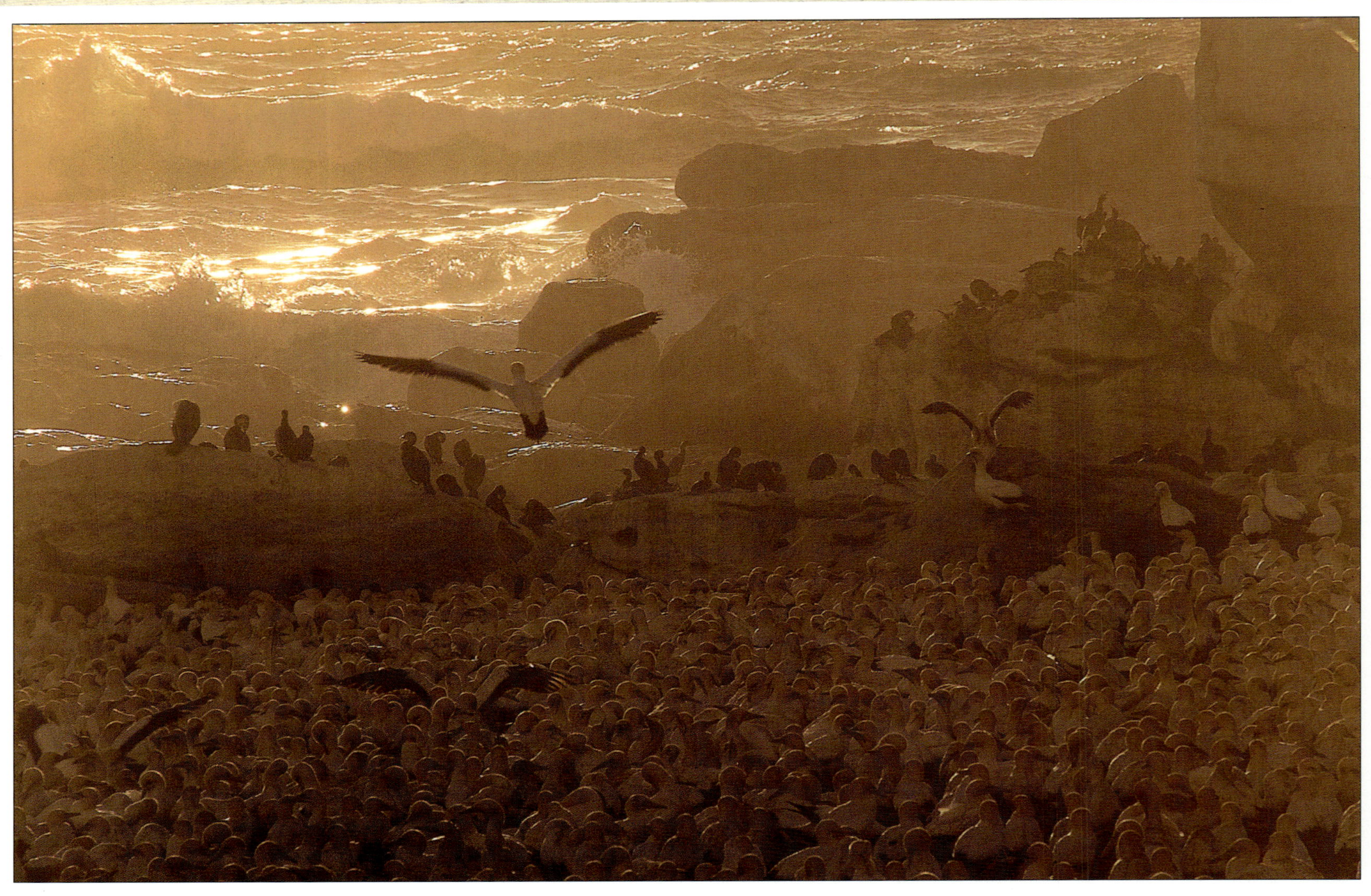

Cornelia Dörr
Germany
HIGHLY COMMENDED

Bird Island

"After a stormy, rainy day on Bird Island, South Africa, the setting sun broke through the dense cloud-cover creating this fantastic light. It was the moment I had been waiting for to take my picture of the Cape gannet and cormorant colony."

Nikon F90X with 300mm lens; tripod; Fujichrome Sensia 100

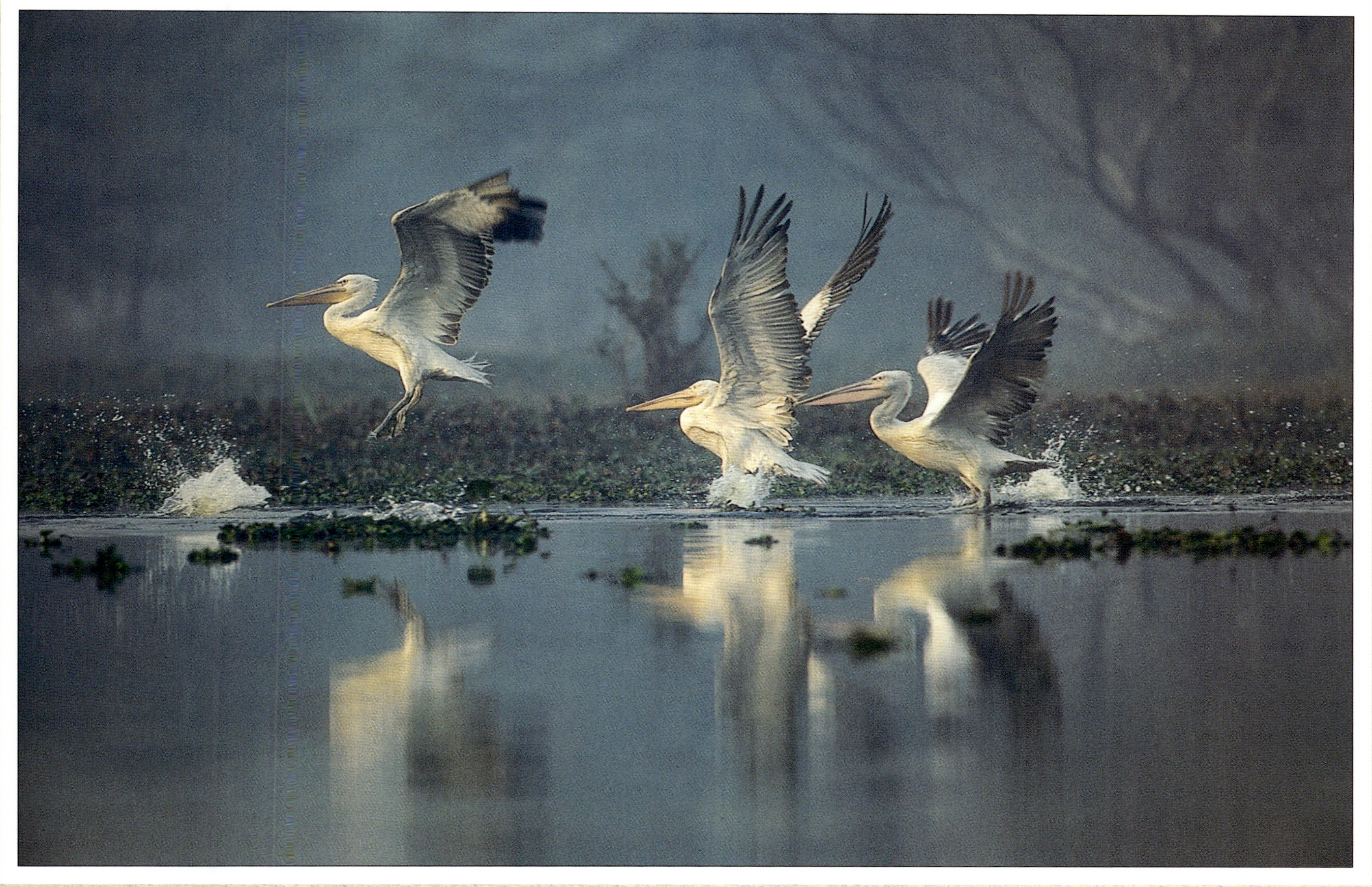

Winfried Wisniewski
Germany
HIGHLY COMMENDED

Dalmatian pelicans at dawn

"The sunrise in Keoladeo National Park, India, was rather marred by fog. But I managed to take a few pictures of these three pelicans as they rose from the water. This was the only time I saw the species during my 11-day stay."

Nikon F5 with 600mm lens; tripod; 1/250 sec at f4; Fujichrome 100

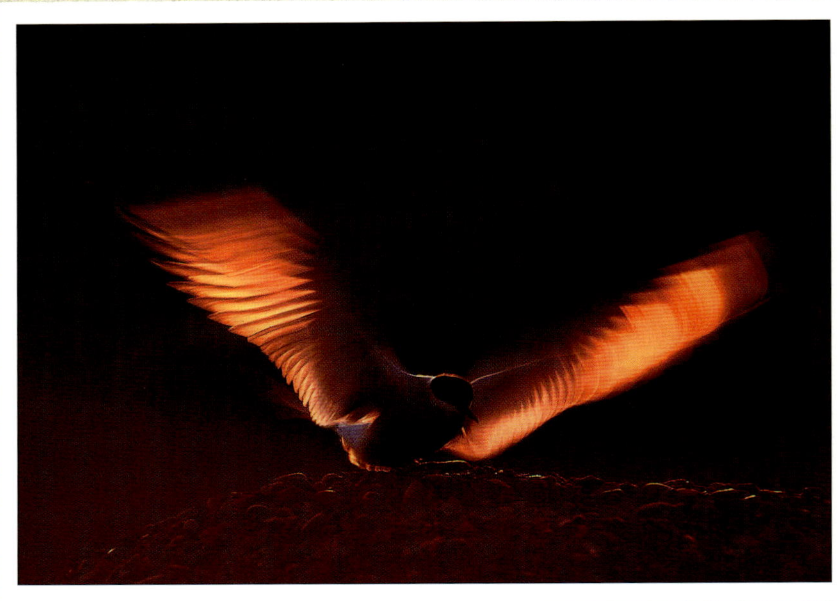

Anders Geidemark
Sweden
HIGHLY COMMENDED

Arctic tern landing

"On my fourth trip to Iceland, I finally photographed an image I had seen many times before and dreamed of capturing on film – an Arctic tern landing with the evening sun reflected in its wings. Thanks to a long shutter speed, there was time for the wings, like large brushes, to paint numerous reflections of the setting sun on the film."

Canon F1 with 500mm lens; tripod; 1/15 sec at f4.5; Fujichrome Velvia

Cliff Beittel
United States of America
HIGHLY COMMENDED

Cormorant reflected

"It was getting darker by the minute at Ding Darling National Nature Reserve, Florida, when the bird stretched up, just staying in the frame, and called before flying off to its roost. The flexibility of its upper beak amazed me."

Canon F1N with 800mm lens; tripod; 1/500 sec at f5.6; Fujichrome Velvia rated at 40 and pushed one stop

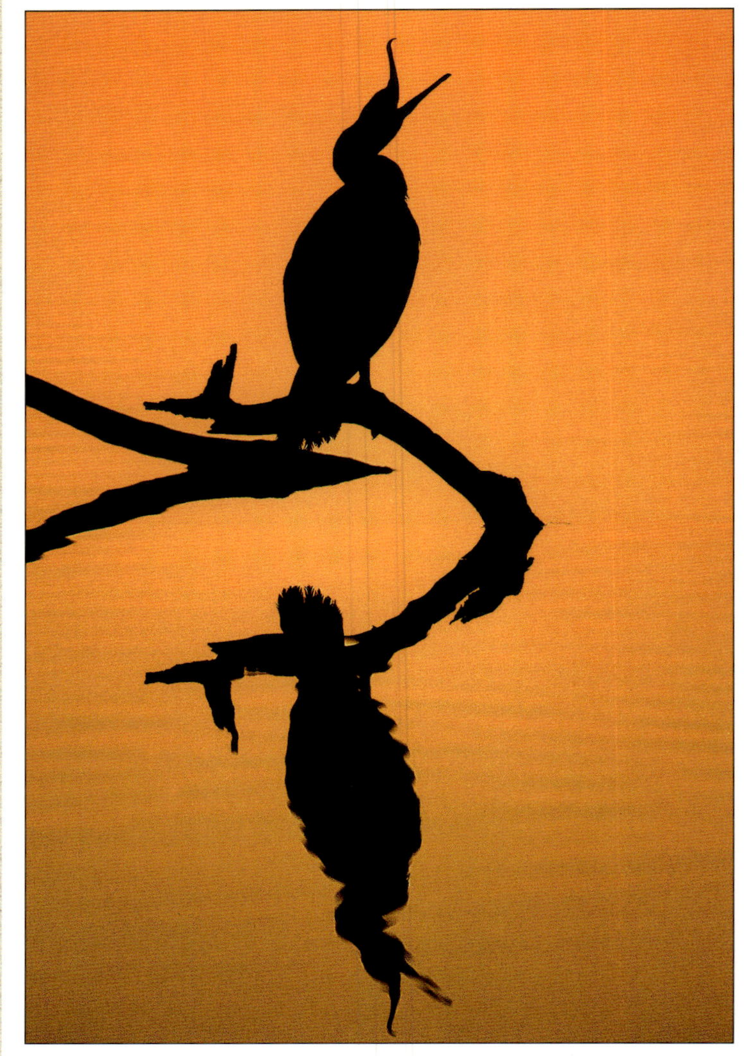

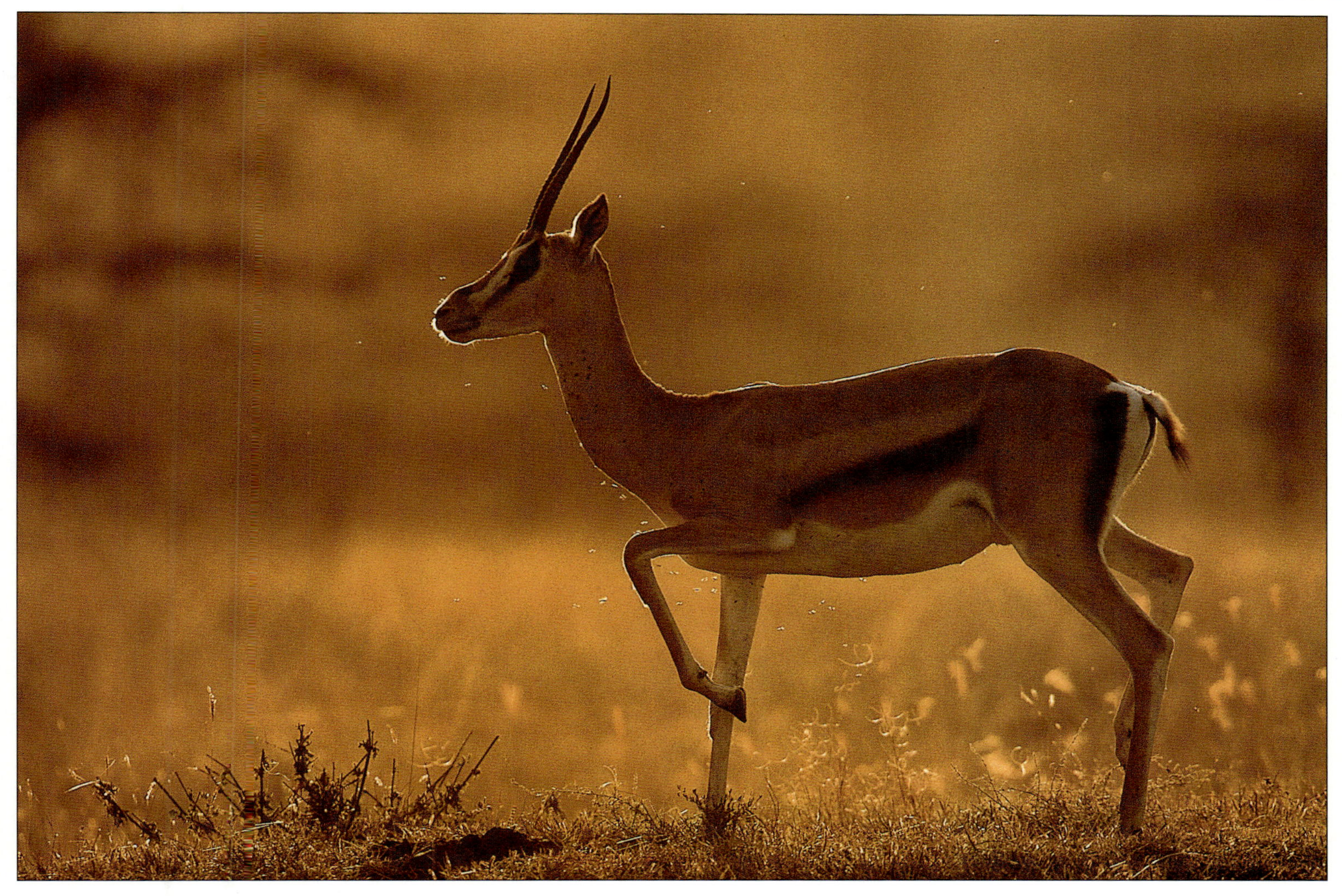

Anup Shah
United Kingdom
HIGHLY COMMENDED

Grant's gazelle

"This gazelle was snorting and stamping its foot in alarm as a cheetah passed by in the Maasai Mara, Kenya."

Canon EOS 600 with 600mm lens; 1/125 sec at f5.6; Fujichrome

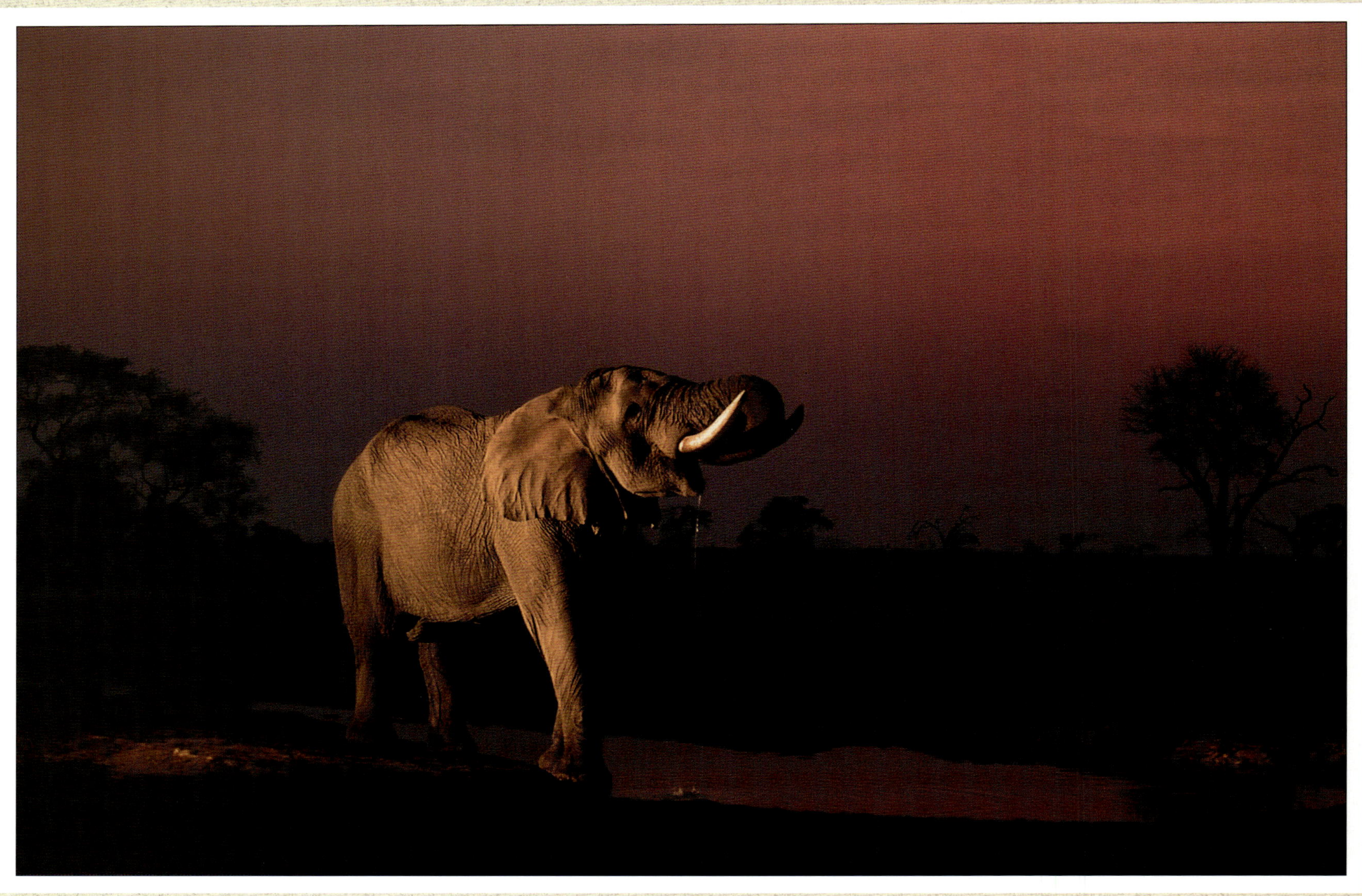

Beverly Joubert
South Africa
HIGHLY COMMENDED

Elephant at waterhole

"Water is very precious to all in the bush during the very hot summer months. This elephant had come to quench his thirst as the first signs of dawn were breaking in Chobe National Park, Botswana."

Canon EOS with 70-200mm lens; tungsten fill-in light; 1/60 sec at f5.6; Fujichrome 100

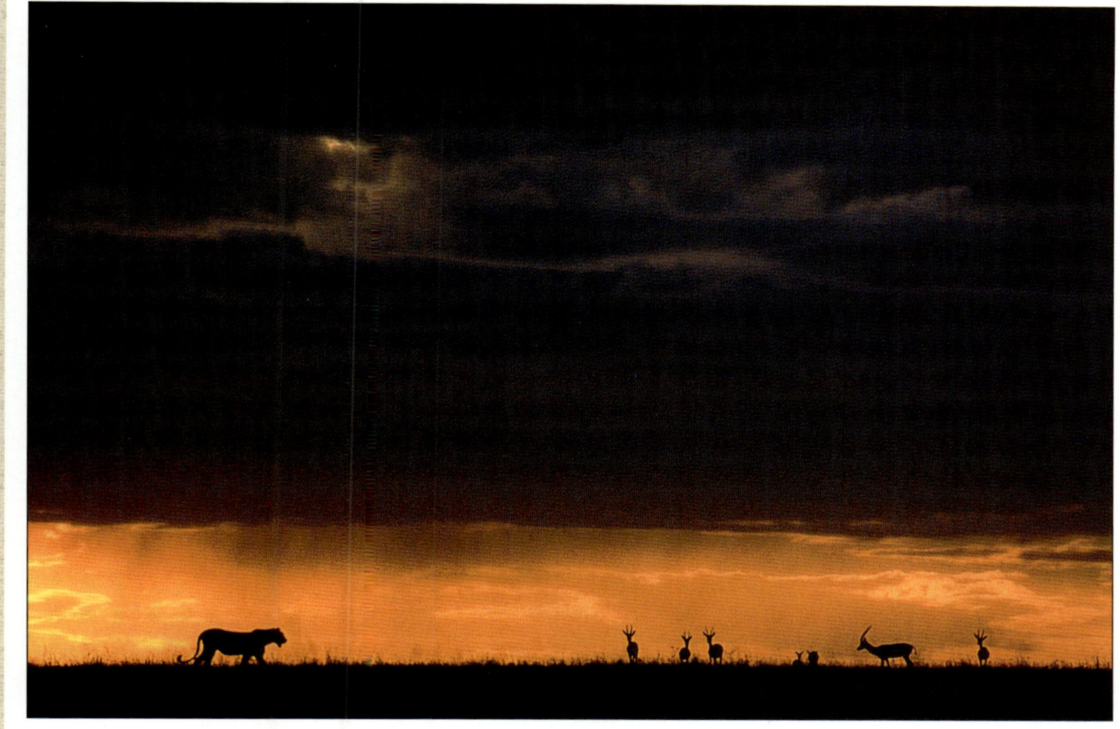

Michel Denis-Huot
France
HIGHLY COMMENDED

Lioness with gazelles

"The gazelles showed no fear of the lioness as she walked alone through the darkness across the open grasslands in Kenya's Maasai Mara Reserve."

Canon EOS 1N with 70-200mm lens; Fujichrome 100

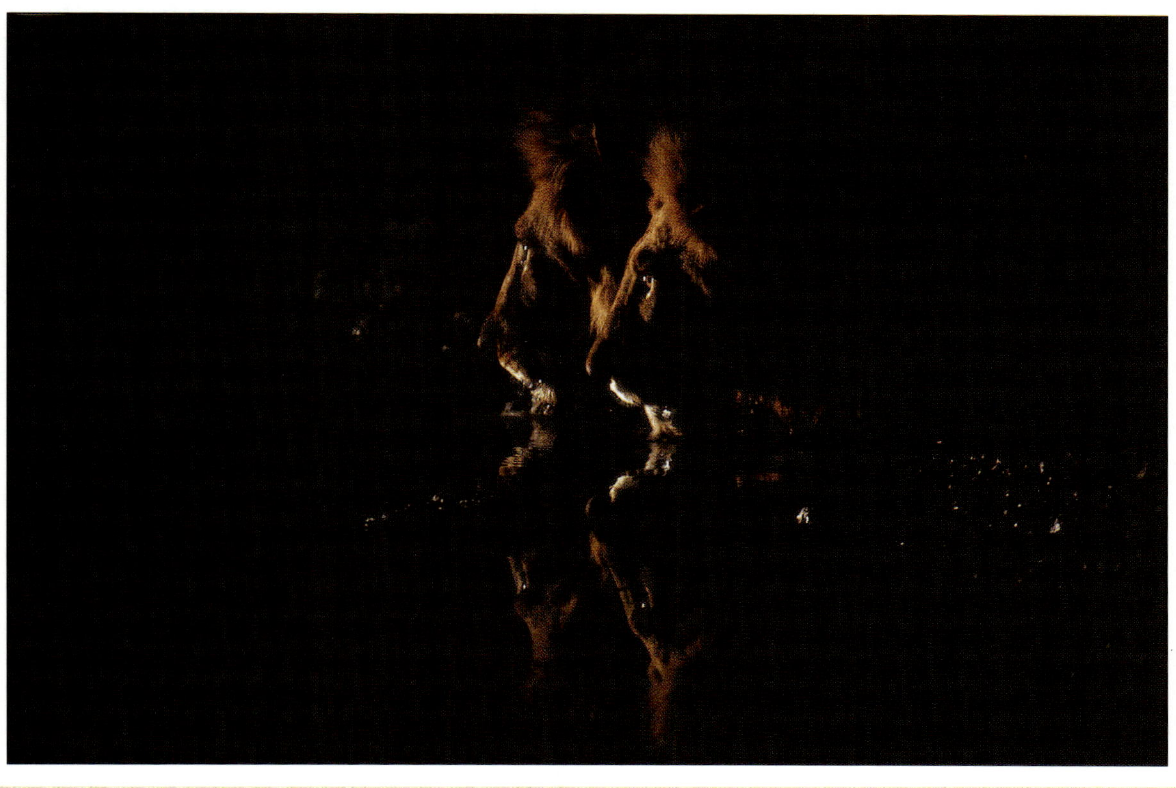

Kim Wolhuter
South Africa
HIGHLY COMMENDED

Lions drinking

"It was the dry season in Etosha National Park and waterholes were few and far between. A pride of male lions came down to drink after a large meal."

Canon EOS 1 with 35-350mm lens; tungsten light; 1/60 sec at f5.6; Ektachrome 320T

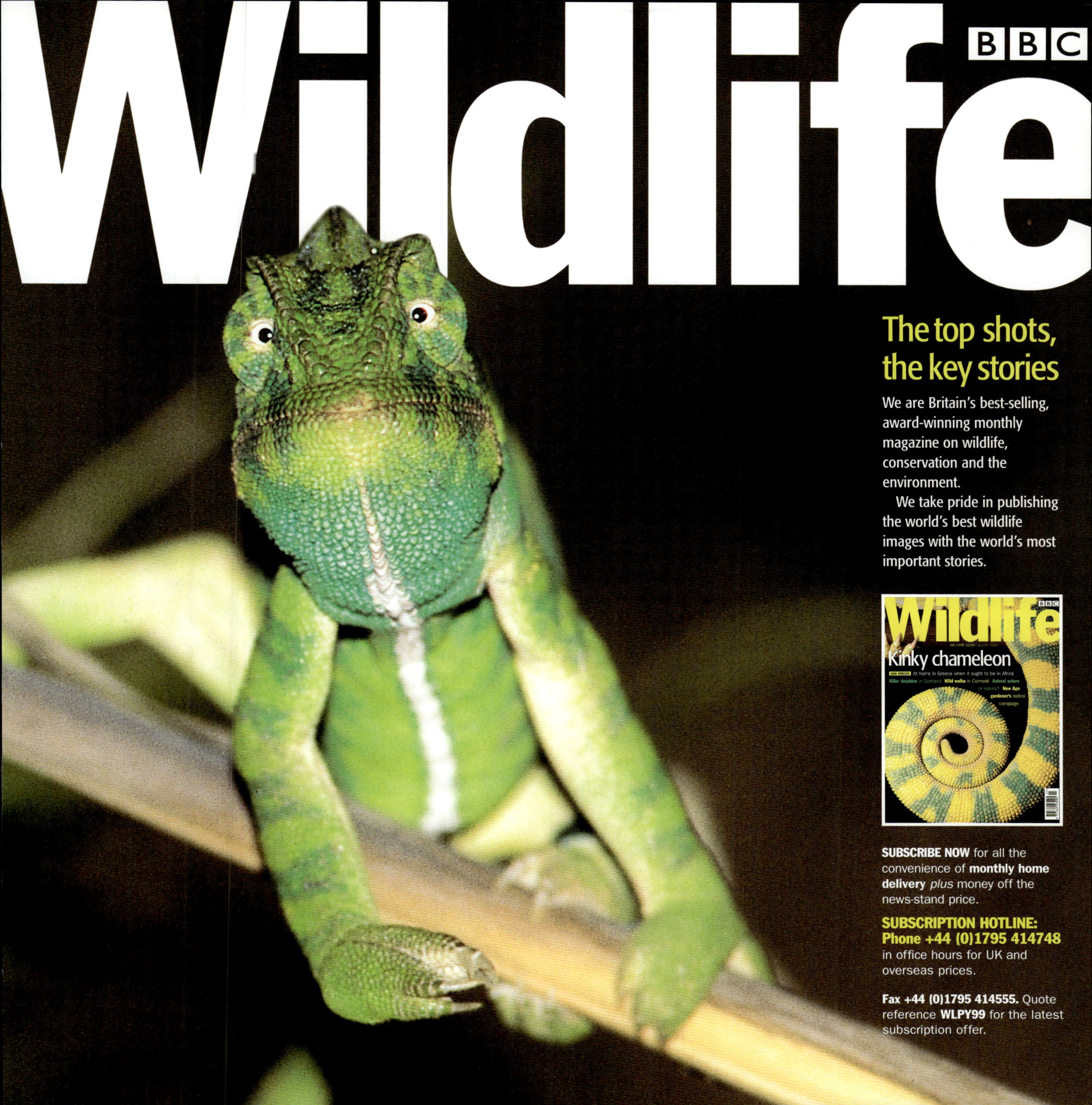

Wildlife
BBC
The top shots, the key stories
We are Britain's best-selling, award-winning monthly magazine on wildlife, conservation and the environment.
We take pride in publishing the world's best wildlife images with the world's most important stories.
Wildlife
Kinky chameleon
SUBSCRIBE NOW for all the convenience of monthly home delivery plus money off the news-stand price.
SUBSCRIPTION HOTLINE: Phone +44 (0)1795 414748 in office hours for UK and overseas prices.
Fax +44 (0)1795 414555. Quote reference WLPY99 for the latest subscription offer.

Index of Photographers

The numbers after the photographers' names indicate the pages on which their work can be found.

Telephone numbers are listed with international dialling codes from the UK in brackets - these should be replaced when dialling from other countries.

Overall Winners 1984-1997

Cherry Alexander
(Overall Winner 1995) 5
Higher Cottage, Manston,
Sturminster Newton, Dorset, DT10 1EZ
UK
Tel: 01258 473006
Fax: 01258 473333
Email: arcticfoto@aol.com

André Bärtschi
(Overall Winner 1992) 4
Bannholzstrasse 10, 9490 Vaduz
LIECHTENSTEIN
Tel: (004175) 232 0338
Fax: (004175) 232 0339
Email: 106224.2041@compuserve.com

Rajesh Bedi
(Overall Winner 1986)
Bedi Films,
E-19 Rajouri Gardens, New Delhi
INDIA 110 027

Jim Brandenburg
(Overall Winner 1988)
c/o Minden Pictures,
24 Seascape Village, Aptos, CA 95003
USA
Tel: (001) 408 685 1911
Fax: (001) 408 685 1913

Martyn Colbeck
(Overall Winner 1993) 4
c/o 33 High View, Hempstead,
Gloucester GL2 5LN
UK
Agent:
Oxford Scientific Films Ltd,
Lower Road, Long Hanborough,
Witney, Oxfordshire, OX8 8LL
UK
Tel: 01993 881881
Fax: 01993 882808

Richard & Julia Kemp
(Overall Winner 1984)
Valley Farmhouse, Whitwell, Norwich,
Norfolk, NR10 4SQ
UK
Tel: 01603 872498

Frans Lanting
(Overall Winner 1991) 4
1985 Smith Grade,
Santa Cruz, California 95060
USA
Tel: (001) 408 429 1331
Fax: (001) 408 423 8324

Thomas D Mangelsen
(Overall Winner 1994) 5
Images of Nature
PO Box 2935, 2nd Level, Gaslight Alley,
Jackson, Wyoming 83001
USA
Tel: (001) 307 733 6179
Fax: (001) 307 733 6184
Email: stockphoto@mangelsen.com

Tapani Räsänen
(Overall Winner 1997) 5
Tasalantie 27, Fin-54100 Joutseno
FINLAND
Tel & Fax: (00358) 54 5344929

Jouni Ruuskanen
(Overall Winner 1989)
Ratakatu 31 As 14, 87100 Kajaani
FINLAND
Tel: (00358) 86 133026

Jonathan Scott
(Overall Winner 1987)
PO Box 24499, Nairobi
KENYA
Fax: (00254) 2 891162
Email: jpscott@swiftkenya.com
Agent:
Planet Earth Pictures,
The Innovation Centre,
225 Marsh Wall, London, E14 9FX
UK
Tel: 0171 293 2999
Fax: 0171 293 2998

Wendy Shattil
(Overall Winner 1990)
PO Box 37422, 8325 E Princeton Ave,
Denver, Colorado 80237
USA
Tel: (001) 303 721 1991
Fax: (001) 303 721 1116
Email: wshattil@compuserve.com

Charles G Summers Jnr
(Overall Winner 1985)
Wild Images,
6746 N Yucca Trail, Parker, CO 80138
USA
Tel: (001) 303 840 3344
Fax: (001) 303 840 3366

Jason Venus
(Overall Winner 1996) 7
24 Central Acre, Yeovil,
Somerset, BA20 1NU
UK
Tel & Fax: 01935 706834

Portfolio Eight

Theo Allofs 54, 90
PO Box 5473, Haines Junctions,
Yukon, Y0B 1L0
CANADA
Tel: (001) 867 634 3823
Fax: (001) 867 634 2207
Email: allofsphoto@yknet.yk.ca

Karl Ammann 21
Box 437, Nanyuki
KENYA
Tel: (00254) 176 22448
Fax: (00254) 176 32407
Email: kamman@form-net.com

Terry Andrewartha 82
The Old Rectory, Cockley Cley
Swaffham, Norfolk, PE37 8AN
UK
Tel: 01760 725740

Adrian Bailey 25, 110
PO Box 1846, Houghton, 2041
SOUTH AFRICA
Tel: (0027) 11 486 1474
Fax: (0027) 11 486 1394
Email: aebailey@global.co.za
Agent:
Oxford Scientific Films Ltd
Lower Road, Long Hanborough
Witney, Oxfordshire, OX8 8LL
UK
Tel: 01993 881881
Fax: 01993 882808

Erwin & Peggy Bauer 49
Box 3730, Sequim, WA 98382
USA
Tel & Fax: (001) 360 683 1300
Email: epbauer@olypen.com

Fred Bavendam 92, 98
18 Woodside Lane, Wenham, MA 01984
USA
Tel: (001) 508 468 2354
Fax: (001) 508 468 2365

Cliff Beittel 150
287 Brookwood Drive N, York
Pennsylvania 17403
USA
Tel & Fax: (001) 717 843 3645
Email: CBeittel@aol.com

Gerry Bishop 70
324 Sherwood Drive, Vienna, VA 22180
USA
Tel: (001) 703 790 4283
Fax: (001) 703 790 4035

Dan Bool 123
East Images
26 Queens Road, Kingston Upon Thames,
Surrey, KT2 7SN
UK
Tel: 0181 546 2033
Fax: (0062) 361 732171 (Indonesia)
Email: eastimages@hotmail.com

Simon Booth 80
13 Blackburn Brow, Chorley
Lancs, PR6 9AG
UK
Tel: 01257 234838

Bartomeu Borrell 72
C/Matas 24, St Cebria de Vallalta
08396 Barcelona
SPAIN
Tel & Fax: (0034) 937 630 588

Dr Hermann Brehm 76
Speilbach 90, 74575 Schrozberg
GERMANY
Tel: (0049) 7939 389
Fax: (0049) 7939 1346

Whit Bronaugh 89
7969 200th Street NE #55
Arlington, WA 98223
USA
Tel: (001) 360 435 6082
Fax: (001) 800 987 3036
Email: whitbron@gte.net

Barbara A Brundege 38
PO Box 889, Groveland, CA 95321
USA
Tel: (001) 209 962 4321
Fax: (001) 209 962 4323
Email: shtgstar@sonnet.com

Marcello Calandrini 65
Via Pietro Maffi 74 Pal A, 00168 Roma
ITALY
Tel: (0039) 063 550 9212
Email: M.Calandrini@flashnet.it
Agent:
Panda Photo, Viale Pinturicchio 13
00196 Rome
ITALY
Tel: (0039) 6 323 1447
Fax: (0039) 6 323 1472

Laurie Campbell 79, 84
Rosewell Cottage, Paxton
Berwick-upon-Tweed, TD15 1TE
UK
Tel & Fax: 01289 386736

John Cancalosi 83
1532 Maplewood Drive
Slidell, Louisiana
USA
Tel: (001) 504 641 3870
Email: Cancalosi@compuserve.com

María Cano 138
Hernando de Acuña 3-2° A
47014 Valladolid
SPAIN
Tel: (0034) 983 336619
Fax: (0034) 983 261750

Peter Chadwick 40
12 Churchill Avenue, Seaforth
Simonstown 7995
SOUTH AFRICA
Tel: (0027) 21 7861671

Paolo Cortesi 106
Circonvallazione Ouest 5
40050 Castello D'Argile, Bologna
ITALY
Tel: (0039) 051 976 152
Fax: (0039) 051 812 697

Michael Cufer 37, 96
30 Como Road, Oyster Bay, NSW 2225
AUSTRALIA
Tel & Fax: (0061) 2 9528 6128
Email: mwcufer@ozemail.com.au

Shaun Cunningham 126
567 Carnation Place, Victoria
British Columbia, V8Z 6G6
CANADA
Tel: (001) 250 479 7806

Manfred Danegger 8/9, 34
Hasenbühlweg 9, D-88696 Owingen
GERMANY
Tel: (0049) 7557 8765
Fax: (0049) 7557 8970

Rebecca Dean 145
Tall Trees, Ellesmere Road
Weybridge, Surrey, KT13 0HY
UK
Tel: 01932 847418

Michel Denis-Huot 62/63, 153
1 Bis Rue des Fermes
F-76310 Sainte Adresse
FRANCE
Tel: (0033) 2 35 46 29 70
Fax: (0033) 2 35 48 04 30
Email: DenisHuot@aol.com

Geoff Doré 28, 121
56 Jumpers Avenue, Christchurch
Dorset, BH23 2ER
UK
Tel: 01202 304248
Fax: 01202 485174
Email: gdp@geoffdore.demon.co.uk
Agent:
Getty Images, 101 Bayham Street
London, NW1 0AG
UK
Tel: 0171 267 8988
Fax: 0171 722 9305

Cornelia Dörr 149
Merowingerstrasse 63, 40225 Düsseldorf
GERMANY
Tel: (0049) 211 3190425
Fax: (0049) 89 66617 43590
Email: cdoerr@mail.online-club.de

Georgette Douwma 94
139 Bedford Court Mansions
Adeline Place, London, WC1B 3AH
UK
Tel & Fax: 0171 636 6477

Wynand du Plessis 20
PO Box 13, Okaukuejo, via Outjo
NAMIBIA
Tel & Fax: (00264) 67 229 813

Richard du Toit 57, 131
PO Box 547, Witkoppen 2068
SOUTH AFRICA
Tel & Fax: (0027) 11 465 9919

Martin Edge 101
238 Rempstone Road, Merley
Wimborne, Dorset, BH21 1SY
UK
Tel: 01202 887611

Fredrik Ehrenström 86
Gunnilse Ljungbacke 11
SE-42456 Gunnilse
SWEDEN
Tel: (0046) 31 943792
Fax: (0046) 31 943393
Email:
fl.ehrenstrom@partille.mail.telia.com

Edmund Fellowes 30
West Isle, Islesteps, Dumfries, DG2 8ES
UK
Tel: 01387 262094

Fabian Fischer 142, 144
Reuthstrasse 3b, D-91099 Poxdorf
GERMANY
Tel: (0049) 9133 4960

Timothy Gallagher 60
PO Box 341, Freeville, New York 13068
USA
Tel: (001) 607 804 4475
Fax: (001) 607 254 2415
Email: twg3@cornell.edu

Howie Garber 124
Wanderlust Images, 3926 Feramorz Drive
Salt Lake City, UT 84124
USA
Tel: (001) 801 272 2134
Fax: (001) 801 277 0687
Email: hgphoto@ix.netcom.com

Brandon T Garland 136, 141
13801 N Riverbluff Lane
Spokane, WA 99208
USA
Tel: (001) 509 466 0579
Fax: (001) 509 466 3383
Email: Trango17@aol.com

Anders Geidemark 150
Enköpings Näs, Nybyholm
74592 Enköping
SWEDEN
Tel & Fax: (0046) 171 449599

Adam Gibbs 113
Unit 83 7501 Cumberland Street
Burnaby, British *Columbia*, V3N 4Y6
CANADA
Tel: (001) 604 520 0263

Rolando Gil 61
Oña 9-5°, 28050 *Madrid*
SPAIN
Tel: (0034) 91 766 8644
Email: *rolandog@ctv.es*

Lorne Gill 128
Yew Tree Cottage, *Wolfhill*
Perthshire, PH2 6DA
UK
Tel: 01821 650455
Fax: 01738 8274 11
Email: *lorne@redgore.demon.co.uk*

Roy Glen 78
257 *Eagle Park Road*
Marton-in-Cleveland
Middlesbrough, TS3 9QT
UK
Tel & Fax: 01642 310644

George Gornacz 75
8 *Wesley Court*, *Noosa Heads*
Queensland 4567
AUSTRALIA
Tel: (0061) 7 5447 5743
Fax: (0061) 7 5448 0284

Olivier Grunewald 104
37 *Rue Montcalm*, 75018 *Paris*
FRANCE
Tel: (0033) 1 42 54 30 43
Fax: (0033) 1 48 06 48 71

Verena Hahl 139
Goethestraße 13*a*, D-68623 *Lampertheim*
GERMANY
Tel & Fax: (0049) 6206 56421

Richard Hamilton Smith 114
The PictureSmith Ltd
2242 *University Avenue*, *Suite* 304
St Paul, MN 55114
USA
Tel: (001) 651 645 5070
Fax: (001) 651 645 8263
Email: *studio@picturesmith.com*

Russell Hartwell 32
34 *Whitepit Lane*, *Flackwell Heath*
Buckinghamshire, HP10 9HS
UK
Tel: 01628 527996
Fax: 01753 887496

Martin Harvey 36
PO *Box* 8945
Centurion 0046, *Pretoria*
SOUTH AFRICA
Tel & Fax: (0027) 12 664 2241
Email: *mharvey@icon.co.za*

Brent Hedges 55
71 *Arabella Street*, *Longueville*
NSW 2066
AUSTRALIA
Tel: (0061) 2 9428 4156
Fax: (0061) 2 9418 6949
Email: *bhedges@curwood.com.au*

Pål Hermansen 91, 135
Brubråten Siggerudveien, N-1400 *Ski*
NORWAY
Tel & Fax: (0047) 6486 5515
Email: *paherman@online.no*

Richard Herrmann 100
12545 *Mustang Drive*, *Poway*
California 92064
USA
Tel: (001) 619 679 7017
Fax: (001) 619 679 3346
Email: *rbherrmann@aol.com*

Mike Hill 27
PO *Box* 25005, *Awali*
BAHRAIN
Tel: (00973) 756292
Fax: (00973) 753624
Email: *hillm@batelco.com.bh*

Rachel Hingley 143
19 *Mount Pleasant Road*, *Norton*
Stockton-on-Tees, *Cleveland*, TS20 2HX
UK
Tel & Fax: 01642 531724

Andy Horner 124
Kulla, *Fin*-22220 *Emkarby*, *Åland*
FINLAND
Tel: (00358) 18 42425
Fax: (00358) 18 42339
Agent:
Naturfotografemas Bildbyrå AB
*Box*90, S-74822 *Österbybruk*
SWEDEN
Tel: (0046) 295 20780
Fax: (0046) 295 21100

Carola Huhn 22, 73
MarbacherStrasse 26
71691 *Freiberg a* N
GERMANY
Tel: (0049) 7 141 27 17 29

Ernie Janes 62
Park House Studio
Northchurch Common, *Berkhamsted*
Hertfordshire, HP4 1LR
UK
Tel & Fax: 01442 871342

Beverly Joubert 146, 152
Wildlife Films, PO *Box* 55, *Kasane*
BOTSWANA
Tel: (00267) 650 384
Fax: (00267) 650 223

Janos Jurka 120
Storängsvägen 5, S-77160 *Ludvika*
SWEDEN
Tel & Fax: (0046) 240 39087
Agent:
Bruce Coleman Ltd
16 *Chiltern Business Village*
Arundel Road, *Uxbridge*, *Middlesex*
UB8 2SN
UK
Tel: 01895 257094
Fax: 01895 272357

Tony Karacsonyi 52
PO *Box* 407, *Ulladulla*, NSW 2539
AUSTRALIA
Tel & Fax: (0061) 244 554552
Email: *tonyk@shoal.net.au*

Frank Krahmer 90
Bahnhofstrasse 13F, D-82024
Taufkirchen
GERMANY
Tel: (0049) 89 612 2974
Fax: (0049) 89 612 09243
Email: *fkramher@compuserve.com*

Melanie Krebs 43
Seelhorst 10, 49191 *Belm*
GERMANY
Tel: (0049) 541 131876
Fax: (0049) 5472 2726

Klaus Kretzer 112
Marktstrasse 31, D-35327 *Ulrichstein*
GERMANY
Tel: (0049) 6645 212

Richard Kuzminski 23
476 *Highland Avenue*
Wood-Ridge, NJ 07075
USA
Tel: (001) 201 507 0368

Tim Laman 68
26 *Drummer Boy Way*
Lexington, MA 02420
USA
Tel & Fax: (001) 781 676 2952
Email: *tlaman@oeb.harvard.edu*
Agent:
National Geographic Society
Image Collection, 1145 17*th Street* NW
Washington DC 20036-4688
USA
Tel: (001) 202 857 7537
Fax: (001) 202 429 5776

Andreas Leemann 118
Zürichstr 113, 8123 *Ebmatingen*
SWITZERLAND
Tel: (0041) 1 980 3163
Email: *andreas.leemann@empa.ch*

Dennis H Liberson 99
12020 *Hamden Court*, *Oakton*
Virginia 22124
USA
Tel: (001) 703 716 1937
Fax: (001) 703 716 5719

John Liddiard 74
56 *Oakfield Road*, *Clifton*
Bristol, BS8 2BG
UK
Tel: 0117 973 6770
Email: *john@liddiard.demon.co.uk*

Erik Stavseth Lornie 97
43 *Dalmahoy Crescent*, *Balerno*
Midlothian, EH14 7BZ
UK
Tel: 0131 449 3981

David Lyons 111
Scroggs, Loughrigg
Ambleside, Cumbria, LA22 9HQ
UK
Tel & Fax: 015394 37233

Gustavo Banhara Marigo 144
Rua General Glicério 364/604
22245-120 *Rio de Janeiro*
BRAZIL
Tel: (0055) 21 285 4606
Fax: (0055) 21 556 1832
Email: marigo@muiraquita.com.br

Mary Ann McDonald 19, 35, 66
McDonald Wildlife Photography Inc.
73 Loht Road, McClure, PA 17841
USA
Tel & Fax: (001) 717 543 6423
Email: hoothollow@acsworld.net

Neil McIntyre 85
Ballinluig Cottage, Kinrara, Aviemore
Inverness-shire, PH22 1QB
UK
Tel: 01479 810545
Agent:
Planet Earth Pictures
The Innovation Centre, 225 Marsh Wall
London, E14 9FX
UK
Tel: 0171 293 2999
Fax: 0171 293 2998

Robert McKemie 87
1980 Central Point Road, Cantrall
IL 62625
USA
Tel: (001) 217 487 7753
Email: McKemie@aol.com

John Mielcarek 29
PO Box 130, Washington, MI 4809-
USA
Tel: (001) 810 677 4167
Email: photojohn@i-is.com

John J Mullin 31
5116 Carita Street, Long Beach
CA 90808
USA
Tel & Fax: (001) 562 425 2108

Amos Nachoum 53
2000 Broadway, 1204
San Francisco, CA 94115
USA
Tel: (001) 415 923 9865
Fax: (001) 415 776 8489
Email: amosphoto@aol.com

Tim Neal 39
Deansbrook, Neals Lane, Chetnole
Sherborne, Dorset, DT9 6PF
UK
Tel: 01935 872759
Fax: 01935 873586
Email: jvenus@dial.pipex.com

Ewald Neffe 105
Raaballee 284, 8181 St Ruprecht/Raab
AUSTRIA
Tel: (0043) 3178 3189

Michael Nichols 18/19, 133
525 Grove Avenue, Charlottesville
Virginia 22902
USA
Tel: (001) 804 295 8549
Fax: (001) 804 296 5369
Email: NickNPhoto@aol.com

Jun Ogawa 88
LT 2313, 77-1 Sezaki-cho
Soka-shi, Saitama Prefecture
JAPAN
Tel & Fax: (0081) 489 27 2213

Fritz Pölking 56, 77, 130
Münsterstraße 71, D-48268 Greven
GERMANY
Tel: (0049) 2571 52115
Fax: (0049) 2571 97098

Kari Reponen 58
Säklänmäentie 141, Fin-52100 Anttola
FINLAND
Tel: (00358) 500 154 298

Hugh Rose 50
620 Yak Road, Fairbanks
Alaska 99709
USA
Tel: (001) 907 479 8984

Andy Rouse 46, 47, 81
Email: andy@andyrouse.co.uk
Agent:
NHPA, *57 High Street, Ardingly*
W Sussex, RH17 6TB
UK
Tel: 01444 892764
Fax: 01444 892168

José B Ruiz 122, 134
PO Box 58, 03080 Alicante
SPAIN
Tel: (0034) 96 524 3913
Agent:
BBC Natural History Unit Picture Library
Broadcasting House, Whiteladies Road
Bristol, BS8 2LR
UK
Tel: 0117 974 6720
Fax: 0117 923 8166

Carlos Sánchez 67
Padilla 38, 2° 1
47400 Medina Del Campo, Valladolid
SPAIN
Tel: (0034) 9 8380 0891
Fax: (0034) 9 8381 1215

Kotaro Sano 45
1429-83 Hatsusawamachi
Hachiouji City, Tokyo 193-0845
JAPAN
Tel & Fax: (0081) 426 65 5573
Agent:
Animals & Earth
3-14-14-103 Minami-Aoyama
Minato-ku, Tokyo 107-0062
JAPAN
Tel: (0081) 3 3401 5858
Fax: (0081) 3 3401 3737

David Scott 140
PO Box 24499, Nairobi
KENYA
Tel & Fax: (00254) 2 891162

Jonathan Scott
(Overall Winner 1987) 42
PO Box 24499, Nairobi
KENYA
Fax: (00254) 2 891162
Tel & Email: jpscott@swiftkenya.com
Agent:
Planet Earth Pictures
The Innovation Centre, 225 Marsh Wall
London, E14 9FX
UK
Tel: 0171 293 2999
Fax: 0171 293 2998

Roland Seitre 23, 52
1 Rue du Commerce, 37370 Marray
FRANCE
Tel & Fax: (0033) 2 4756 3636
Email: seitre@lenet.fr
Agent:
BIOS, *31 Rue de Chanzy, 75011 Paris*
FRANCE
Tel: (0033) 1 43 566363
Fax: (0033) 1 43 566517

Anup Shah 41, 151
29 Cornfield Road
Bushey, Herts, WD2 3TB
UK
Tel & Fax: 0181 950 8705
Email: S.Shah@herts.ac.uk

Roberto Siniscalchi 107
Via Mercato Vecchio 34,
39042 Bressanone BZ
ITALY
Tel: (0039) 0472 836498
Fax: (0039) 0472 836510
Agent:
Panda Photo
Via Flaminia 167, 00196 Rome
ITALY
Tel: (0039) 06 323 1447
Fax: (0039) 06 323 1472

Raoul Slater 40, 102
Box 32, Kenmore, Qld 4069
AUSTRALIA
Tel: (0061) 7 3202 6583
Fax: (0061) 7 3202 7009

Marc Slootmaekers 115
Kijkuitstraat 17, B 2920 Kalmthout
BELGIUM
Tel & Fax: (0032) 3 663271

Ian Stephen 73
The Georges, Station Road
North Thoresby, Lincolnshire, DN36 5QS
UK
Tel: 01472 840540
Email: Ehou294668@aol.com

Michel & Yannick Stoffel-Willame 26/27

Avenue Gossiaux 15/5, 1160 Brussels
BELGIUM

Tel & Fax: (0032) 2 673 3561

Agent:
BIOS, *Rue Chanzy* 31, 75011 *Paris*
FRANCE

Tel: (0033) 1 43 56 63 63
Fax: (0033) 1 43 56 65 17

Juan Tébar Carrera 24

Apartado 469
San Fernando 11100, Cádiz
SPAIN

Tel: (0034) 956 123719

Jamie Thom 10–15

PO *Box 763, Strathavon,* 2031
SOUTH AFRICA

Tel: (0027) 13 7355661
Fax: (0027) 13 7355686
Email: maincamp@iafrica.com

Jan Töve Johansson 125

Prästgården, Härna
S-52399 Hökerum
SWEDEN

Tel & Fax: (0046) 33 274028
Email:
jt.johansson@ulricehamn.mail.telia.com

Agent:
Planet Earth Pictures
The Innovation Centre, 225 *Marsh Wall*
London, E14 9FX
UK

Tel: 0171 293 2999
Fax: 0171 293 2998

Adriano Turcatti 108

Via A Turcatti 1, 23100 Albosaggia
Sondrio
ITALY

Tel: (0039) 0342 510644

Heinrich van den Berg 44, 56

HPH *Photography*
PO *Box 13244, Cascades* 3202
Pietermaritzburg
SOUTH AFRICA

Tel & Fax: (0027) 331 472728
Email: hphvdb@mweb.co.za

Philip van den Berg 45, 69

As above

Dr Freek van Eeden 16/17

PO *Box 38328, Faerie Glen* 0043
Pretoria
SOUTH AFRICA

Tel: (0027) 12 9960046

Jan Vermeer 117

Planetenlaan 10, 7314 KA Apeldoorn
NETHERLANDS

Tel: (0031) 55 355 5803
Fax: (0031) 55 355 7268

Agent:
Foto Natura, *Krommenieîrpad 38 a*
1521 HB *Wormerveer*
NETHERLANDS

Tel: (0031) 75 628 0764
Fax: (0031) 75 640 3409

Bernhard Volmer 59

Rheiner Landstr 82, 49078 Osnabrück
GERMANY

Tel: (0049) 541 432072
Fax: (0049) 541 47148

James Warwick 103

4 Elder Close, Portslade, Brighton
East Sussex, BN41 2ER
UK

Fax: 01273 706030

Agent:
Papilio, Natural History & Travel Library
44 Palestine Grove, Merton, London
SW19 2QN
UK

Tel & Fax: 0181 687 2202

Dan Welsh-Bon 94

8480 Sunny Oak Terrace
Salinas, CA 93907
USA

Tel: (001) 831 663 3134
Email: welshbon@prodigy.net

Christof Wermter 105

Am Stemmersberg 21
D-46119 Oberhausen
GERMANY

Tel & Fax: (0049) 208 892826

Staffan Widstrand 50/51, 134

Smedvägen 5, S-17671 Järfälla
SWEDEN

Tel & Fax: (0046) 8 583 51831
Email: photo@staffanwidstrand.se

Thomas Wiewandt 116

PO *Box 5118, Tucson, Arizona* 85703
USA

Tel: (001) 520 743 4551
Fax: (001) 520 743 4552

Alan Williams 64

30 Fairfield, Ingatestone
Essex, CM4 9ER
UK

Tel: 01277 354981

Winfried Wisniewski 148

Nordring 159, 45731 Waltrop
GERMANY

Tel: (0049) 2309 77116
Fax: (0049) 2309 77117
Email: W.*Wisniewski@t-online.de*

Kim Wolhuter 153

PO *Box 1550, White River* 1240
SOUTH AFRICA

Tel: (0027) 13 750 0868
Fax: (0027) 13 750 1486

Robert Wong 48

1720 Mt Rushmore Road
Rapid City, South Dakota 57701
USA

Tel: (001) 605 341 3888
Fax: (001) 605 399 3203

Konrad Wothe 132

Maenherstr 27a, D-81375 *München*
GERMANY

Tel: (0049) 89 717 453
Fax: (0049) 89 714 7141

Tsutomu Yamabe 71

3-1-802 Tsukushino,
Abiko Shi, Chiba Ken
JAPAN

Tel & Fax: (0081) 471 83 3897

Dr Mamoru Yoshida 33

746 Cambridge Way, Lake Wales
FL 33853-2806
USA

Tel & Fax: (001) 941 676 8939
Email: DrYoshida@juno.com

Daniel Zupanc 127

Haidingergasse 28/12, A-1030 *Vienna*
AUSTRIA

Tel: (0043) 1 710 5204
Fax: (0043) 4239 2707